FROM BEETHOVEN
TO SHOSTAKOVICH

From Beethoven To Shostakovich

The Psychology of the Composing Process

By
MAX GRAF

GREENWOOD PRESS, PUBLISHERS
NEW YORK

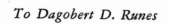

To Dagobert D. Runes

TABLE OF CONTENTS

PART I.

Sources of Musical Imagination

Chapter I.

The Magic in Music

THE AVERAGE music lover, listening to one of the great music works, does not give a thought to how these compositions may have originated.

He enjoys their grand musical constructions, the symphonies, sonatas, chamber music, songs and choruses. He derives pleasure from the tonal beauty and from the musical expression and feels his whole being elevated, his sensual powers augmented and his entire personality transformed.

The world in which he ordinarily moves, and which is the scene of his activity, seems to vanish. He feels himself transplanted to another world wherein everything that would normally catch his interest ceases to exist: his work, his human relations, his worries and hopes and fears, his plans and his everyday sentiments.

In this new and exalted world there are only sounding forms, and within the tones only the lustre of beauty; a lustre that has always been sensed by all susceptible individuals (by some more clearly than by others) as a light coming from a loftier region.

Even those who seek in the enjoyment of music merely the sensual pleasure of sounds, still sense in music firm order and a lawful form which elevate the simplest melody far above the tumult of everyday life.

The attitude of musical audiences in the concert hall demonstrates most effectively the transformation of a crowd of people from its commonplace conduct to a new form of existence.

Before the program starts, the audiences gossip and discuss their private affairs; they laugh, exchange pleasantries, flirt, tell one another vicious or witty or meaningless matters about life and society. As yet there is no audience in the concert hall, and no unity; only groups or individuals.

Then the conductor or the soloist makes his appearance on the stage, and as if at a given command, the conglomeration of listeners changes to a single audience that listens as if with a single ear.

At the first sound of a tone or chord the attention of thousands converges in one direction. The listeners are transformed into a single being whose entire emotional life is changed. It seems as though the souls of thousands would merge in a new, uniform soul that permits music to penetrate. There is a new tension in the souls of all those present; sensations take on a higher degree of warmth; emotions move more rapidly than in ordinary life.

At this moment an event takes place in the concert halls similar to that in Catholic churches when, at the moment of "Transubstantiation" the music becomes silent as the little bell rings through the high room. At this point the pious kneel down as the priest raises the monstrance, and out of hundreds of devout there emerges a single congregation in whose collective soul lives the identical mystic awareness of the presence of their God.

One can observe something similar at every theatrical show, every mass meeting and at every sports event: the transformation of a gathering of people, and of life and sentiments of thousands into a new, more strongly braced, intensified emotion. From time immemorial music has been one of the most powerful means of producing such intensification of feeling and of expanding and enhancing it, and of directing the magnified tensions of the soul toward one goal.

Following the last chord, the pent-up emotions caused by the music give way by means of applause and calls of "bravo." Whereupon the unit disintegrates into its individual groups and component parts. Everyday life again takes hold of the individual listeners who then continue to discuss ordinary matters. Again one exchanges banal courtesies, talks of restaurants one plans on visiting, arranges appointments, discusses business and falls from a lofty sphere back into the commonplace world in which one's life is usually spent.

The magic of intensified emotions produced by one beat of the music has evaporated. The more brilliant world of beauty, of spiritual order, of enhanced emotional life and augmented sentiments submerges. The shining eyes of enthusiastic young people, and the pensive silence of scattered concert-goers who quietly go their ways, are the sole reminders that some part of the soul transformation evoked by the music echoes within them.

Nor is this observation confined to the concert halls. It is noticeable at private musicales as well, how the enjoyment of music captivates the souls and enhances and concentrates their forces. During every performance of chamber music in a private home one observes individual music lovers sitting in a corner, often closing their eyes or covering them with their hands as though trying to forget their ordinary surroundings in order to be alone with the sounding forms.

While the music plays they live in a different world; a world in which forms are more brilliant, patterns more ideal; where the associations of objects are less deranged than in everyday life. Just a simple song such as Schubert's "Heideroeslein" or the Brahms "Lullaby" is able to produce this enchantment. The sentiment expressed in these songs by even the simplest melody is of such purity and beauty that it appears to be idealized, free of all the sediment that adheres to emotions in ordinary life, and detached from earthly by-sounds.

True, the melody expresses sensations known to all of us; but in a form that is clear and pure as a day in spring, the kind of day that gives even the most banal person a feeling of an awakening new life. And the tone arrangement is one that not only enhances the sensations but reproduces them in a new form of beauty.

If a single simple song is capable of elevating human emotions to the level of a pure picture, how much more so the augmented music work. Every music piece is within itself its own world of forms and legitimate life. It is purer and more brilliant than the figures in every-day life and is developed according to laws that are akin to the rules governing the growth of nature and living organisms.

The listener who feels himself transformed by music, who feels that he is elevated by it and transplanted to a different world, knows instinctively that the intensification of his emotional life is caused by his entry into a new world, compared to which the world of profession, business and industry appears dull and chaotic.

*   *   *

When music first touched mankind at the inception of human cultural development, it already showed—albeit in low and elementary forms—this power of transforming souls, of enhancing emotions and of placing the primitive man in a mood wholly different from that of every day.

Music was a magic medium. The world was filled with demons and spirits; stones and trees, moon and stars, water and earth, storm and rain, birth and death, sleep and dream: all were swelled with sinister character that reached menacingly and terrorizingly into life.

The animals hunted by the cave man, and their pictures scratched by him onto the dark walls of his cave; the birds with whose feathers he adorned himself in order to appropriate their magic power; the snakes that slithered out of mud holes and disappeared, and the fish—they all were filled with magical forces.

Music was a means of scaring off demonic powers by dispelling them with loud noises, thus magnifying one's own personality. The primitive man would construct a pipe from the bones of birds or wild game that gave off a shrill sound. Drumsticks and rattles whined and blared and sounded like rain and thunder; hollow logs were stamped upon or beaten with wooden sticks and gave off an eerie rumble.

All of these were magic instruments, designed to frighten off demons·because they themselves were filled with sinister voices. The noisy singing of the witch-doctor in high piercing tones, or murmured litanies which he emitted excitedly, sometimes accompanied by the stamping, jumping and marching of the whole tribe, purported to augment his own spiritual forces, demonstrate his power and elevate his personality.

It was a long way from these primitive beginnings of music through the millenia of world history to the great formation of nations in the regions of the Euphrates and

the Nile. That which was magic in the days of cave-
man tribes now became religion, and its hymns were
sung in the temples of Ur and Babylon, Luxor and
Memphis, to the accompaniment of flutes, castanets,
gongs or harps.

Everywhere great music was mainly religious music:
prayer, exorcism, ecstasy, invocation of the gods. It
was per se something sacred that freed man from everyday life and joined him to the Beyond.

The choruses of the Levites who sang solemn psalms
in the Temple of Jerusalem; the choruses of young
boys and girls in Greece who danced around the altars
of their gods and sang hymns; the hymns that were
sung during the meetings of the Christians at agapes, in
the catacombs and churches; the temple hymns in China and the songs of the priests at the Soma sacrifices
in India: they all enhanced the emotional life of the
devout, magnified the sense of their existence and elevated them to ecstasy. The religious man felt himself
detached from the earth by means of music tones, at
the same time being brought closer to Heaven and the
Divinity.

In Europe music was for the greatest part religious
music even in the moyen age. The masses and motets
of the Netherlanders resounded in their Gothic
churches and, like the structures themselves, were a
flowing current from earth to heaven; a circling of
voices in an element that was lighter than the atmosphere on earth.

The peak of artistic music in the moyen age was
reached by the masses and motets of Ockeghem and
other Netherland composers who had spent their youth
in churches and cathedrals as choristers and who later
became clergymen themselves; by the golden lustre of

Palestrina's masses; the agitated penitential moods of Orlando di Lasso's motets; by the festive pealing of chorus and instruments in the sacred music of Gabriele Gabrieli.

Like paintings by Jan van Eyck and Memling, Giotto and Massacio; like Raphael's Madonnas and Michelangelo's fresco paintings, they were heralds of divine power, religious sentiments, exaltation of prayer.

The magic belief of primitive man had turned to the religion of the Christian man, who was led to the loftiest spheres by saints and confessors, by angels and the Virgin Mary. In his great poem—which itself is the grandest Gothic cathedral—Dante, the most famous of mediaeval poets, described the path from Hell through Purgatory to the bright spheres of Heaven. And even Goethe, in his "Faust" epic, took the same gradation from earth to Paradise, where the Virgin Mary and hosts of angels received the soul of the battling, wrestling Faust, and where the choruses proclaim the credo of the moyen age: "Everything that is transitory is but an allegory."

Four centuries separated the two poems. Yet how little has the religious sentiment changed which, in all great art, remains the animating force. We even find ancient magic powers in great present-day art.

*   *   *

From the 16th century on the religious world of the moyen age had been penetrated increasingly by secular forces that molded modern culture and learning, modern art, natural science and technics.

Mediaeval world philosophy believed in a fixed earth around which the sun revolves and above which a divine heaven arches like a shining bowl to which all living matter ascends after having slipped off its mortal covering.

Galileo exploded this world philosophy. God had grown smaller; man, greater. He had become more conscious of his individuality in love and hate, in fact and performance.

Nature and world changed to atoms and motion, to something that could be calculated and measured. The movement of planets and the descent of bodies in space, the radiation of light, the chemical structure of matter were transformed into laws that could be reduced to mathematical formulas. And when Newton and Leibnitz discovered differential calculus, everything could be calculated, no matter how small or how large, whether it flowed or whether it was just beginning to exist.

Since the days of Hobbes even state and society were subject to the same mechanical laws that governed all occurrences in nature. The various religions became phases of the same religious sentiment that was rooted in the soul of man as moral sentiment is rooted therein.

The state became something mechanical, something turned historical. Gigantic poets such as Cervantes and Shakespeare presented man as being great in passion, hate and love, in dreams and illusions; as the master of his fate and stronger than the tragic forces that destroyed him. Gargantua and Don Quixote, Hamlet and King Lear, Romeo and Falstaff became portraits of the new man who found the divine within himself, rather than in myths and religions which consider him merely a dependent being whose life has some relationship with a higher world, whence it derives meaning.

In this changed spiritual attitude music became expressive of mood and sentiments of the individual. In

operas it was passion that sang, and hate, love, ambition, grief and happiness. In the cantatas all human
emotions sang. Secular instrumental music developed
new art patterns in symphonies and concertos, in orchestral and in chamber music. It culled its powers
from worldly life.

The new instrumental music combined energetic motion, strong pathos, the gaiety of popular and courtly
dance melodies, masterful and brilliant tone play with
refined elegiac moods. No longer does it contain the
spiritualism of the moyen age; only worldliness, enjoyment of life, pleasure in virtuosity, pleasure in art, a
festive pathos, ingenious play.

The baroque era of the 17th and 18th centuries then
made a magnificent attempt at employing the new art
values of secular music for the Catholic reactionary
movement, in the same manner as, in the church paintings by Rubens, it enlisted all sensual color glory, all
radiance and brilliancy, all the virtuosity of the brush
to serve Jesuit piety.

In addition, baroque Protestantism transformed the
mass singing of the people into its devout chorales and
elaborated richly upon these folk tunes in organ variations and organ preludes, in cantatas and passions.

Worldly lustre and worldly tone motion, popular
dances and songs, virtuosity and pomp merged with religious moods. Out of this merger there arose, from the
middle of the 18th century on, classical music: popular
when written by Haydn, romantic from Mozart's pen,
revolutionary and belligerent in Beethoven's compositions. Any music lover, listening to such works as
Haydn's Adagios, or Mozart's "Magic Flute", or Beethoven's Ninth Symphony, must sense, in these great
moments of creation by the classical masters in human-

istic or philosophical exaltation, that the religious tone again becomes audible—the religious tone which is the heritage of great music in mediaeval times.

Following historical and mythical music dramas, Wagner returned to his boyhood impressions of Catholic Mass with his "Parsifal". The "faith motif" that ascends solemnly in the scenes of the Grail is the Gregorian melody of the "Amen" as it was sung in the Catholic court chapel in Dresden in Wagner's youth.

The Brahms "Deutsches Requiem", and his motets, are a revival of Protestant cantatas and motet music of the 17th century. The Lutheran bible was always Brahm's favorite book.

Bruckner's symphonies are Catholic Mass celebrations and almost always end with brilliant choral music that cannot deny its association with baroque music.

Mahler in his pessimism was a religious meditator who, in mediaeval poetry, in the Latin hymn "Veni Creator Spiritus" and in the mystic ending of "Faust" sought the meaning of the Beyond.

Richard Strauss, a professed free thinker, is the greatest modern musician to be free of every religious mood; he is completely a man of the earth, of worldly splendor and sensual virtuosity. However, even while enjoying the gayly colored descriptions of the world, and happenings therein, as presented by Richard Strauss; and while admiring the color fantasy, the splendor, pomp, wit and esprit accumulated in Strauss' symphonic music from "Don Juan" to "Alpensinfonie"—is there anyone who does not realize that in such masterworks of color and performance he is enjoying merely a brilliantly colored surface?

Tiepolo was another such master in his art. In his frescoes—even though they were church frescoes—he conjured onto the walls strongest color glory, the most liberal imagination and gayest play of shapes and figures. Yet this wonderful fantasy, with all its brilliancy, means so little compared to the pious look of a saint following with his eyes the figure of the vanishing Mary, as portrayed by any mediocre mediaeval painter; or compared to the fervour of Fiesolo, or the transfigured expression of Raphael's Madonna whose earthly mother love turns to divine purity; or compared to the contours of Michelangelo's prophets in which is combined the whole magnitude, the grief, or the resigned contemplation on the proclamation of eternal values.

There was a time in the Greek age also, when an epoch of magnificent art initiated an era of virtuosity that no longer was governed by religious standards but by worldly values. It was an epoch that released free subjectivity and turned music into a dazzling virtuoso art. This was the era of Alexander the Great, the era in which Alexandria became a metropolis. In her streets the Orient met and mingled with Hellenism; in her theatres luxurious ballets, colorful shows and mass concerts replaced the great Greek tragedies; poets sang theatrical odes to the accompaniment of chromatic music. And in sculpture ancient solemnity was replaced by passionate, theatrical agitation that filled the altar of Pergamus with pathetic and baroque figurines

Here, too, one may ask: what does this mean to the world, compared to the religious solemnity that flows broadly from the tragedies of Aeschylos or Sophocles; or that, in tragedies by Euripedes struggles spiritually with new ideas; what does it mean compared to the majesty of a Zeus bust, or the Phidias statue of Athene? What does it signify next to the majesty of the Athene temple atop the Acropolis, where marble pillars string along solemnly like the verses of a hymn?

The organizing of scientific work in the museum of Alexandria accomplished great things in the fields of astronomy, philosophy and technics. Yet all this is trivial compared to the fantasy, greatness and religious depth created by Plato's shining sphere of ideas which, like the sun from behind clouds, emerged from Egyptian temple wisdom, from Orphic doctrines, from the mystic precepts of Pythagoras, and shone through the millenia.

Plato was a poet supreme; and without his vision, the philosophy of the moyen age is unthinkable, as is Spinoza, Leibnitz and Kant. By the same token there would never have been a Schubert, a Richard Wagner, a Berlioz and a Brahms without Beethoven.

*   *   *

The fact remains that all over the world great art productions were the result of religious sentiments and religious notions, whether they were Indian dramas, Chinese music, Greek tragedies and Pindaric odes, or mediaeval music, the music of Bach or the best works of the classicists. Neither the boldest architecture of a secularized era, nor the proudest skyscraper of a technical age can compare with a Gothic cathedral. Religious faith gave the Gothic cathedral the outline of a cross. Its pillars ascend from earth to heaven, and inspire mankind. Its windows glow and shine like symbolic pictures of the Hereafter, and its window rose is an allegory of celestial spheres. Even the gargoyles, projecting from the edifice, in the shape of snarling beasts, are unthinkable without the religious beliefs of the

[14]

moyen age. They are the evil, satanic spirits that flee from the sacred building.

So far there has never existed a truly great art era that was not nourished by the strength of religious sentiment and a world philosophy of religious import. A great world of myth as it existed in the Greek epoch and in mediaeval times, can be created only by such sentiments.

This religious sentiment may undergo a change, as was the case with the Humanism of the expiring 18th century. There, the enthusiasm for human dignity and for the magnitude of man had been proclaimed with fanciful exaltation that resounded mightily from the choruses of Mozart's "Magic Flute" and the Sarastro arias, from the jubilation of the Ninth Symphony and from the stanzas of Schiller's dramas.

Religious sentiment may assume a philosophical guise, as in the myth in which Nietzsche creates the prophet Zarathustra; or it may, coming from Dostojewsky's pen, glorify the poor, the downtrodden, the criminals; in Tolstoi's writings the Russian muzhik. Or religious sentiment may have established a religious system, as it did in the moyen age, that carries art in its entirety and that lives in creations of architecture, sculpture, painting, music and poetry; it may only be common faith in something divine, as evinced by Goethe and Beethoven; it may be a solid property of the soul such as Dante possessed, or a battling and struggling as shown by Michelangelo. Always the great art epochs of olden times had been of a religious purport and of a sentiment that inspired man and united him with the divine above, or in, the world.

One comes across this phenomenon quite regularly: In times when religious forces weakened, technics, scientific analysis, rationalism and materialism changed, as far as art is concerned, to virtuosity, to brilliancy without spiritual depth, to theatrical subjectivism, to empty, dazzling display of the arts. Such had been the case toward the close of the classic Hellenistic age, at the end of the Renaissance and in modern time. The gods forsook the world, and the priests who had proclaimed their greatness were replaced by magicians, witchdoctors, actors and tradespeople.

*　　*　　*

One has to survey the entire historic development that leads from the age of primitive hunting tribes to the epoch of modern civilization before one is able to comprehend properly which were the spiritual forces and talents that molded music. It is always the agitated emotion, a state akin to intoxication, that elevates man above the normal mode of living and isolates his personality from the surrounding world; an intensification of his emotional life that seeks an outlet in tones. The primitive witchdoctor who swings the rattles to dispel evil spirits is the ancestor of the modern conductor and concert soloist.

The men of primitive tribes, readying themselves for the hunt, or for war, to the accompaniment of monotonously rolling drums, painted and adorned with feathers, bones and skins of animals, are simply trying to enhance their strength with dances and songs. They are the forerunners of our choruses. The ceremonial dancers, their faces hidden by grotesque masks, conjure rain, transform themselves into demons and re-enact the life of the gods or animals. These are the ancestors of our opera singers. And the drumsticks, the hollow tree logs upon which they drum, the stone-filled pumpkins and bones provided with apertures, are the ancestors of our instruments.

Primitive instruments, primitive choruses and songs and dances are filled with magic significance at the very inception of mankind; just sounds alone are charms. The jingling of amulets, the humming of drumsticks, the rumbling of the rattles, the dull droning of the drums, the shrill whistling of the fifes, are ghostly voices which primitive man thought he heard in the howling of the storm, in the rolling of the thunder and in the splattering of raindrops.

Thus in primeval times music already links the world of phenomena everywhere with an exalted world that causes people to be afraid; the world of man with the world of spirits and demons; the visible with the invisible.

For this reason all primitive music-making is associated with an enhancement of sentiments, with excitement, with a flaring up of emotional life. The fear of demonic powers translated itself into the desire to change oneself into such demons and to transplant oneself to a state of ecstasy and insensibility that lifts the barriers of the personal and augments the intrinsic powers of man. In all primitive music rhythm is the most effective expedient for stimulating the emotions, whipping them up and bringing them to the boiling point.

It is not just the droning of the primitive drums that sounds like a ghostly voice. The monotonous, hypnotizing rhythm is a demonic force that subdues the individual, gathers groups of people into a unit without willpower. It regulates emotional life, which otherwise is free in its motions and flows unhampered, so that it no longer is able to flare up and die down at will. By means of the automatic change of rhythmic accents it is seized as by a machine, concentrated and worked into a uniform mold. The forces thus arranged, augmented and collected by rhythm convert to dance and march steps that still have their religious and symbolic meaning among all old tribes.

As cultural development progresses, rhythm becomes spiritualized, becomes verse, ornament, rows of columns. In verses, rhythm makes lawful order out of a sequence of words, thereby intensifying emotional effect and co-ordinating and elevating it. In ornaments and in columnar rows, rhythm gives the effect of an ingenious parable of a higher order. And in serious music rhythm ties the changing tonal forms, elevates them to a higher rank, joins them to form a unit of mood and, in a resounding, multiform world, it causes the law of their movement and their life to shine through.

Between the music of primitive man and the symphonies of the classic masters and the compositions of the romantic and modern eras lie thousands of years of human cultural evolution. But even in today's enlightened civilization, and despite the business trade that transformed today's music into an entertainment industry, music did not quite lose its old magic enchantment. The everyday world still vanishes at the first chord of a Haydn, Mozart or Beethoven symphony during a modern concert. The emotional life of the individual is changed. Out of thousands of listeners there emerges a unified gathering that is in higher spirits, its emotional life enhanced to such an extent that, after the final chord, it has to give vent in applause and cries of "bravo".

The thousands of listeners who gather in a concert hall after the day's work is done are all modern metropolites: educated newspaper readers, men and women of various professions, with varying interests and different philosophies; they are business men, society women, intellectuals, young folks from colleges, universities, offices. At the sound of music they receive a new soul, a collective soul.

The reaction of each single person may be individual, tinged by education, habit and inclination; but these are only the topmost waves in a sea of sentiments and emotions, of tension and enhanced moods, in a sea that oscillates in a great rhythm. As is usually the case when an individual is incorporated into a mass gathering, it means that the surface of inhibitions and conscious limitations, set up by civilization, is pierced by elemental emotions and instincts, reactions and passions. The sensuality of the tones causes elemental emotions to surge.

The masses react like a primitive being; they are more violently agitated than a man of civilization. They are more passionate, less controlled by conscious thinking, the very foundation of the soul is in turmoil. Irrational sentiments, moods and passions emerge from the dark passage of the soul and take possession of the people, an overwhelming mass of unleashed emotions, of liberated sensuousness, of strong effects that expand, free of every constraint, and inundate the individual.

History and civilization have built up the soul life of man in layers; and every new era has added a new layer. Thus we find in the soul ancient and long-forgotten things: primeval times, ancient times, moyen age, modern time; primitivity and artificialness; primitive man, and the man of progressive cultural development.

The modern person who lives in huge cities in which skyscrapers tower above the sea of houses; the man who is surrounded by all the wonders of the new technical age of science, the man who soars through the air, who talks over the telephone to other continents; the man who drives a car, who keeps himself informed of all events all over the world by reading his newspaper; the citizen of a rationalistic scientific age actually contains, deep down in his soul, the primitive human being.

Every individual, from childhood on, lives through the entire human culture evolution, and all civilization plunges primitive emotions and primitive perceptions into the depth of the soul where they go on living in the dark. Even the greatest works of art take root in this depth, and in all great artists this dark substratum of soul life is rich and of greater power than in other people.

Among all the arts, music has the greatest ability to shape and mold the most profound, subconscious soul life, which is the oldest layer of sentiments.

The primitive enjoyment of sound, primitive pleasure in rhythm, the primitive enjoyment of play with emotions, the emotional power of music—all take root in the deepest layer of soul life and from there ascend to the strata that have been created by the conscious work of civilization.

To this day music, as any evening in a concert hall teaches us, is magic enchantment, a visionary voice. To this day it works a change in man. Even today, in a scientific and technical era, the emotion inspired by great music is related to the primitive religious sentiment of mankind. Present-day business may use great musical works as objects of an amusement industry. Listening to music may have become a social function that is governed by fashion. The manager, the brilliant virtuoso, the advertised musician, the star, the conductor who affects the motions of a fakir—all of them may control musical life. The need for relaxation in the concert halls may look for gratification, or sensation, or topics for gossip. Publicity may create musical fashions. But let there be a performance of a cantata or organ solo by Bach, or of a symphony by Mozart, or Beethoven or Bruckner or Mahler, one of Beethoven's last string quartets, or one of Schubert's great songs in a music hall, and there is added to the mood of the hall something purer and fuller, something deeper and more solemn that does not quite belong to this world and is never felt in equal strength and duration in the distracting machinery of business.

This mood is isolated from everything that would otherwise occupy the people's mind. It is in itself a condition that is richer than the state of the soul in everyday life; it is unity of emotion, an expansion of life, a concentration of all human powers that glow like wine in a golden goblet.

The sensual pleasure in the play of tones alone, the changing figures of sounds cannot create such a state that penetrates the whole person down to the very roots. Whoever listens to the circling of voices in a Bach fugue, to the chorales of the Mattheus Passion, to the merry or serious tone pictures of a Haydn symphony, to the "Magic Flute" choruses, to Mozart's Sarastro arias, or to the struggling, wrestling aspiration, to the tragic or heroic adventures of Beethoven music, and hears only lovely or magnificent tones—that person has never heard or understood music. He is like a child that plays with colorful pebbles lying on the beach: he has enjoyed a gayly colored surface. But he did not learn why composers put the import and the work of a whole lifetime into musical works. Nor is he aware that music creations such as the Bach fugues, the Magic Flute, the Ninth

Symphony, Wagner's "Parsifal" and Stravinsky's "Rites of Spring"; the symphonies of Anton Bruckner and Mahler, Hans Pfitzner's "Palestrina," are among the most magnificent spiritual accomplishments of mankind.

He will never comprehend that behind its shining surface, music has profundity, and above its surface, a Heaven. "Am farb'gen Abglanz haben wir das Leben", Goethe wrote. But with this life is meant not just earthly life that gives great musical works its lustre and sensuousness; it means, too, heavenly life that provides them with spiritual significance.

Just as in a dusky Gothic cathedral the glass portraits in the windows shine colorfully when the sunlight strikes the paintings, and makes them glow—symbolic figures that hover between heaven and earth—just so, in great music, the resounding, colorful appearance is illuminated by a loftier light. Even the most apathetic listener feels that he is being lifted out of the earthly world when the music begins.

CHAPTER II.

Artistic Fancy

IT IS the artistic imagination of composers that creates the great master works of music capable of changing the proportion of spiritual forces at the first downbeat. There is a change in the distribution of emotional powers and rational forces, as well as in the organization of passion and sentiments, moods and thoughts, of the conscious and the unconscious, of sensuality and intellect. The process resembles that of rock being thrown into a smelting furnace, where the red heat reduces it to its component parts. The rock dissolves, and assumes new shapes.

Similarly, tones are purified and begin to shine. Sentiments flow unstemmed. New forms are created. The emotions usually lying chained in the dark of the unconscious break loose from their prison.

The borders separating the various layers of the soul disappear. The forms grow. The tone figures unite, new combinations come to life. Sound patterns are endowed with reproductive and procreative powers. They produce new organisms that take their nourishment from the combined forces of man. The mind supervises this process of forming, re-shaping and living, and itself is made to glow by the flames of the process of imagination. It is, and remains, an artistic mind and, unlike that of the scientist, the logician and the philosopher, it is not an abstract mind. It is the assistant of imagination.

All this procreation and growing, forming and shaping assumes a rhythmic aspect. Rhythmic life fills all tone figures, which are then joined together by musical imagination to form a stream of rising and sinking and alternating accents, a stream that carries all changing shapes.

In the days when glowing masses were shaped into heavenly spheres and planets, it was a similar rhythm that regulated the movements of the universe. It is effective in the rotation of day and night and of the seasons, of high tide and low tide, and in the circling of stars and planets. Musical rhythm is but a part of the great world rhythm, and with the latter's help music is joined to the infinite.

Every movement of a symphony and a sonata has its own rhythm. However, rhythm does not pulsate only through the individual works of the composers. The rhythm of Haydn music differs from that of Beethoven music. The Palestrina rhythm is different from that in Bach compositions. While Beethoven utilizes Haydn's musical form in his first and second symphonies, his heroic, advancing rhythm, by discharging itself in stronger accents, nevertheless is completely different.

When Bach uses Vivaldi's violin concertos for organ or piano concertos, or re-forms an oboe concerto by Benedetto Marcello into an organ concerto, the Bach rhythm permeates the old music.

The theme of Mozart's overture "Bastien and Bastienne" retains the same notes that were used by Beethoven for his "Eroica"; but the fundamental rhythm changes from the idyllic-pastoral quality that it receives from Mozart to the heroic, to strength and energy. It becomes Beethoven rhythm that is derived from his particular personality, from his attitude toward life, from his energy; from physical as well as spiritual qualities.

It is rhythm that puts order in the process of musical fantasy. Without this rhythmic animation, all tone patterns created by the imagination would remain in a chaotic state. And it is rhythm that imparts to music not merely life and unity, but also the power to arrest the audience, to keep them tense, to hold them in an exalted mood.

One has only to hear the first two chords with which Beethoven begins his "Eroica" and which indicate the rhythm. With just these two beats one is removed to a shining tone world in which there is battle and victory. The two beats are sufficient to make a monument of the music, to impart power and majesty to its forms and to elevate it to a higher level. The rhythm of the first two bars alone is enough to stamp the music "Eroica" music.

It is this same heroic rhythm that makes all tone phenomena of the first movement in their triumphal advance a sequence of sounds that have as grand a style as the reliefs adorning Roman triumphal arcs. If the listener hears this first movement as an epos filled with a procession of armed fighters, with battles, flags and swords, with fanfares and march music, it is because the rhythm, in its first two bars, takes possession of him and will not release his eager attention.

Occasionally, in Schubert's orchestral music, the composer starts to dream, or falls into lyric moods, or begins to saunter leisurely. Such a slackening of rhythmic force immediately causes the tension of the listener to weaken. Schumann spoke of the "divine length" of Schubert's C Sharp Symphony.

Interruptions of the rhythmic flow always mean a

lowering of suspense for the audience. Such interruptions occur occasionally in Bruckner's music when, in the midst of the lustre of symphonic music, the composer looks up to heaven and quietly begins to pray before proceeding. Always it is the rhythm of music, rather than its melody, that lifts the listener out of the everyday world to an exalted world, and holds him there.

The musical process of imagination not only produces sounding figures that emerge from the shaft of the unconscious, but also subjects these figures to the law of a rhythm that creates the higher units. It creates and it organizes.

No one pictured more beautifully the work of artistic fantasy than did Friedrich Nietzsche. In speaking of the origin of his "Thus Spake Zarathustra", he describes the creative state in "Ecce Homo": "Does anybody at the end of the 19th century have any idea what the poets of a stronger age called inspiration? If not, I will describe it.

"If one had the smallest vestige of superstition in oneself, it would hardly be possible to set aside the notion that one is merely the incarnation, mouthpiece or medium of an almighty power. The idea of revelation in the sense that, with indescribable certainty and accuracy, something becomes suddenly visible and audible which profoundly convulses and upsets one, simply describes the true state of the matter. One hears—one does not seek; one takes—and one does not ask who gives; a thought suddenly flashes up like lightning, it comes with necessity, unhesitatingly—I have never had any choice in the matter.

"There is an ecstasy such that the immense strain of it is sometimes relaxed by a flood of tears, along with which one's steps either rush or involuntarily lag, alternately. There is the feeling that one is completely out of hand with the very distinct consciousness of an endless number of fine thrills and quiverings to the very toes; there is a depth of happiness wherein even the most painful and the gloomiest do not operate as antitheses, but as conditioned, as demanded in the sense of necessary coloring within such extravagance of light. There is an instinct for rhythmic relations which spans wide areas of forms (length, the need for a wide-embracing rhythm is almost the measure of the force of an inspiration, a sort of equalization to its pressure and tension). Everything happens involuntarily to a high degree, as if in a tempestuous outburst of freedom, of absoluteness, of power and divinity. . . . This is my experience of inspiration."

In every artistic inspiration it is characteristic to find an arousing of the whole emotional life that can be enhanced to an intoxicating rapture, and a deluge of pictures, ideas and figures in inconceiveable abundance.

The artist himself feels this intensified heat as being filled with higher forces. In gigantic music personalities, as for instance Beethoven, this heat could be intensified to a degree of complete detachment from the world and the accustomed surroundings. The pictures of his sounding inspiration confront the artist as something that is not invented by him, but given to him, a strange world that overpowers his imagination. Titanic artists—among them Beethoven, Michelangelo, Lord Byron, or young Goethe—did not feel that they were the ones who created works of art, but rather that within them were stronger, mightier powers that flowed into them.

While Beethoven was composing the "Missa Solemnis", he resembled a man enraptured. "In a living room, behind closed doors"—reports his friend Schindler in 1819—"we heard the maestro singing, yelling, stamping over the fugue to the "Credo". Having listened to this almost horrifying scene for a long while, we were about to leave when the door opened and Beethoven appeared before us with distorted features that caused us anxiety. He looked as though he had just fought a battle of life and death with an entire host of contrapuntalists, who were his perennial enemies. His first remarks sounded confused, as though he were unpleasantly surprised by our eavesdropping."

It was no different when Wendelin Weisheimer visited Richard Wagner while the latter was composing the 'Meistersinger.' Wagner was pale and disturbed, and fled, hiding in his bedroom, from where he yelled out: "Don't bother me, I am in heat".

If Bach and Haendel walked through life great and strong without any outward signs of the storm of their fantasy, concealing the secret of their great creative work behind a bourgeois surface—as Johannes Brahms did in the Wagner era—then it was due to the taming powers of a staunch Protestant faith that gave them this strength. Only the outbursts of fury to which Bach as well as Haendel were occasionally subject revealed the passion within them, and the demonic forces without which great work is unthinkable.

In Bach these forces manifested themselves in the passionate storm of the D-Minor organ prelude, in the tragic recitatives of the "Chromatic Fantasy" and in the raging of the pedals in some organ fugues.

In writing above his scores: "Soli Deo Gloria", or "Jesu Juva"; and in teaching his pupils that the "finis and final cause" of all music is nothing other than "in honor of God alone", or in writing above his "Orgelbuechlein" the words: "In honor of the Highest God alone", the religious Bach said quite distinctly that he considered his creative inspiration a divine presentation.

Haendel's innate passionateness manifests itself in every one of the great biblical figures and in the folk scenes of his oratorios, as well as in the musical descriptions of his operatic arias. It would be just as ridiculous to believe that such passionateness could be possible without overpowering inspiration, as it would be to imagine that Michelangelo's visions of world creation and world perdition, prophets and sybils, redemption and final judgment could have been possible without the arousing of fantasy and the inner turmoil of the entire man.

When, in Michelangelo's "Judgment Day" the Supreme Judge jumps up from His seat in the clouds and, with a gesture of the hand that frightens even the saints, resurrects the dead and hurls the sinners into the abyss —the inspiration of the artist himself was in a similar turmoil of rage, might and terror that lent power to the prophets over a period of more than 2,000 years.

The one composer who thought differently about inspiration was Igor Stravinsky. Says he, in the "Chronicle of my Life": 'For me as a creative musician, composition is a daily function which I feel compelled to discharge. I compose because I am made for that and I cannot do otherwise ... The uninitiated imagine that one must await inspiration in order to create. This is a mistake. I am far from saying that there is no such thing as inspiration; quite the opposite. It is found as a driving force in every kind of human activity and is in no wise peculiar to artists. But that force is only brought into action by an effort, and that effort is work. Just as appetite comes by eating, so work brings inspiration if it is not discernible at the beginning.'

Frankly, this is but an ingenious play of words. Never has "effort" alone produced a work of art, or the world would abound with art works. And, fortunately, it was not "effort" alone that produced masterpieces such as Stravinsky's "History of a Soldier", "Petrouchka", or "Rites of Spring". Even Stravinsky's greatest masterpieces are begotten by inspiration. They are visions, world creations of fantasy, selected figures, as for instance the soldier, the princess and the devil in "History of a Soldier"; the marionettes in "Petrouchka"; or the barbaric era, the roundelays and dances, the ceremonies and trumpeting words of the priest, the sacrifices and ecstasy in "Rites of Spring".

It could be possible that the ingenious constructions of Stravinsky's later compositions were produced by an "effort" of the mind and by intellect. It is not possible, however, for visionary pictures to be created by intent and purpose. As is evident from Beethoven's sketch books, artistic work is able to excavate the buried gates of the imagination, but it cannot create them. It can merely clear the path of fantasy, and clean it.

In olden times, therefore, the artist was always regarded as a man instilled with divine powers. In primitive times the witchdoctors were the original musicians. The temple priests in Babylon and Egypt, in India and China, in Asia Minor and in Greece were the composers and poets of hymns dedicated to the gods. Plato considered the poet as being inspired by God. In the first stanza of his "Comedia Divina", Dante supplicates Apollo; Milton calls to Urania in "Paradise Lost".

Even in modern times poets like Blake, Wordsworth, Victor Hugo, Alfred de Vigny and Arthur Rimbaud look upon a poet as a seer who proclaims divine wisdom in a realistic world.

ARTISTIC FANCY

To Beethoven music was "a more exalted revelation than wisdom and philosophy"; he was "Bacchus who treads the luscious grapes for man and provides him with spiritual intoxication". Music is "the entrance to a higher world of knowledge", he himself a man who is "aware that God is closer to him than to others."

It happened often enough, from time immemorial, that inspiration of artists was compared to other mental conditions which fill people with stronger emotions, attacking them with pictures and visions, and isolating them from the world . . . : with the state of intoxication or mental illness. Aristotle maintained that no great genius existed without some kind of madness, and Democritus declared that the gates of the Helicon, the mountain of the Muses, were closed to sane poets.

The similarity between artistic fantasy, and inebriation and certain forms of insanity, is certainly only superficial, for the imagination of the artist is creative and is converted into great spiritual accomplishments. The forty huge volumes that contain the works of Bach; the scores written by Beethoven and Wagner, and Haendel's works represent the intellectual strength of giants; the frescoes of Michelangelo in the Sistine Chapel are by themselves a summation of gigantic strength in design, arrangement and execution.

Even the imaginative achievements of artists with pathological traits, such as Edgar Poe, or Baudelaire, originated through productive spiritual strength and were not due to temporary heat of intoxication or effects of illness. In some musicians—among whom we find Robert Schumann, Hugo Wolf and Beidrich Smetana—the incipient mental illness weakened their fantasy even before it completely destroyed the soul of these artists, and rendered it tired and colorless. In Robert

Schumann's later works this weakening of the artistic imagination is easily discernible.

Imagination is one of man's primary forces. At the start of human evolution it was stronger than it is today. Primitive man considered the entire universe as having a soul. Everywhere he saw himself surrounded by spirits. The whole sky, sun, moon and stars were filled with gods. Animals were possessed of demonic life. Man's thinking was not logical, not an association of ideas according to set rules; it was a fantastic thinking. His art, poetry, painting, bodily adornments, music, were all means of magic. His emotions were strong, confused, and changed rapidly.

The souls of children to this day represent this stage in the development of mankind. Every nursery is a realm of fantasy. Each object is animated, each doll is an ancient idol, every children's dance a mythological presentation. All the child instruments: rattles, little bells, pot covers that are noisily struck together, are the instruments of primitive men. The fairy tales that are the same the world over contain primeval mythologies. They tell of giants and dwarfs, of animals that change to humans, of evil spirits and of fairies, of birds that can speak, and talking trees.

Children's songs contain melodies, rhythm and scales that belong to a prehistoric past. The child's soul itself that animates everything and is spoken to by everything is, by virtue of its rapid change from crying to laughing, still the soul of the musing, primitive man.

It took thousands of years of human evolution to repress fantasy. Scientific thinking restrained the free flow of pictures, ideas and emotions. It destroyed the myths, transformed magic to religion, celestial tales to astronomy, fantasies about the body to chemistry; it changed the stories of primeval days to history and the fables of the universe, of man and God, to philosophy. Into the place of the irrational, which set the imagination of primitive beings in motion, there stepped everywhere the rational, the logical; that which could be measured and calculated. Out of the mythical world, created by fantasy, there stepped a scientific world.

Following the Greek age, the scientific world expanded more and more. Among the Greeks themselves there was still complete balance of mythical and scientific thinking. Every river in Greece, every spring, each group of trees was still surrounded by legend and was the habitat of gods and demons. Nature was animated. The Acropolis was tenanted by Erechteus and Athene, Pan and the dew daughters. In the rocky chasm fronting the Acropolis lived the Furies; satyrs ran up and down the slopes. The hill of Colonos contained the entrance to Hades. On the mountaintops of Messinia Hermes cared for his sheep, and goat-footed Pan blew his fife. In the mountain ravine of Delphi lived the earth dragon. Zeus resided atop Mount Olympus together with the other Homeric gods. In the Olympian woods rode Chiron and sylvan spirits.

However, in the great philosophies of the Greeks mythical thinking was already changing to science. Despite all the forces of Plato's dialectic thinking, his myth-creating fantasy is still quite strong. The dark stream of mysticism rustles under the surface. How much fable is contained in Herodotus' history books, how much religion in the tragedies of Greek poets!

But after the 16th century, the victorious advance of science is not to be checked. Mythical fantasy had to retreat before the picture of nature and universe created by Galileo and Keppler, by Newton and Huyghens. It was replaced by mathematical thinking; and following Cardano and Decartes, Leibnitz and Newton, mathematics and geometry developed more and more as a tool of scientific analysis.

With Faraday came the beginning of modern chemistry, Volta initiated the study of electricity. The world became increasingly a world of technics, of logical, clear, accountable reasoning.

This development repelled to a smaller territory the imagination that created myths, religions and great works of art. It is quite significant that a modern representative of calculating, analyzing, rational science—Hobbes—calls fantasy "a decaying sense." From a universal emotional power that re-cast all phenomena of world and nature to myths, fantasy was limited to the field of art.

During the evolution of rational and logical thinking that created modern science and modern government, as well as modern technics and modern civilization, one part of the imaginative powers was assimilated for the prosaic purposes of reasoning and was—to use a phrase of Sigmund Freud's—"sublimated". Another part was precipitated into the deeper strata of the soul where the ancient, primitive instincts, ideas and sentiments lay chained.

Just as every big building has its foundation deep in the earth, so, too, does the structure of human culture on which construction work was done by the millenia. In these dark chambers of the soul are the powers of imagination that once governed all mankind, the titanic family of old wishes and old dreams. When they break out of the depth, they emerge as architectural structures, paintings, poetry and music.

[34]

CHAPTER III

Classical and Romantic Fantasy

MUSICAL FANTASY has its roots in the recesses of man's emotional life. These roots reach much deeper into the soul than the roots of other types of fantasy. They extend into the night where the physical and the emotional meet, where the roaring of the blood can be heard, where the rhythmic beat of the heart pulsates, where sensuality glows and elemental emotions storm.

A great musician without an unusual wealth and strength of these deepest strata of the soul is unthinkable. The force of musical fantasy ascends from this underground of the soul to its higher layers. As it passes each stratum, it takes along some of its constituent parts: memory, old sentiments, things long past and forgotten. The sounds take nourishment therefrom, grow, assume larger proportions, until everything that originated in this manner reaches the light of consciousness. Here, the last artistic formation takes place, and that which is engendered by the night becomes clear and light.

The outbreak of musical fantasy power in a musician of Beethoven's personality is liable to have vulcanic force. It may proceed in eruptions, the artistic forming of which requires extremely sound thinking and tremendous moral energy. Or, it may be a broad, even stream that flows powerfully through the various layers of the soul, as was the case with Bach and Haendel. Then again, it may be a harmony of various imaginative powers such as Mozart possessed, in whom we find tragic sentiments and humor, earnestness, solemnity and gracefulness in perfect balance. Or, finally, it may consist of one sole power, as it did with Chopin, who sings the same melody of the soul over and over again in ever new forms.

The power of imagination may be wild and fantastic, as shown by Berlioz; or it may permit the composer to play with it seriously or gaily, as in Haydn's works.

After years of intensified action, it may cease over a period of years. Such was Hugo Wolf's experience. Or, it may continue to work in uniform abundance like Nature herself. It may possess the strength to build great architecture or, in the guise of a lyric mood, move the soul, as is the case with Schubert and Schumann.

Again, imaginative power may carry along a world of colorful pictures—compare Richard Strauss—or glowing masses of sensuousness, as one finds in Richard Wagner's operas. No matter what form they assume, musical fantasy forces always emerge from the depths where they have been nourished by heredity and disposition.

Even the most ethereal rhythm in a great symphony is governed by the physical being of a composer: by the movements of the blood stream, by the rapidity of nerve vibration, by the motion of his spiritual and physical forces. Even the idealized tone is colored by the sensuality of the composer. The fantasy of the musician is the only form of artistic imagination that extends so deeply into the total human being as nature created him, and as history and culture developed him.

The impetus of artistic fantasy most important to musical creation is erotic power. The perceptive faculty of the ear shapes the musician to the same extent as the sensuality of the eye creates the painter, as the sense of touch makes the sculptor, while it takes a mixture of all the component parts of eroticism to form the poet, who sees, sculptures, and sounds. According to which of the individual erotic forces preponderates, there develops within the poet either the epic poet as the "eye" man who sees figures, actions, events, scenes of nature and human life, and describes them; or the lyric poet who luxuriates in moods—the word itself is taken from music—and for whom words and rhythm have above all musical meaning.

Of course there are borderline cases, and between the two there are all kinds of nuances. In his "Birth of Tragedy from the Spirit of Music" Friedrich Nietzsche described with keen spiritual elan how the tragedy of the Greeks came into existence through a combination of the "Apollonian" poet, who has graphic and plastic visions, with the "Dionysian" poet, who is a musician. The Greek tragedy resulted from choruses, and "in several successive outbursts this primal basis of tragedy radiated the vision of the drama"; satyrs dance and sing and they behold the gods and their fates and sufferings.

The best example of how the perceptive faculties of eye and ear, how painting, plastics and music blend and join hands in one great poet, is Goethe. Goethe was chiefly a "seeing" poet who beheld forms and figures as Homer did. But in his youth, residing in Strassburg, music broke out of him. In bold hymns in the style of Pindar, it involved singing words along with its flowing, streaming and whirling. It was music that imparted its gripping force to the emotional descriptions and reveries in "Werther". It was music that lent the

[37]

poems of his Strassburg sojourn and his love for Friedericke von Sesenheim the singing atmosphere and the musical mood that later awakened the genius of Franz Schubert.

But later, in Weimar, when Goethe would have repressed all the storm, gloom and passion that was within him and that had animated his new lyrics and filled it with song and rhythm, his seeing sense awakened, the sense of lucid forms and distinct figures, and he thought himself a painter. He drew landscapes; he saw the solid lines in nature, the definite shape in tree and bush, field and stream.

It was his graphic and sculptural eye that caused him to travel to Italy.

In his letters, he described Italy, Italian landscape and Italian art as a painter would. The scenery at the Brenner Pass appears to him like a picture by Everdingen; the cattle fair in Bozen like a painting by Heinrich Roos. When, in Bologna, he saw Raphael's picture "St. Cecilia", he wrote that he would put no words into the mouth of his Iphigenia that were not suitable to this painted saint.

Influenced by such impressions, he changed his drama "Iphigenia" from musical prose to plastic verse and transformed the tones into pictures and plastic form. He wrote his "Nausikaa" in the Homeric style. He stood in pious admiration before great works of Greek sculpture such as the Ludovisic Hera, and he saw the forms of nature in idealistic purity as architectural and monumental. Painting led him to optics and chromatics; the glance of the landscape artist induced him to study the motion and form of clouds; the study of sculptor's materials led him to mineralogy and geology.

Thus Goethe became the greatest "eye" man among

CLASSICAL AND ROMANTIC FANTASY

German poets. The whole sensuality of his fantasy was
gathered in his large brown eyes, the shining of which
was described by every one of Goethe's visitors. He
was the classical poet.

The whole difference between classical poetry and
romantic poetry depended, even in Goethe's time, upon
whether the sensuality of the eye or the ear preponder-
ated in a poet. Novalis, the romanticist, fancied "stories
without coherence, but with associations like dreams",
and "poems that are merely euphonious and without
rhyme or reason". The romantic poet Wackenroder
heard "in the garden of poetry the roses sing, the tulips,
the birds and the blue sky, the springs and the storm,
the stream and the spirits". And the romantic poet
Tieck wrote of the flowers: "The color rings, the form
resounds; each one, according to shape and color, has
tongue to speak."

The world that, to classical poets, is picture, sculpture and plastics, suffused with bright sunlight, becomes music in deepest night for the romanticists.
Novalis, in his "Hymns to the Night" (which inspired
Wagner in the nocturnal colloquies of 'Tristan') was
the first to celebrate the magic of night; but for the
romanticists the night is filled with musical sounds.

"Keiner der nicht zum Myst 'schen Fest gelassen
Kann den Sinn der dunklen Kunst erfassen . . .
Dem im innern Herzen nicht das Siegel brennt . . .
Woran ihn der Tonkunst Geist erkennt"

wrote the poet Tieck. (No one not admitted to the
mystic festival can comprehend the sense of dark art . . .
in whose inner heart the seal does not burn, that the
spirit of music may recognize him).

[39]

The whole world dissolves in music. Above Schumann's Piano Fantasy in C Major are written the verses of Friedrich Schlegel, one of the leaders of German romanticism: "Durch alle Toene toenet im dunklen Erdentraum ein leiser Ton gezogen, der fuer den der heimlich lauscht". (Through all music is sounding in the dark dreams on earth a low sound for him, who listens secretly). And Eichendorff, another romanticist, wrote similarly:

> "Schlaeft ein Lied in allen Dingen
> Die da traeumen fort und fort,
> Und die Welt hebt an zu singen,
> Triffst Du nur das Zauberwort"

(There sleeps a song in all things that dream on and on, and the world begins to sing if you find the magic word).

The boundaries of art begin to blur for the romanticist, and poetry and music emerge as fragments from the stream of music. Friedrich Schlegel considers romantic art a "form of general art". "What", asks Tieck, "should it not be permitted and possible to think in tones, and to make music in words and thoughts? Oh, how badly off would the arts then be? How poor the language, how poor the music."

And August Wilhelm Schlegel proclaims: "One should approximate all the arts and seek transitions from one to the other. Statues may become enlivened to portraits, portraits to poems, poems to music and— who knows?—some glorious church music might ascend again as a temple."

From such romantic ideas did Richard Wagner derive his thoughts of a "universal art work" that reunites all arts.

[40]

CLASSICAL AND ROMANTIC FANTASY

In his "Vorschule der Aesthetik" (Introduction to Aesthetics—1804), Jean Paul Richter correctly defined the ancient, classic ideal as the "plastic" ideal; the romantic as the "poetic-picturesque-musical" ideal. And August Wilhelm Schlegel is equally correct when he writes: "Antique art and poetry insists upon strict separation of the dissimilar; romantic art delights in combinations. It is the expression of the secret attraction to a chaos that is forever striving for new and miraculous births, a chaos that lies concealed among the orderly creations, even in their womb."

In France it was Baudelaire who proclaimed the new gospel of romantic combinations with the following verses:

"Comme des long echos qui de loin se confondent
Dans une tenebreuse et profonde unité
Vaste comme la nuit et comme la clarté
Les parfums, les couleurs et les sens se repondent."

Paul Verlaine proves that he has accepted the romantic precept by writing as follows:

"La musique avant toute la chose
Et pour cela je préfère l'impair
Plus vague et plus soluble dans air
Sans rien en lui qui pèse et qui pose."

One gains the impression that the ability to subject the various component forces of sensuality to a single dominating power is weaker in romantic art than it is in classic art. That explains the many combinations and the fluctuation, the crossing of talents and promiscuous vibration of the erotic ingredients of fantasy found among romantic artists in all countries.

When Theodor Amadeus Hoffmann began his career, he was painter, poet and musician, and he wrote as fol-

[41]

lows: "A motley world of magic apparitions glitters and flares around me. It is as if something great may happen—some work of art must come out of this chaos —it may be a book, an opera, a painting, God knows."

In Bamberg Hoffmann painted murals in the old castle in which he lived, and conducted opera performances in the little theatre described in his novel "Don Juan".

Later on, his creative work separated into music and poetry. He composed an opera "Undine" which in many respects became the forerunner of Richard Wagner's operas. He wrote fantastic stories, forerunners of those by Edgar Allan Poe and Barbey d'Aurevilly, as well as marvelous essays on music.

Robert Schumann also wavered between poetry and music. He started as a poet. Living amongst the books piled high upon the shelves of his father's bookstore, he wrote poems, dramas ("Coriolan", "The Two Montalti" and "The Brothers Lanzendoerfer") and stories ("Juniusabende und Julitage"—June Evenings and Days in July).

A youthful infatuation for two girls, Nanni and Lilly, lent warmth and exalted mood to the poetic work of Schumann when he was seventeen. But it was not until a year later that he finally made up his mind to devote himself to music exclusively and, under the influence of a new love (Ernestine von Fricken) he composed his variations on the theme "Abegg".

Shortly prior to this he had entered in his diary: "I do not know quite clearly myself what I really am. I believe that I have imagination, and nobody disputes that. A deep thinker I am not; I can never follow logically the thread which I may have started well.

Whether I am a poet—for one can never become one —posterity shall judge."

However, even after Schumann turned to music altogether, his poetic talent merely receded to his musical ability. He became a poetic musician, a novelist in his symphonies and in much of his piano music. The music pieces in his "Papillons" are joined with poetic interpolations. And in his "Intermezzi" opus 4, Number 9 is prefaced as follows: "With that, Florestan concluded, and his lips quivered painfully". And the last number is prefaced: "Quite superfluously Eusebius makes the following statement; at the same time, however, much bliss shines out of his eyes".

The "Kreisleriana" and "Nachtstuecke" take reference to Hoffmann's poetic figures. "Carneval", with its Pierrot, Harlequin, Pantalon, Columbine, Clara Wieck, Chopin, Paganini, Estrella and with the Davidsbuendlermarsch, is invented by a poet who writes words with notes and who, from the letters "A.S.C.H." (Asch, birthplace of his beloved Ernestine) develops music pieces.

Richard Wagner also started off as a poet. He composed poems, and for two years worked on a Shakesperian tragedy before he wrote: "I decided to become a musician".

Literary and philosophical interests gave Franz Liszt's musical creation its impetus, the grand style and the theatrical pose. In the case of Claude Debussy, it was picturesque fantasy, nourished by English Pre-Raphaelites, French impressionists and Japanese etchings, that inspired his musical fancy.

Scriabine, Russia's romantic mysticist, saw music and colors simultaneously, and his symphonic poetry "Prometheus" is accompanied by colored lights. Arnold

Schoenberg, in his monodrama "Die Glueckliche Hand" likewise combined music and colorful lights. Before Schoenberg turned from the romantic program music of his first stage to expressionism, he began to paint pictures that were invented in the style of Kandinsky and Kokoschka, visions of the soul in figure and color. While in his first works poetic fancy had the lead ("Verklaerte Nacht", "Gurrelieder", "Pelleas and Melisande"), it was later replaced by the painter's fantasy in the form of abstract lineal art.

The Austrian poet Grillparzer was a composer who wrote music in the Mozart style. In his novel "Der Arme Spielmann" he gave a description of himself. His artistic imagination divided itself into two streams. Sensuality incited both his eye and his ear.

All great classical music concentrates all sensual forces of tones, embraces them with powerful hand and subordinates them to a single main force.

The finest example is Johann Sebastian Bach. Bach's mighty fantasy consisted not only of musical powers but of graphic forces as well. In many of his works he paints in tones. For instance, in the "St. John's Passion" the tearing of the curtain in the temple and the earthquake at the death of Jesus—Bach himself inserted these incidents in the Gospel text where they are missing—or the heaving of the sea in the cantata "Siehe, ich will viel Fischer aussenden".

With the strength of a great etcher he paints the fog which "arises one moment, disappears the next"; waves, steps, the writhing of the serpent in Paradise, the hovering angels, elevation and humiliation and, with particular beauty, painful downfall and joyful exaltation.

The Bach biographer Albert Schweitzer called attention to the fact that in the Bach family painting talent went side by side with musical talent. Samuel Bach, who studied with Johann Sebastian, was an organist and portrait painter; and Johann Sebastian's grandson, the son of Emanuel, deserted music altogether and became a painter.

But all picturesque descriptions by Bach were merely a part of his imaginative work, just as a graphic ability in Beethoven, which breaks through in the "Pastoral Symphony" and, quite realistically, in the "Battle of Vittoria," is subjugated to his general musical talent.

Franz Schubert, too, paints in his lieder: the little brooks and the river, the city emerging out of the fog, the humming of the spinning wheel, the barrel organ, the flight of the crow. But here, too, these drawings of nature and the universe are just a component part of his musical fancy.

Felix Mendelssohn-Bartholdy forms the transition from the harmony of the classical musicians to the romantic combination. Although he painted aquarelles with a firm hand and a fine eye, this composer still looked upon music as the roof under which his graphic fantasy lived. In the character of his creation he is absolutely the classicist, almost Mozart-like in the grace of his musical form, in the sureness and beauty of the musical line.

As a child, Mendelssohn had been admired in Goethe's house, and he absorbed the latter's old-age wisdom. Accordingly, the method of his creation was influenced by Goethe, and he composed in clear forms and pure tone figures. His extremely fine aesthetic sense regulated the tone patterns: formative musician that he is, he is less profound than elegant and ingenious.

However, in his romantic music fantasy the picturesque is no longer just a part. Mendelssohn's Scotch and Italian symphonies are not idealized and spiritualized landscapes (like Beethoven's "Pastoral Symphony"); they are real, imbued with the atmosphere of the environs. They are already air and color. In the "Hebrides" overture one finds already the Nordic fog and the Nordic sea. Richard Wagner, who admired this overture, called Mendelssohn "the greatest landscape painter among the composers".

The overture to "A Midsummer Night's Dream", the miracle work of the seventeen year old boy, contains in its narrative of the nocturnal magical forest a totally impressionistic array of color, sparks, spots and dots which paved the way for the art of Claude Debussy.

To an even greater extent than Mendelssohn, Hector Berlioz uses completely the fancy of a romantic painter as a stimulus for his musical creative work. It abounds in multiple colors and, in fantastic descriptions, allows the colors to run down the canvas, similar to Delacroix and Delaroche, his intellectual next-of-kin.

In trying to establish which scenes from Goethe's "Faust" Hector Berlioz used for his "Damnation of Faust", one finds only those which permit of graphic portrayal. The color fancy of Berlioz, and his translation of poetic spheres into painting, colorful description and portrayal, is totally different from the tonal narratives of Franz Liszt, which were inspired by literary and philosophical culture. It also differs from the masterful narrative art of Richard Strauss, and from the graphic strength of Richard Wagner, which was set in motion by the theatre and serves the tragic stage.

Classic music fantasy always means the accumulation of all forces in music and in music figures. It means the erection of fantasy from a musical center, and it means that intellect, painting, poetry, sensuality and sentiment overflow into music.

Romantic music fantasy emanates from the poetic, the picturesque, from the theatrical, from philosophy.

In the classical musician all the perceptive faculties: those of the ear and the eye, the plastic sense and sense of color, join forces with the sensuality of music. In the romantic musician the musical fancy is a colorful garden where the earth is not so deeply saturated with music, and where poetry, painting and philosophy are introduced from the outside so that the exotic flowers and vines may grow.

The classic musicians went through life big and strong. Men of strong sensuality and passionateness, they all organized their lives and their imaginative powers in uniformity. It is not until the era of the romanticists that we come across the novel-like life stories of the artists, artists' lives full of unrest and motion; surprising fates, eccentric lives such as that of Hector Berlioz or Richard Wagner. Now begins the age of novel-like love stories: Chopin's friendship with George Sand; Liszt's relations with the Countess D'Agoult and Caroline Wittgenstein; Wagner's romances with Jessie Laussot, Mathilde Wesendonck and Cosima Buelow; the fantastic love of Berlioz for Henriette Smithson.

The romantic era is a period of erotically inflamed, ingenious, or flaring women with whom every romantic artist surrounded himself.

The file of these women, who either fled the bourgeoisie or blazed through it, begins with Bettina Brentano. At once a capricious child and a fanciful woman, she charmed Goethe and Beethoven, like a dark-eyed witch, with esprit, ecstasy and sensuous artfulness.

Berlin boasted of three intellectual Jewish women who were surrounded by romantic artists: Mendelssohn's beautiful daughter, Dorothea Veit, who gave up her own shabby marriage to follow Friedrich Schlegel; Henrietta Herz, adored by the two Humboldts and by the romantic religious philosopher, Schleiermacher; and Rahel Levin, who had the great statesman Friedrich Genz at her feet.

At the age of 23, the romantic poet, Novalis, fell in love with thirteen-year old Sophie Kuehn and, when his beloved passed away, he pined for her until he, too, died of longing.

Another romantic poet, Hoelderlin, (his "Parzenlied" was set to music by Brahms) carried on an elegiac, soulful love affair with the wife of Banker Gontard in Frankfurt.

In the romantic era dawns the epoch of nostalgic, ecstatic, visionary artists' loves which no longer recognize the laws of the world. Erotic love begins to glow, to flame, to dissolve in hot vapour.

With Friedrich Schlegel's novel "Lucinde" erotic anarchism penetrates art; in Baudelaire and Oscar Wilde this anarchism touches the region of morbidness and perversity.

In comparison with romantic eroticism—which is either unleashed sensuality or unleashed desire—how natural and strong does the life of Bach appear! He had two wives, with whom he begot 22 children and with whom he lived in simple wedlock that was in no way different from other bourgeois marriages.

Classical sensuality is strong and healthy; romantic sensuality is restrained and either driven to the spiritual by inhibitions, or divided and diverted onto sidepaths.

When sensuality of classical musicians is transformed

into tones, and penetrates the musical imagination, it becomes wholly sounding patterns, melodic figures, purely musical play of fantasy. In romantic sensuality this concentration is lacking, as is the uniform strength. Romantic sensuality branches out into various paths; it is divided into different parts, it causes oscillations in spiritual life without being able to assemble it in a focal point. The composers begin to philosophize, or to paint or to narrate.

Like their art, their lives are without firm roots. This accounts for the unrest in the lives of the romanticists, the many changes and vicissitudes. It explains the adventures that are reminiscent of motion picture plots, and the many abnormal personalities: the bizarre appearance of Th. A. Hoffmann; Baudelaire, Paul Verlaine and Edgar Poe, the alcoholics; Dostojewsky, the epileptic. It accounts for the suicides of romantic artists, two of which were Kleist and Raimund; Paul Verlaine's assassination plot; Chopin's pulmonary disease and his death on a Mediterranean isle; it is the cause of Oscar Wilde's confinement in the jail of Reading, as it was responsible for the commitment of Robert Schumann and Hugo Wolf to an insane asylum. It explains Hector Berlioz flaring up like a comet. And it accounts for Lord Byron storming through the world, sailing across the Mediterranean in a barge during a tempest; galloping across the Lido after nights of wild love; swimming across the Hellespont and, finally, dying in battle near the blue mountains of Missolonghi.

The crown of romantic life is that of Richard Wagner with its adventurous vicissitudes: the flight from Riga to Paris, from Dresden to Switzerland, from Vienna to Switzerland, always hard-pressed by his creditors, always changing residence, always enmeshed in passionate love affairs, finally to be saved from greatest misery by an insane king who took nocturnal rides on Bavarian lakes, dressed in silver armour, and erected fantastic castles in the Bavarian woods.

Among great artists the pattern of their lives are always created by their personalities and is the expression of their inner natures. Unlike mean, average people, they are not subjugated to life, nor are they molded by life itself. They are not—to use the biblical term—clay in the hands of their creator who makes vessels out of them. They are themselves creators. The stormy life of Richard Wagner, with all its surprises, crises and romances, is the reflection of his stormy interior where, in the depths, as in every genuine dramatist, the forces of the soul are in battle.

Richard Wagner's own fantasy, which erected the contrasts between Venus and Elizabeth; Lohengrin and Telramund; Siegfried and Hagen; Parsifal and Klingsor, also was shaped by stormy, fantastic life.

The same might and strength that molded Haendel's biblical heroes can be found in Haendel's life which, whether it be in Rome or Vienna, in Hanover or in London, was always equally great, free and forceful.

Bach was adjusted to bourgeois life and its conventional rules to the same extent as he adjusted his passionate fantasy to the traditional arrangements of the fugue, the concertos, the cantatas and the Passions, without wanting to create new forms.

Whether the life of a composer is a life of work, such as Haydn's, or of play, as was Mozart's, or a life of struggle, as in the case of Beethoven, or reverie, like Schubert's, depends upon the personality of the artist.

Whether it is the life of a classicist who adapts himself to life because his is a balanced, strong personality;

or whether it is the life of a romanticist who seeks to break the bonds of conventional rules because his imagination drives him beyond life, is determined by the nature and strength of the artist's imagination and his energies.

The root of all fantasy, however, is sensuality that seeks to penetrate the finest ramifications of spiritual life; it is Eros who, according to Plato, sees and creates beauty. Among classical artists this sensuality is gathered in one main force, among the romanticists it is divided into its component parts.

CHAPTER IV.

The Erotic Forces of Fantasy

THE EROTIC powers of musical imagination work in two directions. They are the ones that lend lustre, fullness and color to the tonal performance. The sensuality that collects in the ear causes the tone, and combinations of tones, to shine. It provides the tone with intensity.

If the creative musician hears the tones purer and richer than other humans, so that he devotes his entire life to the cultivation of these tones, it is because the sensuality of the tones captivates him and sets his fantasy in motion.

Musical sensuality has a history. In the course of thousands of years the sensuality of musical sounds, as well as sensuality proper, has changed. Both became something different due to transformation of elemental erotic forces into intellect.

In prehistoric times, and in primitive conditions, tone and sensuality of tone have something elemental. The piercing sound of a whistle made out of stone or animal bones, (unearthed by the hundreds in regions of primitive settlements), or the droning of a drum excited the primitive man in his entire being. It inflamed him and made his blood boil. His own voice, intensified to a scream, represented a charm which he produced by exerting all his strength. Among most primitive tribes music making, singing, beating and blowing of instruments to this day possess the same elemental, stunning, exciting character.

There is created a condition of being beside oneself, a condition that drives the blood through the body, a sensual stupefaction, an ecstatic intensification of all elemental powers, including erotic forces, which transmuted part of primitive music into a charm of fertility.

All over the globe, in prehistoric times, the kettle drum was associated with the cult of goddesses, whose pictures are now being unearthed everywhere: the goddesses of birth, of growth, of fecundity.

Beginning with the period when hunter tribes turned to agriculture, more and more kettle drums are found in the tombs, many of them adorned with symbolic, magic drawings, with ornaments that are as regular in their rhythm as the rolling of the drum. Even much later, the temples in Asia Minor contained the tympanum of the great Earthmother, of orgiastic and erotic cults that promote fertility. The beat of the tympanum stunned and excited; cymbals and castanets reinforced this elemental sound which accompanied the religion of fertility everywhere with its drone, and stormed into Greek life together with the Dionysian armies.

The Greeks were the ones who spiritualized the primeval erotic life of tones, thereby creating the foundations upon which European music was erected.

The Greeks arranged musical tones intellectually, polished them and brought them into the line of the scales. They subordinated music to the word. Their chief instrument was the kithara which, with its gentle, thin tones, pushed the Oriental pipes into the background.

They looked upon music as spiritual and moral

value, not as an elemental power. They spiritualized the rhythm, repressed the chromatic scales and organized the tones as clearly as they did the columns of their marble temples, their poems, their dances and processions and their idols.

During the reign of Alexander the Great, when Alexander's armies marched into Asia, colorful, exciting Oriental music once more pervaded Greek culture in the form of shrill chromatics and blaring instruments. But upon the foundations of classical Greek music was built Christian music. Tones became prayer and exaltation. Sensuous instruments were banned from the church. The Gregorian chant attached itself to words, and declaimed and recited. The elemental, primeval tone became sounding spirit. The original erotic forces in tone turned to spiritualized ringing.

This evolution started with the rudiments of the classical Grecian tone scales, which had become church tones, and had been continued by the European moyen age. The tone of mediaeval masses and motets, encased in polyphonous lines, artistically built like mediaeval cathedrals, was a sublimated tone.

Sacred music, in which the new tone patterns were developed, assumed a heavenly glow; it expressed religious sentiment as perfectly as did sacred images and statues at the portals of Gothic churches. It possessed a new spiritual magnitude and a new spiritual and moral value.

The tone of Palestrina's masses shine like silver—just as the sound of Mozart's tones has a golden glimmer. In this Palestrina tone, and in the fanciful, sentimental expression of the Roman master's "Hohe Lied Motets", there is a gleam of sensuality. The glowing expression of the "Hohe Lied Motets" is even intensified in the

"Buss Psalmen" of Orlando di Lasso, but this sensuality and ardour are something entirely new. The light is spiritual rather than material.

With increasing secularisation of life after the epoch of great exploring expeditions, and in the age of growing cities, economy and business, secular music waxed ever more personal and richer. The Renaissance, according to Jakob Burckhart, "discovered man and the world". Instrumental music became the musical expression of the new sense of living. It was then that the changed sensual tonal feeling no longer went astray. That which had been newly created by mediaeval musicians: tone as soul and spirit, was adopted by the new era.

The sensual charm of tones no longer was the old, elemental magic, no longer a primitive power. It was not intensified animal-like, or something that resembled the cries of animals in heat. It was now a magic power of modern life, cultivated and tamed, lucid form and life-filled figure, a symbol of spiritual emotion and pure sentiment. The tones no longer proclaimed the magnitude of natural life, but the greatness of man's personality.

All sensuality, all the rippling and all the pomp of the baroque tone, which became ever richer from Corelli and Scarlatti to the era of the classicists, and from there to Wagner, Liszt, Bruckner and Richard Strauss, were the ringing of a spiritual man who, in the "age of enlightenment" made humanity his religion.

Coming from Arnold Schoenberg's pen, this tone—which in "Verklaerte Nacht", in "Pelleas and Melisande", and in the "Gurrelieder" expands its full sensual wealth—becomes increasingly abstract. Intellect, construction and thought had completely devoured sensuousness.

And yet even the most abstract music, and artificially constructed music, is unthinkable without the sensuality of the tone performance; just as there is sensuousness in the aesthete, although it is subdued and subjected to the mind by willpower.

Progressing civilization altered the sensuality of tonal performance, but it did not destroy it. Everything that lends color, lustre and splendour to the tone; everything that distinguishes it from other presentations, everything that gives the tone a finish and makes a body out of it that shines and gleams—all that is the work of erotic forces.

All the spiritual and intellectual value of tone performance has changed the presentation of the tone, but not its kernel. These values are something like the atmosphere that surrounds a glowing centre; a part of the heat emanating from this centre that has turned to steam.

From the era of primitive man to our time winds a long road of cultural work, of thinking, of civilization. But the natural foundations of man remain the same. The chief impetus of human life, the power which creates life, and generates and shapes, which changes to love, friendship and social feelings, still is sensuality. And without sensuality there would be no fantasy and no art, both of which derive their main nourishment from erotic forces.

*　　*　　*

Among all musicians, none had tonal visions of such beauty, purity and clarity as Mozart. Each composition shows the tone to be enhanced to such a fullness of sensual beauty that not one second of dimness occurs, and of a purity equalled by that of a free-swinging bell. Every instrument in Mozart's chamber music, or in an orchestral composition, is employed in keys that produce the most sensual tone. This is true whether it be the mighty peal of the trombone in the "Dies Irae" of the Requiem which possesses nobility and majesty; or whether it be the singing of the violin in the G-Minor Symphony, or the gleaming sound of the trumpet at the entrance of Donna Anna and Ottavio in the sextett of "Don Giovanni", or clarinets and bassoons in chamber music pieces.

Tone combinations have a great abundance of tone-color, for instance in the trombone choruses of "Zauberfloete", or in veiled, refracted, shaded colors similar to those in the slow movement of the D-Minor Piano Concerto, or in the seraphic tones of "Ave Verum."

Beethoven's piano sounds more powerful, bulkier, more tempestuous; Liszt's piano more brilliant, dazzling with esprit and virtuosity. Schubert imparted his own lyric warmth to the piano; its harmonies ascend unexpectedly from the dark depth, and it has romantic charm. Chopin's piano has its nocturnal moods, its Italian singing, its chivalrous or fanciful lustre; Debussy's piano has its picturesque color specks that hover in the air, in the fog, in the rain. But no piano ever sang more beautifully in melodies and passages than did Mozart's.

If one takes a middle voice out of a choral movement by Mozart, either from "Magic Flute" choruses, or from "Requiem Aeternam", it has the same pure tone as the melody-carrying treble.

Only Palestrina's choral phrase may possess a similar light in its tones; but Mozart hears the musical tone in its greatest perfection not just in choruses and in arias, but in orchestral and chamber music as well. As he hears it, it is glowing with sensuality, gleaming in a light that shines through the tone like the sun through a crystal.

Compared to this shining of the Mozart timbre, even the heroic, or tragic, or spiritualized tone of Beethoven appears as material as gleaming ore. His tone was molded by intellect, willpower, spiritual energy, while that of Mozart was shaped by nature itself. Even Schumann's orchestra has some spots that are tonally dim, and Brahms music contains much autumnal grey. But in Mozart's works there isn't a moment in which the timbre of the orchestra does not gleam.

That Mozart as a child already sensed the musical tone almost physically, becomes known from a letter written by Schachtner to Mozart's sister Marianne, (Salzburg, April 24, 1792) wherein he states that Mozart, up to his tenth year, had an insuperable fear of the trumpet. . . . "Wolfgang no sooner heard the crashing tone than he turned pale and started to sink to the floor, and had I continued, he surely would have had convulsions."

With such nervous irritability of the auditory senses Mozart combined the most perfect tone memory. The announcement of a concert given by the seven year old boy in Frankfurt stated: "In addition he will, from a distance, name accurately all tones that can be given either individually or in chords on the piano or on any imaginable instrument, bells, glasses or clocks."

Added to this is the general sensitivity of the boy, whom psychiatrists today would analyze as a "nervous child."

We hear often that Mozart wept easily. He wept when Schachtner asked him whether he liked him

(Schachtner); he cried upon awakening in the mornings because he did not see his Salzburg friends (letter of his father to Hagenauer dated August 20, 1763). He wept when he was praised (letter of his father of Feb. 1778). And as late as 1778 Mozart wrote to his father: "Today I can do nothing but weep; I have a much too sensitive heart."

Mozart's juvenile sensibility — "He became easily attached to every object" reports Schachtner in 1792— his tone memory, his sensitivity for sounds (according to Nissen "music gripped his whole emotion and staggered him") gave lustre and light to his tone visions.

To this was added the erotic sense, which had been awakened in the boy at an early age and which probably nourishes and enhances the fantasy of every child prodigy.

The letters that Mozart wrote as a boy are full of erotic puns, jokes and rhymes; and the letters which he wrote to his cousin Maria Anna in Augsburg, also when still a young boy, are to this day not published in their entirety because they contain so many erotic allusions.

The texts which Mozart used for his canons in Vienna are equally blunt. A poem that he wrote for his sister in the Salzburg dialect on the occasion of her marriage (Mannheim, December 20, 1777), teems with enjoyment at expressing naturalia which today would be considered turpitude.

Mozart would never have been able to describe with such great psychological faithfulness the erotic moods of puberty in the first aria of Cherubin, nor the pining and languishing, the attraction to every female if, as a boy, he had not experienced such erotic awakening with such intensity. He was always ready to joke and jest with a female; in later years he spoke of his "chambermaiding," and under date of July 25, 1781 he wrote: "If I had to marry all those with whom I played around, I would easily have 2,000 wives."

The boy's sensuality, which leaned toward music, was quite natural and healthy; it was not the refined sensuousness of the rococo age, which descends from a worn-out sensuality. The cry "Constance" at the start of the opera "Abduction from the Seraglio" certainly sounds longing and delicate enough. However, when Mozart reported to his father that he wanted to marry his Constance, he did not write romantic letters filled with desire and idealistic passion, as did Robert Schumann under similar circumstances. Mozart wrote: "My nature speaks as loudly as anybody's else's, and perhaps more so than in many a big, strong fool. I can not possibly live the way most young people live nowadays. In the first place, I have too much religion; secondly too much love of my neighbor; and my intentions are too honest to betray an innocent girl. And in the third place, I have too much terror and disgust, fear and shame of sicknesses and too much love for my health to romp around with whores." This does not sound visionary, but rather natural and frank. (From a letter dated December 15, 1781).

During his whole short life, Mozart's erotic temperament was tied up with his child fantasy.

When Mozart was composing, his wife had to sit down next to him and tell him children's stories. His letters to his wife are truly child-like, brimming with naive fun, puns and nonsensical rhymes. Like children, Mozart and his wife danced around the stove in the winter when they had no money to buy coal.

The love scene between Papageno and Papagena in "Magic Flute" is an idealized portrait of such childish dances. Mozart's erotic sense was playful, naive and gay. Even the virile eroticists created by Mozart's fancy —the Count in "Marriage of Figaro," and Don Giovanni — are visualized as comics. The romanticists eventually made Don Giovanni a demonic figure; to Mozart, the debaucher who gets into so much trouble with the women is just a buffo figure; the hero of a "drama giocoso."

The erotic tension that was the foundation of Mozart's music creation relaxed itself, while he was composing, to some extent in the same erotic jokes which we know from his boyhood letters. Mozart's brother-in-law, Joseph Lange, described Mozart's attitude while composing: "Never was Mozart less recognizable as a great man in his conversations and actions than when he was busy with an important opus. At such times he not only talked confused, but occasionally made jokes not becoming to him; he even deliberately neglected his manners. Yet he did not appear to be brooding and musing. Either he purposely concealed his innermost exertions under a cloak of extreme frivolity, or it pleased him to bring the divine ideas of his music in sharp contrast with commonplace notions, and to enjoy himself in a kind of self-sarcasm."

The blunt erotic jokes that Mozart told while composing were the sparks that flew from within him as from the wheels of a fast-moving vehicle. They were the surplus of the same erotic forces that turned to tones when he composed.

However, the erotic powers of musical imagination that make tone performance glow, and cause it to shine and radiate, have a second duty to perform.

Together with sensuality, which vibrates in harmony with the tones, these erotic powers do not merely give the tones their particular color, purity and a richer lustre. They also enhance the mood of the soul and of the collective emotions. They stimulate the memory and help to create that delirium-like condition in which the soul of the artist becomes more mobile, more flexible and more receptive.

Even the most pedantic, unimaginative, matter-of-fact man knows those moments when the world appears, as it were, in a new, stronger light; when he has visions and day-dreams; when emotions have more elan. This occurs mostly in the days of youth, when he is in love and in a sensual mood.

Such a condition evaporates rapidly in the barren business man; but when it extends over a life time, that man becomes an artist. For this reason Goethe attributed to the artist a "repeated puberty."

When, at the age of 64, Goethe fell in love with Ulrike Levetzov and, in the tempest of love emotions wrote his passionate "Marienbader Elegie," the aged minister and statesman, the councillor of Weimar, again became the youthful poet who wrote "Werther." He experienced love just as young Werther did, and he wrote the passionate verses of a young Werther.

Nobody described better than Goethe, himself, how love emotions immerse the world in glowing colors and stimulate the fantasy of the soul. He observed the changes in nature when, in 1787, he was in love, with Castel Gandolfo: "I let my glance roam all around, but my eye experienced something different than the picturesque scenery; a tone had enveloped the surroundings that could not be attributed either to the sunset or to the evening breezes alone. The glowing illumination of high spots, and the cool blue shade of the valley appeared more glorious than I had ever seen it pictured in oil or aquarelle: I could not look enough."

In similar manner amorous sentiments cause music to sound richer and fuller in the fantasy of the composer. If one were inclined to discount all the works in music that emerged from creative fancy due to love, love's desire and love's fulfillment, there would be no songs of the minnesingers, no madrigals, no "Abduction from the Seraglio," no Beethoven Adagios, no Schubert lieder, no Schumann music, no Chopin melodies, no "Tristan and Isolde," no first act of "Walkuere," no third act of "Siegfried," no Bruennhilde and no Evchen.

All lyricism would disappear from music as though the earth would suddenly dry up and all gardens would turn to desert. The loveliest melodies and most beautiful tunes would vanish from the world, as would the most beautiful poems of Petrarch, Goethe, Heine, Verlaine, and Lord Byron; as would Shakespeare's sonnets and his "Romeo and Juliet," Dante's Beatrice and the portraits of women painted by Raphael, Titian, Rubens and Leonardo da Vinci. Richard Wagner's tenet: "I cannot conceive the spirit of music other than in love" is well founded.

When Robert Schumann became engaged to Clara Wieck, erotic feelings, the tension, spiritual heat and longing of that period brought forth an abundance of the most beautiful music. The Sonata in F sharp Minor signified to him: "a single cry of the heart for my beloved."

While composing the "Davidsbuendlertaenze" during the same period, he wrote to his beloved: "The dances contain many wedding thoughts — they originated in the most beautiful agitation that I can ever remember." And: "But what is in the dances, my Clara will find out. More than anything else I have dedicated them to her. For the whole story is a nuptial eve (Polterabend), and you can picture beginning and end. If ever I was happy at the piano, it was while composing these dances."

Schumann joked about the "Novelettes," so called because "Wieckettes did not sound good."

And in another letter to Clara Wieck, he wrote: "I have learned that nothing gives wings to the imagination as much as suspense and desire for something. Such was the case in the last few days, when I was waiting for your letter and composed books full—some of it strange, some of it mad and even friendly—your eyes will open wide in surprise when you get to play it. As a matter of fact, sometimes I feel like bursting from all the music within me." . . . "I play my 'Kreisleriana' occasionally! A right wild love is contained in some of the movements, and so is your life and mine, and many of your glances."

"My dear Clara, not to write to you for a whole week —is that proper? But I mused about you, and thought of you with a love that I have never known before. The whole week long I sat at the piano and composed and wrote and laughed and cried alternately; all this you will find pictured in my opus 2 of the big Humoresque, which is already being engraved."

Later on he wrote: "My bride, in the Novelettes you appear in all kinds of positions, and in other things that are irresistible about you! Yes, look at me! I maintain that Novelettes could be written only by someone who knows eyes such as yours, has kissed lips like yours."

From out of these amorous moods Robert Schumann's song spring broke loose with irresistible might. "When I composed them (the lieder) I was completely tied up in you. Romantic girl that you are, your eyes follow me everywhere, and I have often thought to myself that without such a fiancée one cannot write such music."

No great composer employed love and amorous long-ing as fuel for his imagination to the extent that Beetho-ven did. Beginning with his youth in Bonn, when he was infatuated with vivacious, blonde Jeanette d'Hon-rath, and Werther-like in love with Fraeulein von West-erhold, all the way to his Vienna period a line of women from all walks of life accompanies him; some for a short time, others for a longer period, some as passing infatuations, others as the materialization of his dreams. His boyhood friend, Wegeler, reports: "In Vienna, as long as I lived there, Beethoven always had liaisons and he made conquests of women which would have been impossible, or difficult, for many an Adonis." And: "Beethoven was never without love and mostly gripped by love in the highest degree."

Beethoven was not one of those artists who, during their entire lifetime idealized their love in but one woman and made this woman their dream, as for in-stance Dante did with Beatrice Portinari. This dream appears in every one of Dante's works, from "Vita Nuova," where the girl first appears wreathed in can-zonets and sonnets, to his "Comedia Divina," in which Dante leads her to the halo of Paradise.

Nor was Beethoven a lover of Richard Wagner's type, to whom Jessie Laussot, Mathilde von Wesendonck and Cosima Buelow were incarnations of the same situation of his life and emotions: one and the same woman in three shapes. Neither was Beethoven a lover like Goethe, who found a woman in every phase of his life to embody the spiritual and emotional content of each particular epoch.

Again, he did not resemble the Don Juan type of Lord Byron. The eroticism in his personality was free-flowing. Every second of his life it searched for some object, like a fire that devours everything in its path and is nourished by it.

When Beethoven went walking in Vienna he stared at every good-looking woman (so Ferdinand Ries tells us), "particularly at those who had young, pretty faces. He turned around when he had passed a pretty girl, looked at her through his spectacles, laughed and grinned."

The women who appealed to him could just as well belong to the lower classes. Once he fell in love with the beautiful daughter of a tailor. Another time with a frivolous peasant girl. He kept staring at her while she stood on a dung-wagon, shoveling manure, until she finally drove away her admirer with scoffing words. However, he soon returned to have another look at the village beauty. (This was in the summer of 1815).

Still, hardly sensual pleasures were not foreign to the idealistic Beethoven. Sometimes his erotic life, similar to that of Brahms, was divided between earthly love enjoyment and ideal ecstasy. In his diary of the spring of 1817 one reads: "Sexual pleasure without union of souls is and remains brutish. After sexual enjoyment one has no emotion of noble feeling, rather repentance." And his diary of 1817 or 1818 states: "Only love, nothing but love can give you a happy life. O God, let me finally find the one who strengthens my virtue . . . whom I am allowed to love."

Of the women whom Beethoven loved, this contemplation precludes all those who, to Beethoven, were representative of the motherly type and among whom he sought mostly kindness, motherly care and protection.

One such woman was Helene von Breuning, in Bonn, whom he called "Mother". In Vienna it was Christianne von Lichnowsky, in whose house he lived from 1794 to 1796. Of her Beethoven's friend Schindler said: "she became Beethoven's second mother".

Another woman of this type was Countess Marie von Erdoedy, who may have reminded him of his mother on account of her sickliness. It is probably correct that Beethoven, as a friend of his reports, liked "weakly women" who brought to his mind the picture of his mother. Of Countess Erdoedy, Beethoven wrote: "She was a good and charming mother to me, my best friend." For a time Beethoven lived in the house of the petite, refined, always ailing countess. He wrote her philosophical letters and called her his "confessor". To her Beethoven dedicated the two Trios opus 70, and two cello sonatas, all of them music with mysterious and tragic moods.

Of chief importance to Beethoven's creative work were those women who stirred up within him reverie, longing, storms of passion and sentiments, which he needed for his work. One such woman was Therese Malfatti whom he celebrated in "Liederkreis an die ferne Geliebte" while he was unhappily in love with her; another was Therese von Brunswick, yet another Christine von Franck, or Bettina von Brentano and, above all, Giulietta Guicciardi.

Of all these women, no one evoked greater love passion in Beethoven than Giulietta. Of the beautiful, sensuous girl, who at sixteen was fully matured, Beethoven said that "he was deeply loved by her, and that she loved him more than she did her fiance (Count Gallenberg)". "My youth, yes, I feel so", Beethoven wrote during the time of happy love, "begins now. I always had been a sickly man. My bodily forces, however, increased since some time more than ever, and so, too, the forces of my imagination. Oh, it is so beautiful to live thousandfold. I am no more capable of living quietly."

It must have been a gripping moment of passion when Giulietta, fleeing from an unhappy marriage, came weeping to Beethoven and was repulsed by the maestro. "I despised her", his diary of 1823 tells us. Nevertheless Beethoven never forgot Giulietta. Her picture was found among Beethoven's estate.

The passionate letters found in a secret compartment of his desk after Beethoven's death—"letters to an immortal beloved"—were most certainly addressed to Giulietta Guicciardi. They are the three most tempestuous love letters in world literature, filled with ecstasies and passionate exclamations: "Love me—today—yesterday—what longing with tears for you—you—you—my life, my all—farewell—oh love me ever"; with tears, with avowals of love: "eternally yours, eternally mine, eternally us"; and with affectionate phrases: "my loyal, one and only sweetheart", "my immortal beloved", "my dearest soul".

In the C Sharp Minor piano sonata, which Beethoven dedicated to Giulietta, this passion has already given way to resignation which sounds movingly from the lament of the first movement. However, this resignation was already prepared in the love letters to the immortal sweetheart when Beethoven writes: "Why such profound grief where necessity speaks—can our love exist except by sacrifices, by not demanding everything, can you change matters that you are not wholly mine, I not entirely yours?"

This passionate love started off with resignation, and

THE EROTIC FORCES OF FANTASY

Beethoven wrote to his friend Wegeler, to whom he confessed his infatuation for the "enchanting girl who loves me and whom I love": "It is the first time that I feel marrying can make me happy. I am sorry that she is not of my class, and now I could not marry. I have still energetically work to do." (November 1801).

Love—whether it be spiritual, or erotic desire—did not represent to Beethoven material for a work of art as it did to Goethe when the latter wrote "Werther". Only very little music composed by Beethoven is a direct expression of amorous moods. The opera "Fidelio" glorifies marital love and the heroic action inspired by it. Love of liberty, heroism and marital love combined created the music of this opera. Here, love is not passion. It is not Werther reverie nor Isolde rapture. It is morality.

None of Beethoven's symphonies contain love music inspired by encounters, adventures or dreams. In the Ninth Symphony it is the love of mankind that rejoices, not the individual. Even in the more intimate music forms, such as piano sonatas, which contain so much personal love sentiment in compositions by Schumann and Chopin, we find only very little by Beethoven that could be termed love song. (The first movement of the piano sonata in A Major opus 101 belongs to this type of music).

In Beethoven's piano sonatas song means resignation, lament, or prayer, an upward glance to starry skies, or mystic rapture, rather than love. Of all Beethoven lieder, only "Liederkreis an die ferne Geliebte" can be brought into relation with an amorous adventure.

All this is decidedly remarkable for a composer who, according to his friends, "was always in love".

As far as Beethoven was concerned, love simply did

not mean material for tone creation, but enhancement of creative temper and erotic inspiration of the entire being. Love signified elevation to an idealistic world of pure forms. Eros led him to the land of fancy, just as Beatrice had led Dante to the lustre of Paradise. The erotic stream in the creative fantasy that becomes visible in Beethoven's life, imparts to this artistic imagination its energy, its impetus, its creative power.

In Goethe this erotic stream had become apparent in the succession of the women he loved—from Gretchen in Frankfurt and Friedericke von Sesenheim on to Charlotte Buff and Frau von Stein, from Lilly von Tuerckheim to Christine Vulpius, from the beauties of the Leipsic circle to Anna Willemer and Ulrike von Levetzow.

In Richard Wagner, the dramatist, this erotic stream separates into two parts—both equally strong and equally radiant. The one part is a violent sensuality. As he describes it in "Mitteilung an die Freunde": 'The phantastic dissoluteness of German student-life, after some violent excesses, had soon become distasteful to me; woman had begun to be a reality for me . . . The effect of the impression thus received found utterance in my actual life in the only way in which nature can express herself under the pressure of the moral bigotry of our social system as what people call unfortunately to-be-tolerated vice.'

Wagner admits, then, that this sensuality was already quite impetuous when he was a student at Leipsic. During the first stages of his creative work it drove him to write the opera "Das Liebesverbot" which glorified unrestrained sensuousness. Not unlike his Tannhaeuser, Wagner alighted at the Venusberg and caroused with Madame Venus.

[70]

THE EROTIC FORCES OF FANTASY

The strength of this material eroticism in Wagner is shown in "Parsifal", written when Wagner was almost seventy, in the person of Klingsor, who had to mutilate himself in order to curb his erotic lust. In "Parsifal" there is still a Venusberg, in the form of a magic garden with its flower girls.

It was this sensually-glowing erotic half of the Wagner personality that gave his orchestra the flaming colors and stormy rhythms, the voluptuousness of the Bacchanal, the ardour of mythological pictures, the Makartian colors.

The other part of the sensual stream had been transformed into a spiritualized gleaming and celestial purity. It was not enjoyment, but longing; not revelling, but devotion and solemnity: "Longing for gratification in an exalted, nobler element that had to appear to me as a pure, chaste, virginal, inaccessible, unassailable object of love". (Thus Wagner characterizes this part of his personality in the Tannhaeuser period). "What else, after all, could this love desire be—the noblest sentiment that I was able to experience in accordance with my nature—but a desire to vanish from the present, to die in an element of infinite non-existing love. This seemed attainable only in death."

This two-way sensuousness is embodied in "Tannhaeuser" in the persons of Tannhaeuser and Wolfram, in Venus and Elizabeth, in Venusberg dances and the pilgrims' chorus, in pagan and Christian song.

"A consumingly voluptuous excitement kept my blood and my nerves in feverish agitation while I was planning and executing the music to "Tannhaeuser" My true nature had returned to me in my disgust of the modern world and in my longing for something nobler, something most noble. As in a violent and ardent embrace it encompassed the most extreme contrasts of my character, both of which flowed into one stream: deepest love desire."

With such words Richard Wagner himself indicated that even the supersensuous longing in his nature was amorous desire. In the "Lohengrin" period he gave an even stronger indication when he wrote: "In 'Tannhaeuser' I had torn myself out of a frivolous sensuality that nauseated me; with the force of my longing I had swung myself to the desired peak of the pure, the chaste and the virginal. I felt as though I were outside the world, in a clear, sacred, ethereal element that fills me with wanton shudders in the enchantment of my solitude . . . It was just this blissful solitude that awakened within me—after hardly having received me—a new unspeakable longing: a craving to go from the summit to the depth; from the sunny gleam of chaste purity to the familiar shadow of the most human love embrace."

In the person of Lohengrin Wagner realized his longing from the summit to the depth, from the lustre of the Holy Grail to earth, from sacred service to the "familiar shadow of the most human love embrace."

It was the supersensuous half of Wagner's nature that inspired him to the seraphic tones of the Holy Grail in "Lohengrin", to the glistening and gleaming, the solemnity and timbre of religious services. It was this same supersensuous half that created the great moments in Wagner's works where all passion dissolves in tones of transfiguration, in the peace of a loftier world, in rustling and ringing, in ecstasy and oblivion.

In the ending of "Tristan and Isolde," death opens the gateway to heaven, where all love passion unfolds and dissolves in a pure element. In the finale of "Goetterdaemmerung", the old world of greed, power and execration perishes and a new world of love emerges solemnly. Both these endings are created to the same extent by the light components of Wagnerian sensuality, as is the finale of "Parsifal" with the glistening rustle of the harp and the heaven-aspiring choruses.

The same bi-partition of the erotic into an earthly half with sensuous craving, and a heavenly half with holy peace and transfiguration, re-formed by Richard Wagner to dramatico-musical pictures, had originated in Schopenhauer the doctrine of "The World as Will and Idea": the philosophy of the tempest of the will that revolves in Nirvana and thereby is redeemed.

Like Wagner, Schopenhauer had felt the sex demon. A poem, written by the philosopher in his youth, "O Wollust, O Hoelle" (O Lust, O Hell) proves how painfully he suffered under it. A notation of Schopenhauer's at the age of 25 shows perhaps even more distinctly than quotations from Wagner's writings, how the partition of the erotic into a hell and a heaven grows out of a metamorphosis and sublimation of part of the erotic forces, out of a spiritualization of one half of the general erotic stream; and how, through a combination of both, mental activity is enhanced:

"In days and hours when the sex impulse is strongest . . . a burning desire . . . that is exactly when the greatest forces of the spirit, even improved consciousness, are prepared for greatest activity, although the moment consciousness has submitted to desire, they are *latent*; however, it requires merely a mighty exertion to reverse the direction, and instead of that tormenting, necessitous, despairing desire—the realm of the night— it is the activity of the highest mental powers—the realm of light—that fills consciousness."

[73]

FROM BEETHOVEN TO SHOSTAKOVICH

No artistic person remains unfamiliar with the enhancement of the artistic powers of form vision and
form acoustics through eroticism. This intensifies the
lustre of the figures, causes the world to appear in a
magic light and gives the artist a stronger feeling of
power and of the creative, art-producing faculties.

The philosopher Plato, nephew of a poet, and himself a poet, wrote tragedies and dedicated a funereal
poem to Dion. His descriptions of Athenian youths encamped under a plane-tree are poems. In his sympo-
sium he lets Diotima proclaim the secret of the love
consecrations: erotic mysticism, the rule of Eros who
begets spiritual and physical beauty.

Eros signified to Plato agitation, longing, formation
and procreation; love, the path from the sensual world
to the supersensuous sphere. Poetry and music should
plant in the soul love of beauty as the seed of all exalted life, and are themselves one of the forms of Eros.

In modern times no one described better than Friedrich Gundolf the erotic powers that change to art. In
his "Goethe" book Gundolf writes: "Although the
artist finds himself in artistic condition to start with,
nevertheless the great poet distinguishes himself from
the ordinary person by always moving in a passionate
and loving element; he is simply man impassioned. Not
always does he find the objects of his dream, more rarely yet the embodiment of the dreams: still, he always
loves, is always a lover".

However, this too is still metaphorical language and
allegory rather than exact science. It is the language of
myth.

In the modern age it was Sigmund Freud who first
attempted to make a scientific analysis of eroticism and
its transformation into pictures, fantasies and art. To

psychiatrists who probed into the recesses of soul-life, erotic stimulation was one of the basic powers of the soul.

Originally, this basic force pervaded all living matter undivided; later it collected on individual islands, the so-called "erogenous zones": in the eye of the painter, the ear of the musician, in the plastic sense of the sculptor.

It associated itself with the emotional life of man. Some parts of this power sank down to the lower strata of the soul, whence they emerged as fear, as neurosis and hysteria, as phantoms and fantasies; they were subterranean forces that broke through all barriers set up by civilization.

It is probable that new research will alter the Freudian constructions. Such attempts were already made by Alfred Adler and C. G. Jung. However, we have a permanent benefit in the glimpse into the depth of the soul, and in the doctrine of the soul's strata. In the night of the soul live primitive forces, among the mightiest of which are the erotic powers. From the soul they arise, transform themselves, assume new shapes, are spiritualized.

When this path from night to light runs straight; when it is a natural growth, a lawful organizing, then it is that great works of art originate. But when this path is crooked, hemmed in and frequently divergent, the fantasies of the mentally ill are born.

Only in this sense are artistic creation and mental illness somewhat related, just as every type of sickness is a variation in the organization of life's forces. There may well be transitions from health to illness in the artist—even in Beethoven we find morbid traits, hallucinations, the many sudden changes of residence, emotional outbursts, even violence—still, mental illness is quite different from artistic work.

Anyone wanting to describe artistic creation must analyze it as natural forming and as organizing of all mental powers. It must be considered as spiritual shaping of sensuality which, in the musician, imparts color, light and lustre to the tones, creates tone figures and, by heating all emotional forces in a white-hot cauldron, as it were, brings all mental raw materials to the melting point. Thus the mental and the spiritual; sensuality and thoughts, emotions, moods, experiences and memories; wishes, dreams and energy are all made to melt in one single mold.

CHAPTER V.

The Subconscious

MODERN MAN no longer claims that god, a demon or some superhuman force speaks out of the composer. Nor does he say that the forces that awaken tones in his soul and build augmented forms from these tones are inspired by the muse. Neither does the composer consider himself any longer a brother of the prophets who played instruments to conjure visions, pictures and dark words out of their souls and, in a kind of delirium, to receive inspirations from an exalted world.

The powers that inspire his work are in his soul. Schumann, ill, might have believed he heard the angels playing and that an angel had been sent to him by Schubert. This angel is supposed to have sung him a melody which Schubert, dying, could no longer write down, and had given him the order to sketch it. Schumann, in good health, knew that music emanated from his own soul and that it was his mental work, in poetic mood, that patterned symphonies, piano compositions and lieder.

Albrecht Duerer, the painter, used to say: "A painter is inwardly full of diagram." Similarly, a great composer is inwardly filled with sounding diagrams that were created by his imagination. In a mental process in which his fantasy, as well as his thinking, his personal talents and his work participate, these diagrams become tonal vision.

[77]

The enhancement of emotional life which accompanies artistic work; erotic glow, the intoxicating intensification of his mental powers does not signify to the great composer that God speaks to him as He spoke to Moses from the burning hawthorn bush; he sees these phases as an arousing of all his spiritual forces, which is a prerequisite for his creative work because it removes barriers and inhibitions that otherwise would obstruct his fantasy in its free movements.

The path of fantasy leads from the deepest foundations of the soul, past its many layers, to the summit. Only the most perfect organization of all conscious and subconscious part-forces of the mind; harmonic collaboration of inherited traits, experiences and sentiments, memories and instincts, emotions and conscious thought, and extremely strong organizing power of personality can produce musical works of art.

There have been many composers who stopped dead in the middle of this path of imagination and who, from unshapen lumps and fragments, were unable to bring to light a finished piece of art. Just as in nature, so in art, too, there are premature births and abortions. There have also been many composers who succeeded only once, under a lucky star, in harmonizing all the talents necessary for creative work.

It was not originality of imagination that failed to function in other works by these same composers, regardless of how much else they composed; rather it was perfect co-ordination of all the wheels of imagination that was lacking, and which was perfect only in one single instance, in a lucky hour.

But even among the musical classicists, who accomplished such great feats in exemplary organization of the many spiritual and artistic forces necessary to creative work, there are minor works in which the most complicated of all machinery—the mental machine—functions only at half-strength.

Haydn and Mozart composed a good deal of work in commission; music that is certainly Haydnish and Mozartian. But this music does not originate in a fantasy that dissolves all animating substances on its upward flow from the depths of the soul to its peak. Or perhaps such fantasy does not come from the depths at all, merely from one of the higher layers where only technique is at work. Even Beethoven complained, in 1823, that he was not writing what he would have liked to, but, "for the sake of money, that which I have to." Such compositions were also Beethovenic, but not all the smelting furnaces of his fantasy were working, not all cauldrons were lit, not all wheels were in motion.

In works of this kind, composed by the classicists for special occasions—by Haydn as court composer for Count Esterhazy; by Mozart for friends, or to test his technique; by Beethoven in works for his publishers—it was not the imagination that had become weaker, but organizational work. This work did not reach down to the recesses of the unconscious, whence great creation emerges.

That was not necessarily the result of such works having been written on order. Many of the greatest compositions by the classic masters had been commissioned, among them Mozart's "Don Giovanni" and "Magic Flute". Many of the grandest masterpieces were composed for special occasions, one being Beethoven's "Missa Solemnis". Yet these works became mighty creations because the idea behind these works had the strength to conjure visions, moods and sentiments out of the subconscious mind where they had been stored for a long time.

Works of this type affected the whole personality of the composers; they called upon all the forces that led a shadowy existence deep down; they penetrated the soul in all its parts, in its dark and lighter layers, and they set in motion all potentialities of artistic organization. In such works formation, extending over much larger areas of soul-life, was greater than fantasy.

Musical fantasy had a much larger territory to conquer and to manage. Mozart and Beethoven were Mozart and Beethoven in the most minor form. Mozart's small chorus: "Ave Verum" is music that is just as pure, just as transfigured and as beautiful as "Magic Flute"; and Beethoven's smallest "Bagatelle" is swelled with his bold imagination equally as much as each of his symphonies.

But works like "Magic Flute" and a Beethoven symphony occupy a much larger portion of soul-space, extending broadwise as well as in the depth, and are created by the full exertion of all formative faculties.

For purpose of analyzing musical creation, the composers' work can be divided into three phases.

1) The preliminary work done by the subconscious
2) The combined work of unconscious and conscious mental powers
3) The conscious final polishing of the form.

All these three phases converge and mingle; all three are dominated by the same formative instinct, although the range of the three territories and their mutual relation may be different.

The complete harmony of these three consecutive phases of musical work characterizes the classical music work that found most perfect shape in the productions of Haendel and Mozart. Here we find the proportion between unconscious and conscious working forces in the most ideal balance. All the wheels in the factory of fantasy are geared in such a manner that there is never a stoppage.

The preliminary work of the unconscious collects tone material and connects internal and external adventures with the tone figures. Sentiments and passions that are to become melody and tone; personal life that molds the rhythm; the chaos that will become form, and the purification of these unshaped tonal masses by sense of beauty and conscious work, interlock with this preliminary work without any difficulty whatsoever.

Even in the greatest compositions, this melting of unconscious and conscious work is always uniform, a streaming and glowing, a hammering and growing. It is always the same force that carries the whole process of composition.

Haendel (we are told) was perhaps the fastest of all composers. Composition and sketching almost coincide with him, and the first sketch always determines the piece completely in its main traits. In executing the sketch another examination is made. Haendel's drafts offer to the least extent an image of inner development; not even the clues to guess at it. On the other hand we have, in his arrangements of his own compositions as well as of other people's works, an important medium of learning—if not the originating process of an individual work—at least the general conditions on which the formative power of his fancy was based.

Mozart's music grew in his fantasy like a tree in the soil. Rarely was this growth interrupted. We possess only slightly more than 100 of Mozart's fragments that were not completely shaped, in contrast to the many fragments of started works to be found in Beethoven's sketch books, lying there like marble splinters in the studio of a sculptor.

In addition to Beethoven's nine symphonies, we have his sketches to a C Minor symphony dating to the days of his youth in Bonn; also sketches to a symphony in B Minor and to symphonies in D Major, E-Flat Major, F Major (1814) and the draft of a tenth symphony.

From the years 1815 and 1816 we possess quite a number of incomplete fugue themes, the beginning of a double fugue in A Minor and another in D Major. From the year 1808 we have the plan of a piano concerto in F Minor; from the following year a sketch for a piano concerto in D Minor, and from 1815 and 1816 we find, in the midst of preparations to the piano sonata opus 111, the magnificent sketch of a piano concerto in D Major.

Beethoven's sketch books contained designs to the most varying compositions that remained torsos: songs, instrumental compositions, among them drafts of eight sonatas and five quartets, and the many sketches for a "Bach" overture. And Beethoven's "Bagatelles" are nothing else than fragments, designs and ideas that were not further developed or executed.

While the Beethoven composition process often assumed volcanic power, that of Mozart was always a blossoming, and his work was akin to the creation of nature: organic life that sprouts, grows, takes shape and transforms all substances of earth, moisture and air into roots, stalks, branches, leaves and blossoms.

The perfect harmony of all creative, generative and formative mental forces found in Haendel and Mozart, is attained by Beethoven by hard struggling. Only a combination of greatest ethical and moral strength and vigorous logical powers was capable of taming chaos in Beethoven and of subduing, in heavy battles of the soul, the eruptive violence of his subconscious, and molding it. A nature as tragic and heroic as Beethoven's did not convert passion to beauty without a struggle. This is what gives his work and his personality magnitude; but Beethoven's formative process is something unique, personal and inimitable; it is expression of his ethical and logical strength, not innate harmony as in Mozart.

Beethoven has often been represented as having formed the sublime in music, Mozart as having shaped beauty. That is not so. In Mozart, as in every profound nature, there is darkness, agitation and tragedy, too.

Mozart's C Minor Piano Concerto storms dismally, like a Beethoven concerto. Above such compositions as the G Minor String Quartet and the G Minor Symphony, above the C Minor Piano Fantasy of Mozart's and the D Minor String Quartet hover somber clouds. Mozart's feelings for tragic mood, which overshadows even the buffo opera, is quite evident in "Don Giovanni". But in Mozart the dismal, clouded, and deeply agitated characteristics are only a part of a general harmony; not, as was the case with Beethoven, a preponderant and independent part of his fantasy.

Only Mozart, therefore, can be compared with Shakespeare. Although little is known of the latter's method of working, this much we do know: that extreme tragedy, such as the emotional tempests of King Lear, and Hamlet's melancholia, the storms of jealousy in "Othello" and the love-fire in "Romeo and Juliet", was in perfect balance with extreme gaiety as it laughs and jokes in Shakespeare's comedies.

Only an artist of Shakespeare's caliber could,—burying Prospero's magic wand—say farewell to the stage with an ingenious fairytale; just as Mozart parted from the theatre with the kindred "Zauberfloete" rather than with the stereotyped "Titus". Wise Prospero is the next-of-kin to wise Sarastro, Miranda the sister of Pamina, and Caliban a variety of Monostatos. Fairytales, both, in which serious problems of humanity shine through in colorful pictures, and containing gaiety of spirit, smiling reverie, perfect balance of soul. In his great monologue, Prospero invokes "a solemn air, and the best comforter to an unsettled fancy", just as Mozart sounded it in the Sarastro arias and the priest choruses of "Zauberfloete".

Inbetween Mozart's harmony and Beethoven's taming strength stands Johann Sebastian Bach. In Bach— of whom Beethoven said he should be named 'Meer' (Sea, rather than Brook)—as in every mighty nature, there is passion, quaintness and boundlessness. His early compositions show this distinctly enough. That which we admire today as controlled strength, extreme order and concentrated power in the compositions of the Leipsic era is a superstructure above the mental tempests of Bach's subconscious.

Bach acquired his quiet force of forming when, in 1708, he came to peaceful Weimar as court organist and chamber musician and wrote cantatas for church services in the court chapel. The organ compositions of that period are still full of storm and stress. Albert Schweitzer characterizes them as follows: "The preludes are dramatically agitated, partly incoherent, non-uniform; the fugues are frequently confused. "

This youthful style was inspired more by the effects of the unconscious than by clear recognition of the form and conscious modeling ability. Study of works by Legrenzi, Corelli and Vivaldi purified this style and taught Bach how to transform passion, fermentation and exuberance into great, simple style.

The Weimar era meant the same to Bach as it did to Goethe: clarification and moralization of a titanic youth. In the case of Bach and Goethe alike, it was finally Italy that assisted them in their efforts and reared them to greatness.

Bach, himself, indicated in later years what he thought of the romantic compositions of his youth. Not one of his earlier works did he remodel, while he did re-mold his later masterpieces again and again until their form was quite pure—powerful in its simplicity.

Similar to Beethoven, Bach was surrounded by a solid, musical form-world where all storm and passion found its limitation. In Beethoven's work it was the Haydn symphony pattern that absorbed all eruptiveness and distributed it so that, instead of destroying like a stream of lava, it flowed white-hot through strong forms. With Bach, it was the traditional forms of organ music at which the centuries had been building, and the forms of Protestant church music which had an even longer history, that absorbed his agitated emotional world and his romantic mysticism.

Neither Bach nor Beethoven needed to create new forms, or, like the German "Stuermer und Draenger", and the French romanticists, they would probably have become what Goethe termed a 'fragmentary genius'. Beethoven would perhaps have developed as a kind of Berlioz, a subjectivist, a pathetic visionary, driven by passion and circling through the universe like a comet in an eccentric orbit. And Bach might have become in music what Mathias Gruenewald was as a painter in the 16th century: a feverishly excited portrayer of holy stories, the most forceful expressive artist, and an ecstaticist.

Their music would have been propelled by the emotions that erupt in the subconscious of artists, rather than by quietly forming, spiritual forces; it would have been a wild stream, an unending torrent. The collaboration of unconscious and conscious, which produces great style in music, would have remained incomplete. Its domination over the masses of sentiment would have been jeopardized by eruptions from the underworld of the soul.

This is conceivable if one considers how great the power of the visionary and the mystic was extant in Bach even in later years, when he created the 'Crucifixus' of the "Hohe Messe". The latter can compare only to the crucified figure upon Gruenewald's Isenheim altar, which is described by a modern author on art as follows: "A picture of misery, a lifeless figure that has tasted of physical tortures to the bitter end ... Never was the disconsolate feeling of total abandonment by God and man expressed so movingly."

It is further evidenced by individual moments of chaotic outbursts which Beethoven allowed to remain in his last great works, thereby showing the contrast to the great forms that arise victoriously from these works.

Only within the past four and a half decades have we had an insight into the dark recesses of the soul where works of art give their first sign of life. It was Sigmund Freud who descended into the deepest districts of the soul with the watchword: "Flectere si nequeo superos, Acheronta movebo" (If I cannot bend the heavenly forces, I will move the Hades). This is the motto of Freud's "Interpretation of Dreams."

Here was night, but in this night was life. Figures

moved. Emotions, buried under the cultural work of thousands of years, gave signs that they were not entirely destroyed. Primitive life, ancient ways of thinking, old fantasies, were still effective here. Here was the past of the human race. Here was the childhood of mankind. Nothing that had ever touched man had vanished altogether.

All that which was long buried and chained was in motion. It surged to the light of the conscious. It set the bright upper world in motion. Man's feelings were reinforced by old hate and old love ascending from the depths. Every idea of awakened consciousness drew forth, as with a net, whole bundles of figures, forms and tones from the depths. Particularly strong, rich powers of the unconscious motivated artistic creation.

The bright sphere of conscious soul-life is very small as compared to the dark realm of unconscious thoughts and sentiments. It resembles a tiny lamp in a dark cave. This cave is surrounded by a small, bright circle wherein our conscious ideas and inclinations move like moths hovering around a light.

Beneath this bright top layer of our soul is a darker sphere to which our memories descend, and whence they re-emerge. This process was called the "before-known" by Freud. Here we find everything that was at one time conscious but which later disappeared in the night of oblivion and which may again reach the conscious mind.

We like to imagine the artist as being especially well endowed with such visions and emotions which, on the strength of similar or related ideas—"associations"—can again become conscious. A strong sensual memory for body outlines characterizes the sculptor; a keen memory for scenes of nature and universe, for patterns and colors, facial contours and bodily motions marks the painter; a strong memory for experienced emotions that convert to tone and rhythm makes the musician. And it is a memory for both: pictures of the external world and tones and rhythms of the intrinsic world, that marks the poet.

Goethe termed this reminiscing of the poet "Learning nature by heart". Shakespeare employed approximately 1500 words in his poems and plays, while the average Englishman uses three to four thousand words in his colloquial language. This represents a huge amount of ideas, observations and recollections, a wealth of memories second to none.

All great musicians experienced the sensitivity of emotional life in childhood already to a great degree. If so many famous musicians demonstrated their musical ability so early in life, it was not just because their acoustic sense was prematurely strong or their instinct for playing with tones had awakened at an early period. It indicated that their emotional life was in violent agitation.

It was this which made child prodigies of many great musicians. One such was Haendel. When shown the six sonatas for 2 oboes and bass which he had composed in his tenth year, Haendel remarked: "I used to write like the devil in those days".

Haendel's biographer Chrysander describes Haendel's enjoyment of music in his childhood: "He lived and weaved tones from infancy; he listened to them, ran after them and began making music on his own when he was barely able to use his limbs. Horn and trumpet, bassoon and flute, drum and jew's harp, and whatever else Santa Claus used to bring formed the beginning of his orchestra. Haendel spent many secret hours at the clavichord that had been spirited into his parent's house."

"In my fourth year, music began to be my foremost childhood occupation", one can read in the dedicatory prologue of Beethoven's first piano sonatas (1783).

Schubert's musical nature also became apparent at a very delicate age. In his parent's home he liked to busy himself with the old piano, and derived particular pleasure from hanging around a piano workshop where he was taken occasionally by a relative of his who was a cabinet-maker's helper. As a pupil in elementary school, Schubert could already play piano, violin and organ. In the church choir he sang the soli and at an early stage started to capture musical thoughts on paper.

Felix Mendelssohn-Bartholdy began to play piano in his seventh year. Likewise, Robert Schumann who, at the age of seven, essayed little dances and free fantasies. He also portrayed his school friends on the piano in the same manner as he portrayed, in later years, Clara Wieck, Chopin and Paganini in "Carneval"

Of all the child prodigies, Mozart was the most precocious.

When Papa Mozart instructed his small daughter in playing piano, it made such an impression on three year old Wolfgang that he sat down at the instrument and amused himself by trying to locate thirds. "As soon as he began to occupy himself with music (writes Schachtner), all his interests for all other matters were as good as dead, and even roundelays and children's games failed to arouse his interest, unless they were accompanied by music. When he and I carried toys from one room to another, the one who went emptyhanded had to sing an accompanying march and play the violin.

"However, since taking up with music he became so receptive to every kind of childish trick that was spiced with a bit of wit, that he could forget eating and drinking and everything else over it."

Remarkable, too, are the serious traits of the usually gay boy at music. In a letter by Mozart's father one can read: "As a child and young boy you were more serious than childlike, and when you sat at the piano, or were otherwise occupied with music, no one dared to make even the least fun. Why, even in your physiognomy you were so serious that many sensible persons were inclined to worry for your young life because of the talent that was sprouting too early and because of your ever gravely thoughtful facial expression."

When Mozart was in his fourth year, his father had undertaken to instruct the child in piano playing. In his fifth year he was already composing little tunes. He played them for his father, who then set them down on paper. At the age of seven, Mozart gave performances on the piano, at the organ and on the violin, and was admired for his skill as an accompanist. Four sonatas for violin and piano—Mozart's first engraved compositions—date back to that period.

Mozart's enjoyment of tone essence and the sensual forces of music; his delight in playing with tones, as well as his pleasure in improvising with tones, were awakened by the rich emotional life of the boy. His emotional sensitivity manifested itself in the quick transition from mirth to tears, in his easy impressionability, his invention of fables and in his affectionate relationship to his father. Until he reached the age of ten, he never went to bed before standing up on a chair and singing a song for his father which he, himself, had composed, (Oragna fiagata, fa marina gamina fa—a meaningless, Italian sounding text), and then planting a kiss upon the tip of his father's nose.

The memories of childhood moods never left Mozart. He remembered very distinctly the sentiments of that time and could at any time transplant himself to the world of childish feelings. The letters that Mozart wrote to his wife from Vienna are replete with the same jokes and nonsensical rhymes and puns as the letters that Mozart wrote from Italy as a boy. They contain the same gaiety, the same laughter, the same playful happiness.

The Salzburg clown is still inherent in the mature Mozart, who had his harlequin costume forwarded from Salzburg to Vienna because he liked to dance and jest in it. His raillery with women at costume balls, where he embraced the waist of his partners, are real juvenile jests and, following his custom as a boy, so too, in later years, he flies laughing, joking and bantering from one woman to another. As in his childhood days, his mood changes rapidly from laughing to weeping, and he has "black thoughts", of which he spoke during the period in which he composed his three greatest symphonies.

A childlike, fabulous glimmer lies upon all compositions; it is a gay lustre that is the reflection of a blissful youth. No matter how keen his judgment of people, no matter how realistic the characters of "Abduction from the Seraglio", "Marriage of Figaro" and "Don Giovanni"—Mozart never lost his childish naivité. The man who wrote the songs of Papageno and Papagena in "Magic Flute" had always remained a child, with all the sentiments of an innocent childhood in his heart.

In Mozart's life there is no marked distinction between the time of childhood, the time of his youth and that of the adult man. All these periods intermingle, and Mozart is always in a humour to return to his childhood. Thus he was capable of toying even with the tragic, as he did in "Don Giovanni", and of injecting fun into the solemnity of "Magic Flute".

Beethoven, on the other hand, was grave and gloomy as a child. In a report by the violincellist Maeurer one reads: "Even as a child he was introvert and serious; the usual children's games were never entertaining to him." He is described as being "sullen among other people". Doctor Mueller also describes him as "shy and taciturn".

What a difference between Beethoven, who as a child was already a man, and Mozart who, as a man, was still a child because the recollections of a happy youth always surrounded him, even in later life, and the psychic moods of childhood days were alive in the mature man.

The early awakening of strong emotions in childhood is proven among many composers.

Chopin as a child reacted so strongly to tones that at the sound of music, he began to weep. The same is told of Tschaikowsky. He was found in bed, crying convulsively one evening when there had been a lot of music in his parent's home. Questioned as to what was wrong with him, he sobbed: "This music! It is right here, in my head. Free me of it!"

The emotional life of Richard Wagner was especially violent in his childhood. In his autobiography, Wagner relates his fear of ghosts and furniture which, when he was alone in a room, seemed to come alive. He then "yelled out loud in his fright".

In the portraits of noble ladies hanging upon the walls of his bedroom in Leipsic, he saw ghostly beings that filled him with great terror. "Sleeping alone in such a remote, big room, in the antique state-bed, in the proximity of such an eerie picture was terrible to me. Of course I tried to conceal my fear from my aunt when she accompanied me to bed with a light; nevertheless there was not a night that I was not bathed in sweat from having been exposed to the most awful apparitions."

Nightmares were especially violent in Wagner as a child. "Not a night passed, as late as my last boyhood years, but that I woke up from some nightmare with terrible screams that did not cease until some human voice bade me be quiet. The most violent scolding, even physical punishment, then seemed to me a kind relief. None of my sisters or brothers would sleep near me any more; they tried to bed me as far away from the others as possible, not realizing that my ghastly cries for help only became louder and longer lasting. Finally they became accustomed to this nightly calamity."

Pediatricians associate this fear with an early awakening of erotic life in the child. Actually, Richard Wagner's first infatuation did coincide with this period; he was in love with Amalie Hoffmann who "astounded the boy to long lasting speechlessness."

Still greater proof is an episode told by the aging Wagner in his autobiography: "Other times I can recall having simulated insensible sleepiness in order to be brought to bed by the girls with efforts seemingly necessitated by this condition; for I had once noticed to my exciting surprise that a similar condition had brought me in close contact with the female being that pleased me."

Other signs of the unusual emotional agitation in

the Wagner child are his acrobatic inclinations (even as an old man he sometimes stood on his head in moments of excessive gaiety); his "tussling and his pugnacity". To suppress his boyish sensuality, he took refuge in religious moods wherein the boy wished himself in the stead of the Saviour at the cross.

No important composer was in a greater turmoil in his youth than was Beethoven. The harshness and strictness of his father, the father's drunkenness and the pressure of a hard childhood weighed upon the boy's soul. Many witnesses saw the child standing at the piano and crying. When his father came home at night, intoxicated, accompanied by his friends from the tavern, the boy was awakened and chased to the piano.

One witness (Justizrath Krupp) reports that the father, in his drunkenness, often locked the child in the cellar.

Thus Beethoven the boy grew taciturn and uncommunicative—in his Bonn days he was called a "lovable, softspoken man—inclined toward sudden outbursts of rage."

He was pervaded by a fear of becoming consumptive, and morbid thoughts attached themselves to this fear. "It is a poor man who knows not how to die", Beethoven said in 1816 to Fraeulein Giannatsio de Rio; "I already knew it as a boy". Often he was dirty and neglected. His contemporary and classmate Wurzer reports: "Ludwig von Beethoven distinguished himself in particular by uncleanliness, neglect, etc."

Nevertheless the boy was also possessed of a superiority complex; when Caecilia Fischer once called his attention to his untidiness, the boy answered: "What does it matter, someday I'll be a gentleman and then nobody will notice it".

Longing for love, desire for liberty and dreams of happy people must have been present in the boy to counteract sadness, melancholia and depression; and all these contrasts excited the boy with violent emotions that erupted whenever similar feelings and situations arose in Beethoven's later life and brought recollections of juvenile sentiments.

The period of greatest mental agitation in a boy's life is puberty with its storms, its concentration of erotic forces and its transition from child to man. Within this period the childish joy of playing with tones allies itself strongly with emotional life in the composer, and among most composers this is the time when the productive impulse comes to the fore.

Most of Beethoven's "Bagatelles" opus 33 were composed in his twelfth year, and in the same year Beethoven's first piano sonatas were published. Schubert wrote his Fantasy for Four Hands—the first of his early works to be preserved for posterity—at the age of thirteen. Chopin's opus 1, a Rondo in the minor key, was composed at the age of fifteen, and six Fughettes by Karl Maria von Weber were published by his teacher, Michael Haydn, when the pupil was twelve years old. Between the ages of twelve and fourteen, Karl Maria von Weber wrote an opera (The Might of Love and Wine), a large mass, trios and other instumental works; in his eleventh year Mendelssohn composed a violin sonata, two piano sonatas, a small cantata, lieder and male quartets.

True, Mozart's first compositions appear as early as his fifth year, but this is an exception; for in Mozart, more than in any other composer, childhood moods, child play and child joy form the foundation of his fantasy. His genius, more than that of other musicians, was the genius of his youth, and he relates its gay and shining stories in his music.

Mozart's whole life, all his sentiments, his melodies and his tonal plays, his graceful passages and lucid forms, his brilliant mind and spiritual charm, tonal sense and appreciation of beauty: all these were life, emotion and music of a divine adolescence which, during Mozart's entire lifetime, was the real creative power.

All recollections, pictures, figures, landscapes, experiences and sentiments of past times that have descended into the darkness of oblivion, pass colorfully and plastically through the souls of the artists. They can be revived at any given time, and an artist without extreme strength of memory for such recollections is just as unthinkable as the artist without an imagination that is capable of employing such recollections in new associations.

The composers' recollection of sentiments and moods with which their music is permeated, is always alive Joy and grief; fun and earnestness; love and devotion not only possess greater depth in musicians, but greater soul energy as well, which preserves this memory. In the mobile fantasy of the musician emotions are preserved with the most minute gradations of color and rhythm.

More important to artistic creation than the recollections that aim toward consciousness and that are encamped about the halo of conscious soul life, are the spiritual forces that are at home in the "subconscious," in the deep strata of the soul and in the dungeons of the structure of the human soul. They are not, like the "pre-conscious," memories that protrude from the conscious, and they are not able to re-appear at will.

THE SUBCONSCIOUS

They have been forced away from the conscious, and the same power that thrust them into the dark abyss of the soul keeps them prisoner there. They are captives in chains: impulses, emotions, sentiments that have been suppressed by the moral and cultural development of man, albeit not deprived of complete efficaciousness.

These are the impulses and ideas that transform themselves into dream visions and, masked as such, enter the conscious mind. The fear that accompanies so many dreams and which, in Richard Wagner's dreams, recurs regularly in such violent form, reveals clearly enough that the impulses that produced nightmares are considered immoral or evil.

Titanic powers of the human soul: hatred, destructiveness, cruelty, hostility toward close relatives, erotic desires crowd the subconscious. If these powers are transformed entirely into the spiritual, then out of destructiveness can emerge wit, caricatures, revolutionary activity. Cruelty can change to compassion for the trials of our neighbors; animosity toward a father can become scientific criticism and liberality of mind; and eroticism can be elevated to brotherly love, cosmopolitanism, or to love of beauty and art.

Human idealism is a transfiguration and an ennobling of the suppressed emotions of the human soul.

However, when the sublimation of these inclinations does not succeed entirely—and all human culture and all moral progress is based on such success—parts of them are supplanted to the unconscious where they become mental illness, hysteria, neurosis, hallucinations; in the ordinary man they become dreams, in the creative man, works of art.

FROM BEETHOVEN TO SHOSTAKOVICH

"Was dem Menschen *unbewusst*
Oder gar veracht
Durch das Labyrinth der Brust
Wandelt durch die Nacht"

("What is unconscious in men
or even despised, is wandering
through the labyrinth of the soul
during the night.")

Goethe wrote pensively, and "The artist is the knower of the unconscious" Richard Wagner recognized.

The artist possesses the strength of organizing with his imagination the impulses of the unconscious that attack the borders of the conscious, as well as man's psychic underground and the displaced, incarcerated impulses. He transforms them to shapes, patterns, melodies. He makes these impulses, which otherwise would destroy and ravage, useful, and erects barriers and dams that turn wild torrents into placid flowing waters that drive the mills.

That which in mental illness lacerates the soul, or forcibly invades it, or makes it a toy of uncontrolled emotions; and that which in dreams joins one seemingly meaningless picture to another, in the work of art becomes intellectually organized form and logical unity that connect fantasy and thinking.

It is not a rare case that of two brothers, the one who possesses organizing creative talent succeeds in mastering the subconscious while the other one does not.

An example is set by the Grillparzer brothers, the great Austrian poet Franz and his brother Adolf. The former had the talent for transforming the elemental life of the subconscious into tragedies and poems; the

[98]

latter was overcome by the unconscious. True, he had attempted to balance his emotional forces with poetic works, and among his estate was found a tragic drama, "Sodenberg, the Sufferer, or the Salvation," a play in four acts. However, this attempt at unburdening himself poetically miscarried. Less talented in the poetic field than his brother, he committed suicide.

In music, Gustav Mahler and his brother Otto represent a like instance. Gustav Mahler, the great composer, in his ingenuity found the means of changing into musical shape everything that was a violent and oftentimes dark, psychic storm in his subconscious; the result was lieder—which are sketches of his symphonies —and symphonies.

The task was no easy one, and the nervous tension of Mahler's Ahasueric nature often increased to morbid violence in his music. All his symphonies are filled with psychic battles. Outbursts of shrill laughter are not uncommon, convulsive screams break forth, often the music writhes as in a "grand arc" of hysteria. There is satanism in many of his symphonies. In the fourth symphony Death plays upon a violin that is out of tune.

Similar distress and torture of mind is found only in Strindberg when the Nordic poet was grasped in the claws of agitated mysticism. Death and the Devil threaten in both artists. Life appears grotesque, a spectre.

Despite all mental struggles, Gustav Mahler found relief only from time to time, never permanently. No sooner had he reached God and the Angels in Heaven, than he plunged right down again to Hell. No sooner did Eternal Love receive him, than he succumbs to despair. Following the jubilation of the "Eighth Symphony," he again saw distorted nocturnal apparitions. Thus Mahler belongs to the great split personalities among modern artists: Dostojewsky, Strindberg, Huysmanns, Baudelaire, Edgar Poe.

While Gustav Mahler succeeded—at least temporarily—in liberating himself in creative work, his brother Otto did not. This brother was also a musician, and Gustav Mahler valued him as such and took care of his education.

Otto Mahler finally became choir master in several small German towns: a torn personality who envied his brother's greatness and probably felt himself crushed by it. Like Gustav Mahler, he was an admirer of Dostojewsky, and like Raskolnikov he philosophized on life and death before finally seeking death.

Another brother of Gustav Mahler's, Alois, apparently the least talented, turned out to be a lunatic whose mental life was wasted in illusions of grandeur, in lies and fantasies. Finally he forged banknotes to pay his debts, and fled to America, where he disappeared.

Alma Mahler wrote correctly about the composer's brothers: "They are the sheet lightening which portends the real thing, the chaotic element which precedes creation."

Gustav Mahler was capable of organizing artistically the chaos of the unknown in his soul. Otto Mahler lacked this ability and was destroyed by the chaos, while Alois Mahler lost his equilibrium on account of chaos.

In this connection mention can be made that Beethoven's brother, Johann Christophe, was a lunatic, too. The feeling of grandeur that turned to heroic music in the genius became comical folly in the brother. He was conceited about his wealth and rode through the streets of Vienna with four white horses. Everybody called him "Prince Christophe" and laughed about the funny man who sat atop the box of his coach, snapping the whip.

THE SUBCONSCIOUS

In letters to Brother Johann, "Landowner," Beethoven signed himself, Ludwig van Beethoven, "Brainowner."

Artistic work means: "mental unburdening." This was expressed most clearly by the poet Hebbel in his diaries, which constitute one of the most important sources for the comprehension of artistic work.

One entry reads: "The first entreaty with which I venture before the Throne of Eternal Power in this new year, is the request for material for greater portrayal. I require a receptacle for many things that are in upheaval within me if everything that has torn loose from me is not to recede and destroy me."

The same thought is given utterance even more keenly in the prologue to Hebbel's Drama "Maria Magdalena": "A repressed, or impossible, spiritual delivery can result in destruction to the same extent as a physical delivery, be it by death or insanity."

No less intelligently did the tragic poet Hebbel write in his diary on Shakespeare: "That Shakespeare created murderers was his salvation, for he thereby eliminated the possibility of becoming a murderer himself. This may be saying too much in the face of such strength. Still, one can well imagine a broken poetic nature in which elemental life—restrained in other people, and in perfect balance as a matter of course while in the artist it is unleashed and must rely on a balance yet to be acquired—erupts directly in acts because the artistic production is either stifled, or suffers mishaps in delivery."

Of equal significance is a statement made by Brahms that Beethoven, under different circumstances, might have become a master criminal. The masses of repressed emotions were surely very large in Beethoven. They imparted aggressive force to his rhythm, and this aggressiveness in turn distinguished the new rhythm from that of Haydn and Mozart, which had been playful and harmonious. Beethoven rhythm marches forward like an attacking army; it is a rhythm that is vehement and that vanquishes all opposition. It is a prostrating rhythm and, like the main theme of Beethoven's Fifth Symphony, a clenched fist. Of this theme Beethoven said: "Thus fate knocks at the gate!"

Such rhythm possesses elemental power rather than human force. Never before did a composer dare to concentrate a symphonic theme entirely upon the rhythm, as Beethoven did here in attempting to portray tragic might in music—a might that descends upon life and strikes down everything. There is no preparation, no gathering of storm laden moods, as in the beginning of the "Ninth Symphony." Four notes: a crash; a blow.

The aggressive force of the Beethoven rhythm is expanded and enhanced to heroic proportions in the Third Symphony, while it assumes a bright glow in the first movement of the Seventh Symphony.

Even before Beethoven found the theme of the Allegro in his sketches of the Seventh Symphony, the rhythm broke away from him, and the dactylic rhythm took possession of all melodic ideas. Even the melody of the scherzo—which did not receive its ¾ tempo until later —was involved by this rhythm.

Rhythm was the elementary occurrence from which the Seventh Symphony sprang. It had primitive power, tamed by artistic work. It was motion of the soul personified which broke forth from the subconscious and, having reached the higher regions of the soul, first became a musical frame and then a series of sounding pictures.

Beethoven's great achievement is the spiritual domination of the rhythmic. Just as in Shakespeare's "Tempest" Caliban becomes Prospero's servant so, in Beethoven music, do the elemental forces of rhythm (which in the bloody, primeval ages of mankind increased to orgiastic wildness) become the servant of the mind, gay play and the smile of wisdom.

The battles of rhythms in Beethoven music indicate the struggling of mental powers. The Beethoven Piano Sonata in E Minor, opus 70, gives a picture of such rhythm wrestling. The first theme has the jambic rhythm (short—long, short—long) pulsating in all melodies and themes of the first part. This rhythm assumes ever new forms, and appears in energetic and in delicate figures.

The second theme has the rhythm in reverse: (long —short,   )

Between both parts, however, we have a fight of both contrasting rhythms. Resistance meets the first rhythm. In the basses, those of the second rhythm storm against the basses of the first rhythm, which is fighting for its life. Its rhythmic strength lessens increasingly. The weapons are knocked out of rhythm's hands, its accents lose strength.

There follows a final, breathtaking struggle. The first rhythm wrestles despairingly—increasing its last forces in three bars from pianissimo to fortissimo, and then finally collapsing in a diminuendo:

With the menacing beats of the ninth chords, the victory of the second rhythm is won.

However, Beethoven would not have been the great heroic character had he not caused the vanquished combatant to arise once more. Dying, it lifts itself up:

And then the first rhythm breaks down completely with two heavy sighs, and gives up its spirit:

Beethoven dramatized rhythm. But dramatic life with its contrasts, its conflicts and its battles pre-supposes passions which often were visible in the external life of dramatists; so, for instance, in the unrest and stormy movement of Richard Wagner's life, in the excited wanderings from place to place, from the sea to the high mountains, from cities into nature.

The tumult in Richard Wagner's soul repeatedly tore him away from his means of existence. Wagner himself, in his autobiography, speaks of his "restless, often violently erupting inclination to break off with everything that was habitual." This turmoil in his soul is a reflection of his inner conflicts.

These inner conflicts between repressed emotions that storm in the depth of the soul, and conscious forces of will and spirit were so violent even in the fifty year old Wagner, that he often contemplated suicide in order to escape them.

Such conflicts were not strange to any dramatic genius—i.e. any man whose creative work lives upon such conflicts, which he transforms into artistic visions of battle and decline.

Young Schiller's life, with flight, passionate infatuations, debts and catastrophes, resembled Wagner's life. At Sachsenhausen Schiller wanted to end his "useless life" by jumping off the bridge into the river.

Goethe described in a letter to Zelter the resolutions and efforts he made during the period of Werther passion to escape the waves of death. And Beethoven wrote to Frau Streicher: "During the night I thought often of my death; but such thoughts are not foreign to me by day, either," and in 1817 he wrote yet to Zmeskall: "I am often in despair and would like to put an end to my life . . . May God have mercy on me, I consider myself almost lost."

On his fiftieth birthday, Wagner wrote to Frau Wille "I cannot tell of my desire for the final rest, my heart no longer can endure this fraud." And to Weisheimer:

"I cannot go on, and I feel too strange in this world in which I feel inhibited about everything, art and life, design and disposition. I have no desire any more, the shock and recognition of the individual's impotency are too great and definite. Of me it can be said simply—enough of life." (June 18, 1836).

Even Mozart speaks of "black thoughts" which he must "forcibly talk himself out of" (letter of June 2, 1788).

Goethe fled from the tragic when, at the peak of his life, he brought his life into classic pattern. He wanted to suppress the destructive, dangerous forces of the unconscious,. which he termed "the demonic." He told Schiller frankly he didn't know whether he could write a genuine tragedy. Just the idea frightened him, and he was almost convinced "that he might destroy himself in the attempt."

In his mature age Goethe no longer wanted to read "Werther" as the book of tragic passion; nor did he wish to attend a performance of "Tasso," for "what good will the memory do me of the days when I felt, thought and wrote all that?" To such an extent did he fear meeting the midnight forces of his soul.

When Shakespeare retired to Stratford-on-Avon at the age of 49, a celebrated stage poet, to live there as a farmer, it may have been because the poet who brought ever darker clouds of misanthropy and hatred of life onto the stage—from "Hamlet" to "Timon"—and who, in "King Lear" lets nature and human souls erupt in mighty tempests, tried to find rest in the peace of nature. "To be nothing higher than a simple shepherd" seemed to him a happy life even in "Henry the Sixth."

Beethoven withstood all these storms. No matter what volcanic, menacing, ravaging forces arose in his subconscious, he transformed them into great artistic form. Not the Beethoven rhythm alone is the victory of intellect, of creative strength and of moral courage against dark powers which, restlessly, violently and full of aggressive energy, attempt repeatedly to erupt from the gorges of emotional life and which, when dominated less artistically, could have become chaotic or destructive.

Beethoven dynamics give the same picture as the rhythm. Differing from those of Haydn and Mozart, they are not a balance of accents, or harmony in the contrasts between strong and weak, an even distribution of dark and light.

The crescendo and decrescendo of tones in Haydn and Mozart music is always a transition, never, as in Beethoven works, an eruption, a dramatic medium or a tempest, an accumulation of increasingly large masses as in the "Leonore" overture, or at the start of the Ninth Symphony. The dynamics convulse the musical structure from the foundation, like an earthquake. They quiver and jog, threatening to pierce the musical form any minute.

A theme such as the first theme of the Eroica has, within thirteen bars, six dynamic designations, distributed entirely without symmetry. Twice it increases, twice the force that propels its tones decreases in power:

Often enough Beethoven lets outbursts of extreme violence explode at the very moment when he had completely quieted down the tones. Such was the case at
the beginning of the C Minor Piano Sonata opus 111
toward the finale of the introduction. Here, everything
is finally pacified when suddenly, in the moment of
greatest calm—pianissimo—there is a droning deep
down. The drone increases, and from out of the droning there erupts, fortissimo, the theme of the Allegro:

[109]

THE SUBCONSCIOUS

The same thing occurs in grandest style, and on the broadest music surface, at the end of the modulation of the Eroica allegro: powerful outbursts, mighty chords of dissonances, a progressive suppressing of the disturbed tonal masses, an increasing weakening of the tones, gentle vibrating full of tension, stillness and the sounding of the theme as from a distance, then again an eruption of full strength and a joyous advance of the themes.

One of Beethoven's most characteristic forms of dynamic expression is the "sudden piano" following a forte or a crescendo: a controlling of excitement by willpower and spiritual strength. Only a composer like Beethoven—who controlled his emotions so strictly because he recognized the danger of uncontrolled forces in the psychical underworld—could write a phrase such as we find at the beginning of the "Appassionata": Again a calming down and a sudden outburst, a strong chord ("get back") and a 'sudden piano.'

Just like every other musical means of expression, the harmonious ones are music of Beethoven's soul, and the discords are signs of struggling forces. Neither a Mozart nor a Haydn risked beginning a symphony on a discord, as Beethoven did in his First Symphony. Neither did anyone dare to interpose in a symphonic theme the dispersing force of a dissonance, as Beethoven did in the Eroica. (see theme on page 105, from the 5th bar on, where rhythmic discord: syncopation in the treble; dynamic discord: the crescendo; and harmonic dissonance: the seventh chord, meet. A picture of battle in the middle of the theme.)

No one wrote a "Rueckfuehrung" such as that contained in the first movement of the Ninth Symphony, where the agitation of the execution and its struggles pervade the repeat phrase; where dissonant chords rain down and the big pedal-note of the kettledrums holds the dissonant masses together as with a giant fist.

If one hears music as that which it is: soul motion of the composer in sounding forms—one can understand that such music emerges from abysses where the emotions possess impulsive strength and are not yet refined by civilization and human evolution, nor regulated or toned down. They still have the full force of nature. They are uncontrolled and vehement; they erupt from the soul like geysers and often, from the viewpoint of civilized man, they are destructive.

THE SUBCONSCIOUS

There is deep meaning in the words of the poet Hebbel, when he enters in his diary: "Great talents are great phenomena of nature, like all others. A Shakespeare tragedy, a symphony by Beethoven and a tempest are all based on the same principle."

To be sure, great artists like Beethoven also possess the spiritual strength with which to master all the stormy masses of emotions, and to shape that which is excessive. Everything in his soul that had crowded into the subconscious and that threatened to deluge him, was transmitted into great forms and mighty rhythms. All conflicting sentiments are transformed into discords that must conform to the general law of harmonic motion. Whatever glowed and sizzled in dramatic dynamics was made artistic expression.

As a child Beethoven already knew the ardent powers of the soul, the outbursts of hate and fury, of wild, ravaging emotions, of unconscious and suppressed hostility.

His father's brutality, the mental cruelties inflicted by the drunkard, had to instill in the Beethoven child impulses of resistance. If, in this frequently dark period of childhood and early youth, he was described as "softspoken" or as a boy of "good, quiet manners," as "gravely meditating" and as "shy and taciturn," occasionally even as melancholy and unsociable, then it was simply because the boy had withdrawn entirely into his own self.

What a contrast to the boy Mozart who was always ready for fun and laughing nonsense. What a difference, too, between the "dirty and neglected Beethoven boy" and Mozart, always neatly attired, as shown in early pictures. In later years, too, Mozart loved elegant clothes, whereas Beethoven knew periods in later years

[113]

when he neglected himself: the outward sign of depressed moods.

Although a report about Beethoven's youth claims "the customary children's games never afforded him entertainment," one sometimes hears: "he enjoyed being carried piggy-back, and laughed right heartily." But we know how rattling was Beethoven's laugh. It came out of the mouth of a man who forced himself to laugh and who was not accustomed to a gay, untroubled chuckle.

Even though Beethoven's resentment of his father's rough treatment may have been shifted to his subconscious mind, there it remained a dominating sentiment in many forms: as rebellion against any kind of pressure and coercion which often assumed violent forms (for instance, when he cried out "I won't play for such pigs!" in the house of Count Browne); as uncontrolled fits of rage; it showed in Beethoven's enjoyment of the opposition speeches in the English Parliament, and in his admiration for Caesar's murderer, Brutus, whose statue stood in his room.

The extent to which such feeling of hate toward a father in childhood can influence an artist and mold his fantasy, is best shown by Schiller. In his dramas the hatred of a son toward his father returns repeatedly as the main motif (in the "Robbers," in "Intrigue and Love," in "Don Carlos") because Schiller as a child had experienced the same kind of pressure as Beethoven.

Beethoven's longing for universal charity grew out of the same root, likewise his hate of tyrants. Beethoven tore up his dedication of the Eroica to Napoleon when he heard that Napoleon had crowned himself emperor. ("Now he, too, will become a tyrant like other tyrants.")

THE SUBCONSCIOUS

Of the autocratic Bourbon kings in France he spoke only as of the "rotten Bourbons."

His harsh childhood made Beethoven a revolutionary. Austria's emperor Franz, whose police kept all liberals in Austria and Italy under surveillance, was not entirely wrong, despite his silliness, when he sensed "something revolutionary" in Beethoven's music. The composer who, in "Fidelio," drew the minister Pizarro with the sharpest lines and blackest colors; who opened the prison gates and filled them with a gleeful crowd of people; that composer had been made a revolutionary by the brutality suffered as a child.

Beethoven's childhood emotions: resentment of harshness; fury about the impotency of the trodden; hatred against suppression by one stronger and bigger than himself; suffering, silently borne; sorrow at the hurt inflicted upon a sensitive soul—they all were stored up in his unconscious. And they were the emotions that raged in the soul and created tension, aggressive energy and agitated passion. The slightest incident that recalled the childhood situations which had lacerated the boy's soul, sufficed to call forth all the old moods again and to cause injury anew.

In later years Beethoven had many an outburst of rage that spared not even his tested friends. No one regretted them more than Beethoven himself, who humbly begged forgiveness once his anger had cooled off. Usually the occasion for the outburst was all out of proportion to the explosion. It just so happened that the injured part from the past had been touched again.

Upon the old layers of insult, anger and hatred, new layers of the same or similar feelings continued to settle. In the course of the years mine fields were laid that blew up thunderingly whenever a foot touched upon them.

If, later on, Beethoven sensed an infraction of his liberty, his personality or his independence, his whole psychic structure was set in motion; the deep layers of childhood sentiments and the layers of later experiences and emotions that accumulated on top of them began to totter.

Thus in later years the fits of resentment and anger increased in strength, and the Beethoven music that was born from such moods became increasingly greater in passion and power. Only because the moral and spiritual forces that shaped music increased in proportion, Beethoven's style became ever grander.

In the rhythmic power of Beethoven, in the Napoleonic advances of the tone armies; in the attacks and storms; in the passionate agitation of dynamics and in the dissonances is contained not just the strength of a single soul, but of many souls. Many experiences and recollections accumulated in the various layers of Beethoven's soul. Every impulse of creative fantasy emanates from the unconscious soul foundation and collects the individual adventures and memories in a single form that contains everything: the effects of the subconscious, repressed passions, childhood and adult life, the entire man who has developed and grown.

Great artistic fantasy concentrates all this, and gives it clarity. To be a great composer means: to have stronger, richer experiences than other people; to possess a more retentive memory for psychic conditions than other people; and to have the ability to organize all this and transform it into sounding forms.

To create musically means not to be driven by moods, but to be able to concentrate moods and summarize them, be it in an ideal picture as those created by musical classicists, or in a fantastic picture as done by the romanticists, or in a realistic portrait such as Richard Strauss would paint, and in the case of Claude Debussy, with impressionistic technique.

The simplest melody obtains its beauty from the summation of moods. In the folk hymn of Haydn, in Mozart's "Veilchen," in Beethoven's adagios, in Schubert's "Staendchen" and "Ave Maria," it was not just a single sentiment that became musical shape, but a whole bundle of emotions that contains the moods of many generations. Thence the greatness of such simple melodies; for they permit one to listen in to the depth of the soul, as far down as the dark ravine of the unconscious, where one hears rustling as in a deep well.

CHAPTER VI

Forms and Figures in the Subconscious

AMONG THE IDEAS, instincts, emotions and impulses that crowd the subconscious mind of artists, there is particular significance for the composer in mental visions composed of memories and sentiments. Psychiatry calls them "complexes."

Such complexes are forms that took shape in the recesses of emotional life, without the light of consciousness ever touching them. They originate in the womb of artistic fantasy and grow there until they gather enough strength to govern independently the emotional life and the imagination of the artist. In many instances where artists feel themselves overwhelmed by creative forces and imagine that their inspirations come from supernatural sources, it is the strength of unconscious formations that invades their fancy.

"Complexes" of imagination form from the oldest sentiments, inclinations and experiences of the artists, which interweave and interlock and take shape in the dark of the unconscious. They are the crystallization of original life in fantasy.

From infancy on, a child is surrounded by mother, father, brothers and sisters; they are the object of his first emotional relations and experiences out of which complexes develop. In particular it is the mother, whose affection naturally transfers itself to the child, who determines the emotional life of artists from their earliest infancy.

FORMS AND FIGURES IN THE SUBCONSCIOUS

Although in biographies of great musicians it is mostly the father who stands out, as was the case with Mozart and Beethoven, nevertheless musical fantasy, like every artistic fancy, is usually heritage of the mother; and the emotional life of the musicians that displays so many feminine traits is mysteriously bound to the emotional life of the mother. Mozart inherited his tendency to fun comedy and gaiety from his mother, not from his dry, serious father. Even though Mozart's father was a trained musician, Mozart's fantasy has more of his mother's soul than his father's.

Of Beethoven's mother we know little. She is described as being upright and gentle. Under the pressure of an unhappy marriage with a drunkard whose debts she had to pay, she was no doubt as introverted as Beethoven himself. The description of Beethoven as a boy applies to her also: "She was always grave," and "Nobody could remember having seen Madame van Beethoven laugh." But one important trait is reported, namely, that she "could become violent." We can assume, therefore, that Beethoven inherited his tendency to outbursts of fury from her, ergo the tension in his psyche, everything in his music that alternates between soft lament and tempest; in fact, everything that is Beethovenic.

Richard Wagner's disposition and his nervous liveliness are heritages of his mother. In his autobiography Wagner emphasizes her "hasty, almost vehement, loud character" as much as he does the "rare ardour with which she spoke, in almost pathetic tone, of greatness and beauty in art." All of which are familiar Wagnerian traits.

Wagnerian eroticism was also inherited from his mother who (according to a verbatim excerpt from Wagner's autobiography) as a girl "enjoyed the care of a
so-called high fatherly friend." Her affair with Ludwig
Geyer, whom she married six months (Wagner, in his
autobiography, palliates this to one year) after the death
of her first husband, is certainly more than a conjecture.
Wagner himself says in a letter to his sister Caecilie,
dated January 14, 1870 (after having read letters from
his "father" Geyer 'with real shock'): "I have the feeling that our father Geyer thought to atone for the whole
family with his sacrifice."

From Wagner's letters to his mother it becomes quite
apparent that tenderness of a mother can awaken accentuation of erotic feeling in the artist. Wagner writes
under date of October 1834 from Magdeburg: "See,
Mother, now that I am away from you, I am overwhelmed by sentiments of gratitude for your wonderful
love toward your child. You displayed it recently again
so fervently and warmly that I would like to write and
tell you about it in the most tender tone of a lover to
his beloved."

From such impulses, stored in the subconscious mind,
grew such poetic pictures as the scene under the linden
in "Siegfried," when Siegfried sings of his mother:
"Aber wie sah meine Mutter wohl aus? Das kann ich
mir gar nicht mehr denken! Der Rehindin gleich glaenz-
ten gewiss ihre hell schimmernden Augen, nur noch viel
schoener. Ach moecht' ich Sohn meine Mutter sehn!"
(But how may my mother have looked? I can not remember at all! I am sure her lustrous eyes resembled
the doe, only more lovely. Oh, how the son would like

to see his mother.)* It is his mother whom Siegfried thinks he sees when he has traversed the fire and wakened Bruennhilde: "So starb nicht meine Mutter, Schlief die Minnige nur?"

Thoughts of his dead mother pervade two scenes of "Parsifal." And one of the most magnificent scenes of "Parsifal" is that in which Kundry attempts to seduce the pure fool with a mother's kiss: "Als Muttersegens letzter Gruss der Liebe erster Kuss."

In the first setting of the Prize Song in "Meistersinger von Nuernberg," thoughts of his mother twine around the thoughts of Eva: "Traum meiner toericht goldnen Jugend wurdest du wach durch der Mutter zarte Tugend?", and: "Ihr zu weihen mein Glueck, mein Heil, mein Leben, wie Mutter, dankt ich's Dir."

The most beautiful and most instructive example of how the "mother complex," woven with golden threads from tenderness and love, warmth and a physical nearness of nine months' duration, can influence the entire creation of an artist is given by Raphael, whom the whole world admires above all as the portrayer of madonnas.

Innumerable painters pictured the celestial mother in the 14th, 15th and 16th centuries. None of them gave the Virgin-mother the purity, beauty and grace that Raphael did; none of them portrayed the union of mother and child with such delicacy, as Raphael in the "Madonna della Sedia," in the Sistine Madonna,

---

* Compare herewith Wagner's letter of September 16, 1846: "When I leave the smoke-filled city and enter a pretty, green valley, I stretch out in the grass, observe the slim shape of the trees, listen to a wood-bird, till, in cozy comfort, a tear, unheeded, escapes. Thus do I feel when I reach for you through a chaos of oddness and call to you: 'God keep you, my good, old mother'." This was written five years before the creation of the "Siegfried" scene. The "lustrous eyes" are evident in photographs of Wagner's mother.

and in many other pictures in which the Madonna holds the child on her lap, or plays with him, or carries him in her arms, or looks down at the playing infant.

Raphael's mother died when the boy was eight years old, and the longing for his mother always remained alive in him. Raphael's mother was called Maria, and thus his memory of her associated itself with the pictures of the Divine Mother and, as Raphael himself relates, the picture appeared to him in dreams repeatedly.

When, as a boy, Raphael heard the name Maria spoken, he became melancholy, and he confesses that it was his greatest desire to paint the Madonna. Day and night he thought of this desire, and from these desires of the unconscious Raphael's dreams of the Virgin Mary took shape, as well as the pictures that portrayed her. The longing for a mother's affection, for protective embrace; the recollection of life with his mother, and her caresses, her fondling and cradling are preserved in Raphael's madonna portraits in idealized form.

The manner in which eroticism spins its threads in the relationship of son and mother, and daughter and father, is one of the mysteries of human life. Innumerable sons unconsciously sought their mother in the beloved; countless mothers tried to interfere in the relations of their sons. There have been extreme cases, too, that border on the pathological. Rousseau called his mistress, Mme. de Warens, "Maman" and displayed painful candor in writing about her in his "Confessions": 'I felt as though I had committed an act of incest.'

However, psychic material does not deposit itself in the unconscious only around tenderness and love instincts of the child; it also gathers around sentiments of animosity and hate that are no strangers to children. Morbid thoughts of death can result from repressed impulses of hostility that move down into the unconscious mind, whence they return to consciousness in altered form.

The diary of the poet Hebbel abounds in entries about murders, bloody outrages, deaths and bloodiness; and even his dreams, which Hebbel calls the "focal point of all secrets of the soul" are crowded with graves, rivers of blood, dead people, murders and coffins. As a child the poet lived near the cemetery, and the sight of funerals and corpses was a daily routine for him. In his childhood, which he himself called "dismal and barren," fear and hate easily associated themselves with thoughts of death.

Hebbel confesses in his diary: "My father hated me, nor could I love him"; and even as a man he dreamed back to his distressed childhood: "And I trembled before my father."

The adult Hebbel wept when he saw a happy child approaching, for his father "hated happiness" and "could not bear the sight of it on the faces of his children." "He considered laughter a crime" for "the path to joy was obstructed by thorn and thistle."

It is not easy to place oneself in such a trodden, hurt child psyche where fear, hatred and thoughts of death dwelt side by side; but it would be only human if, due to the association of all these sentiments, evil desires developed in the boy, desires that descended to the darkness of the unconscious and later came to light in the guise of tragedies.

While Beethoven's youth can not be compared to the childhood of Friedrich Hebbel that lacked air and light, nevertheless there was the father's harshness, the quarrels and poverty in the parental home, the mental oppression that burdened the boy, and the early tendency to melancholic moods. The child lived alone in a world of thoughts and emotions that separated him from his surroundings. We know that he was often immersed in his fantasies. And Caecilia Fischer describes how the boy often sat at a window, facing the yard, both hands clasped around his head, staring into space, completely lost in meditation. If one addressed him, there was no response. He cared nothing for comrades or company. He was taciturn and introvert. Yet he did not grow hard, as Friedrich Hebbel did. His sense of grandeur elevated him temporarily above depressing morose moods.

In the case of Beethoven the "death complex" is not composed of cemetery adventures and hate of his father, but of melancholy thoughts and the fantasies of future greatness.

The funeral march of the Piano Sonata opus 26, in A-flat Major, is the glorification of a hero (Marcia funebre sulla morte d'un eroe.) The hero, solemnly borne to eternal rest is Beethoven himself. It is also Beethoven in the funeral march of the "Eroica" with which the composition of this symphony was begun (1801.) The first picture that came to Beethoven's mind, when he conceived the heroic symphony, was the funeral music with its lament, its sympathy, its weeping and its transfiguration.

These funeral march fantasies extend far back into Beethoven's youth. The composition which we must consider as having been Beethoven's first—the "Variations on a march by Dressler"—(printed 1783)—was written by the boy at the age of eleven and has as its theme a pathetic funeral march. Beethoven's music begins in a dismal minor key.

Among the last works planned by Beethoven were variations on the heroic funeral march by Haendel. Had Beethoven completed this plan, his creative work would have begun with variations on a funeral march and ended with variations on a funeral march.

Of greater significance still is the "Cantata at the death of Josef the Second," composed by Beethoven in 1790. In none of his youthful compositions is Beethoven so much, and so completely, himself as in this work. "It is all and absolutely Beethoven," Brahms remarked when he was shown the score after its rediscovery.

The first chorus contains a touching piano choral interlude: "Dead! Dead!" that increases in volume until it reaches a fortissimo eruption: "Dead!" This chorus practically wallows in pain. Still more movingly felt is the continuation, when the choir sings unisono: "Dead, it moans through the dismal night" (from here on the music is piano), and then, to make a deeper impression: "the dreary night." The music is insatiable in the portrayal of destitution and pain.

This music of the twenty year old composer is more than just a soulful musical setting, by a talented young composer, of Averdonk's bombastic text. The text aroused emotions in young Beethoven that were completely personal; it touched upon a spot in his emotional life that housed sorrow, solitude and melancholy thoughts.

There is no better proof for this than the fact that the identical musical moods that broke through in this chorus, like a flood of grievous sentiments, show up later in the funeral march of the "Eroica." In bar 29 of the funeral cantata Beethoven accompanies the words: "Und ihr Wogen des Meeres, heulet es durch eure Tiefen" with the following music, written in agitated sextulets of the violin and viola and with a wallowing passage of the celli and basses in the lower registers:

The same musical picture appears again in the funeral march of the "Eroica" (bar 178):

We have the same thing in both works: same instrumentation, same harmony, same movement in violins and violas, the same wallowing bass passage. That this is no coincidence is indicated by a similarity between another passage in the funeral cantata and the "Eroica" funeral march. In the cantata the choir sings in gripping pianissimo (bars 69 to 72):

In the marche funèbre of the "Eroica" we find the same musical expression of extreme destitution at the end (bar 19 from the final bar):

Here, too, the same mood of grief is framed in the same musical picture. It is the same soul complex that produced the music of the years 1790 and 1804.

However, the "Funeral Cantata" produces impressions from yet another direction; impressions that are instructive for the continued efficacy of mental "complexes" in the subconscious, and significant for the recognition of Beethoven's emotional life.

The third piece of the "Trauerkantate" is a soprano aria with chorus and wind instruments. Thayer, in his Beethoven biography, is justified in his praise of it: "The noble dignity of the melody, and the magnificent euphony of the instrumentation spread a wonderful charm over this piece."

One has only to compare this piece with the preceding bass aria in order to appreciate which music is seasonable and which is eternal.

The aforementioned soprano aria with chorus is a vision of happy people aspiring to the light. It must have been visions like this that comforted young Beethoven in dark hours of sadness, just as they appeared before his mental eye years later.

Twenty five years later, when Beethoven wrote his "Fidelio," and the prisoners emerged from their dungeons to the light in exaltation, he remembered the melodies from the funeral cantata and adopted them into the F-Major song of thanks of Fidelio: "O Himmel, welch' ein Augenblick."

It was the similarity of the situation that recalled the music to Beethoven's fantasy: "And the people climbed back to the light, and the earth revolved more happily around the sun, and the sun gave warmth with rays divine," had been the text of the cantata; words that deeply affected Beethoven's religious feelings and his humanity in early boyhood. Words that became great Beethoven music, and words which he recalled when he sounded the jubilation of "Fidelio," where again people ascended to the light.

That which I called the "death complex" in Beethoven, the complex in which moods of sorrow, destitution and melancholia mingle, inspired Beethoven's imagination in the Adagio of the String Quartet in F-Major, opus 18. Beethoven himself relates that while writing this music, in which sadness alternates with passion and founders in helplessness, he had in mind the grave scene from "Romeo and Juliet." One of the sketches to this quartet is captioned: "Les derniers soupirs":

Les dernières soupirs

The tone picture of the last sighs is quite realistic here, but the realistic portrayal was not included in the completed string quartet.

To occupy oneself with thoughts of death certainly is an eternal human problem, and as strong a man as Johann Sebastian Bach never wrote more moving music than when the words of cantata texts include "death" and "dying."

Even Schubert, who loved the world so much and sketched and portrayed all phenomena of nature with so much affection, had his dark hours. In a letter to his friend Kuppelwieser he writes: "Every night when I retire, I hope never to awaken again; and every morning proclaims anew yesterday's grief."

In such dark hours Schubert's lieder of the "Winterreise" were composed.

Much of Brahms' music is darkened by such morbid thoughts. Brahms was quite a young composer when he wrote his dismal "Funeral Song," reminiscent of

[129]

mediaeval woodcuts: "Nun wollen wir den Leib be-
graben" (Now will we bury the body). The "Deutsches
Requiem" is dedicated to the memory of his mother,
whom Brahms commemorates especially in the soprano
aria: "Ich will euch troesten, wie einen seine Mutter
troestet" (I will comfort you as a mother comforts one).
It is a funeral rite. The lieder "Immer leiser wird mein
Schlummer" and "Auf dem Kirchhof" are full of death
thoughts; and Brahms' final work, the "Vier ernsten
Gesaenge" proclaim: "O Death, how bitter art thou."

Still, what we term "death complex" is something
more than just musing about the mysterium of death.
It is a psychic creation that consists of death thoughts,
sensations of fear and destructive forces of the soul. It
originated from the repression of hostile impulses, and
submerged into the unconscious.

The "death complex" presupposes transformations
in the human soul, which created fear out of aggressive
feelings, which opposed sensations of destruction with
heroic reaction (as in the case of Beethoven) and turned
suppressed hatred to affection and antagonistic desires
to love.

The "death complex" is a product of spiritual work,
and its spiritual strength is so great that anything can
develop from it: crime, mental disease and—provided
the creative fantasy controls the complexities of the
soul—works of art.

No great musician was as susceptible to the influence
of the "death complex" as Gustav Mahler. He is what
doctors call the "classic case," which we are able to
study more thoroughly because we have sufficient mater·
ial. The book written by his wife, Alma Mahler: "Gus-

tav Mahler. Memories and Letters" (New York 1946), reports candidly on the family history of the composer.

Let us first state the factors that affected the soul of Mahler as a boy. Mahler's father was "a man of strong and exuberant vitality, completely uninhibited." He ran after every skirt, brutalized his wife, who was sickly and had a game leg, and beat the children. The townspeople of Iglau avoided the brutal, arrogant man. This marriage, contracted without love, and remaining love-less, brought forth twelve children, all of whom were afflicted with the pathological traits that are a matter of course in a home of this kind.

Mahler's sister Justine, who lived in a "nightmare of whipping," as a child placed candles all around her bed, laid down and lit the candles, imagining that she had died. Thus we find the "death complex" inherent in Mahler's sister, too.

Such fantasies were not foreign to Gustav Mahler. While working on the second symphony, the first movement of which was originally titled "Todtenfeier," he dreamed he was laid out beneath flowers and wreaths. The dream and the music came from the same source, the subconscious thoughts of death.

Gustav Mahler had come in contact with death at an early age. Five of his brothers and sisters died young of diphtheria. One brother died of hydrocardia at the age of twelve.

Here we already have all the constituent parts of the "death complex": premature experiences with dying; a prematurely agitated emotional life of the boy*, aggravated by fear due to the shock of a premature sexual experience*; fear of his father's brutality and tenderness for his ailing mother. It was her "face, smiling in profound sadness and as through a veil of tears" that he had in mind when composing the Andante of the Fourth Symphony.

Henrik Ibsen wrote: "Poetry: fighting the uproar of dark forces in oneself." And dark powers were plentiful in the soul of Gustav Mahler. Like Dostojewsky, whom Mahler admired, he portrayed his mental conflicts in works of art.

Mahler was well aware that his artistic work had been predetermined by his childhood. "Composing is like playing with blocks, whereby new structures can be made from the same blocks. But the blocks are all quite ready from childhood on, which alone is destined to collect them and pick them up."

The fourth movement of Mahler's First Symphony was inspired by a picture, "The Hunter's Funeral," which the boy had seen. It showed the forest animals, feigning grief, accompanying the dead hunter. The theme of the alto phrase in the Third Symphony, "O Mensch gieb Acht" was, according to Mahler, adopted from a composition of his school years. The buglehorn solo that ironically disperses the moonshine magic in the third movement of the Third Symphony sounded every evening from the barracks opposite the house where Mahler lived as a child.

Even Gustav Mahler's odd counterpoint, with its in-

---

* He was, involuntarily, witness to a brutal love scene between a young man and the maid which took place in a dark room. "This episode left a deep mark on his mind," we are told by Alma Mahler, who also speaks with great candor of Mahler's panic in the first love night. We can believe her when she says that until then Mahler lived ascetically in spite of the love affairs he had, one of which inspired Mahler's "Lieder eines Fahrenden Gesellen" and the First Symphony.

dependent modulation, owes its form to childhood experiences. When Mahler, attending a national festival, heard the combination of noises from the shooting galleries, the military music, ring-tossing and organ grinder, he exclaimed: "Do you hear? This is polyphonic, and here is where I get it from! In my early childhood in the forest of Iglau it moved me oddly and impressed itself upon me. For I do not care whether the ringing comes from such noises or in the thousandfold song of the birds, in the howling of the storm, in the rippling of the waves or in the crackling of the fire. Just so, from different directions, the themes must come."

In much of his music Mahler expressed his dread of life in sudden outbursts of panic, or in distorted pictures, in shadowy figures or in shrill contortions. This terror was already inherent in the boy when he ran out of the house, sat himself down on a tree stump in the Iglau woods and stayed glued to the spot for hours.

Of course Mahler also described the loveliness and beauty in nature in his Third Symphony and in his "Lied von der Erde." He portrayed the gracefulness of the flowers and the vitality of the animals; meadows glittering in the light of the early dawn, and the evening dusk; the beauty of dancing girls and the virility of young boys on horseback. But the terror that erupts suddenly in all the glory of nature is typically Mahler. Speaking of his Fourth Symphony, Mahler intimates how "terrifying" the sky gets; how, "on the loveliest day, in the midst of brilliantly lighted woods, a panicky fear often overcomes one" and how: "The perpetually moving, never resting, never comprehensible machinery of life becomes horrible—like the rocking of dancing figures in a brightly lit ball room, into which one looks in a dark night—from such a distance that one no longer can hear the accompanying music! Life becomes meaningless then, and a horrible nightmare from which one may awaken with a cry of loathing." (Letter of March 26, 1896).

At one time Mahler also speaks of "the forest with its wonders and horrors" which he weaved into his tone world, and he adds: "I realize more and more: one does not compose, one is composed."

Of such Mahlerian world perception which, similar to that of mediaeval people, sensed something ghost-like and spectral in universe and nature, are the Mahler symphonies composed. The thought of death lurks menacingly behind all of his music.

At the age of nineteen Mahler already expressed his desire for death movingly enough in a letter: "O dearly beloved earth, when, oh, when, will you take this forlorn one into your lap; look! man has turned him away, and he flees from their cold, heartless bosom to you, to you! Eternal mother, admit the lonely, restless being!" (June 17, 1897).

Mahler's First Symphony already contains a funeral march in its third movement that is all scorn and sneer. The first two movements of the symphony were steeped in gay light. The first movement is paradisiacal with its glowing colors, its spring flowers, its dew drops in which the sun sparkles. The second movement is a dance. But in the third movement this world of youthful bliss is devastated, and under the ruins cries an unhappy soul, and the violins sob the Mahlerian song melody: "Da wusst ich nicht, wie das Leben tut".

The death song sounds shrill. Skeletons rattle. No Hieronymus Busch painted more horrible ghosts than those set to music by Mahler; no Breughel painted a more grandiose portrayal of Judgment Day than Mahler in his Second Symphony. The first movement already intones the "Dies Irae" as the opening of the mystery play of death and eternal life, resurrection and judgment. The bird of death sings a gruesome tune at the sound of the trumpets, and the procession of the dead marches to the tribunal while the mystic choruses proclaim: "You will arise".

In the Fourth Symphony the devil plays a dirge on a shrill violin.

The Fifth Symphony opens with a dismal marche funebre. And in the "Song of the Earth" Death arrives on a black horse and offers the farewell goblet. In the Ninth Symphony, too, Death threatens with shadowy tremoli, with trumpet calls and beats of the tamtam, with funeral march rhythms and with demonic figures and grimaces.

To what extent Mahler was imbued with morbid thoughts is proved by his "Kindertotenlieder", which he composed even before his own child died, and from which his Fifth, Sixth and Seventh Symphonies originated.

Another symphony of death is the tenth, which Mahler only sketched. Fear of dying gripped the ailing man when he wrote the notes of this symphony. A man in despair wrote above the notes such words as: "Death! Destruction!" Or: "O God, O God, why hast Thou forsaken me!" Or: "Mercy!"

The fourth movement is superscribed: "The devil dances it with me." And underneath are the words: "Madness seizes me, the accursed! Destroy me, that I may forget that I am! That I cease to be, that I for(get)."

At the close of the fourth movement a muffled drumbeat returns: it is the rolling of a drum in a funeral procession that passed Mahler's New York hotel, and the beat of it moved Mahler to tears.

One can safely say that the thought of death that crystallized into such a variety of symphonic shapes in Mahler was the greatest reality in his emotional life. Mahler saw the universe only as a symbol. The world's phenomena indicated something more exalted. The animal and vegetable kingdoms described by Mahler in his Third Symphony in large scenes are not portrayed realistically, as they are in Haydn's "Creation", where the lion really roars and the reptiles really crawl, but in stylistic form.

In Gustav Mahler's First Symphony the cuckoo does not call in thirds like a real cuckoo, and like the one in Beethoven's "Pastoral Symphony", but in fourths.

Mahler considered everything that was transitory merely an allegory. "Indoors and out he lived in a dream", we are told by his wife. "He dreamed his way through family life and childhood."

The scenes of nature in "Lied von der Erde" are not realistic, either. They possess the sheen of a fairy tale, like pictures by Boecklin or the frescoes of Puvis de Chavannes. Gustav Mahler, contrary to his antipode Richard Strauss, never painted naturalistically. He was a mystic, a philosophical mind; a man seeking God. He shaped an intrinsic world, not external worlds. What he portrayed in music was the answer to questions that arose in his childhood from his innermost being, and that re-emerged again and again from his subconscious, threatening and terrorizing him. The death thought always shoveled more coal into the glowing furnace of the unconscious.

Gustave Mahler built his spiritual world above the "death complex", in pictures and visions that temporarily calmed the Faustian struggle. Mahler flees repeatedly to a gay, shining children's world where everything sings and rings, where, as in a nursery, little bells make joyous noise.

Mahler's First Symphony already has this paradisiacal world. In the Third Symphony the angels sing to the tune of "Ding Dong Bells", and over the Fourth Symphony, too, the children's heaven arches.

Another of his visions is the universe, in which the planets revolve around the sun, and Eternal Love pours down from the Most Exalted Heaven. Such visions were common to all mystics, and to Spinoza. Even the angel choirs that sing in Mahler's Third and Fourth Symphonies become silent, then, and only the instruments sing of Eternal Love, which is also glorified in the massive choruses of the Eighth Symphony—"Accende Lumen sensibus" Then the unredeemed soul that was Mahler plunges back into the abyss of death thoughts in the Ninth and Tenth Symphonies.

Soul "complexes," which are the first formations of fantasy, set the whole world of sentiments and moods in motion among all great musicians. These complexes are embryonic forms of the soul that take nourishment from all the juices of the mother organism and thrive thereon. They produce the typical artistic pictures that always re-appear in so many great artists.

One of these typical artistic pictures can be found in Anton Bruckner's symphonies, the finale of which is always a brilliant gleaming of the tonal masses, a veritable apotheosis of tones, often in the form of a chorale that is pealed by the wind instruments; brilliant fanfares like those of church festivals, where trumpets and trombones resound.

Whoever heard Anton Bruckner improvising at the

organ knows that Bruckner always finished off his fantasies with a raging intensification that unleashed all the festive masses of the organ tone at their climax. Often fugues paved the way for this climax of the "organo pleno". The final movement of Bruckner's Fifth Symphony—wherein toward the end the great orchestral fugues are crowned by a shining chorale—gives us a good idea of the manner in which Bruckner planned his organ fantasies. The finale of the Fourth Symphony, too, is a Pentecost of tones in which the main theme of the first movement returns with "fiery tongues".

When Bruckner toyed with the idea of writing an opera, he wanted a libretto in which the finale of the opera would have a huge mass of people hoping for the Saviour, who settles down upon them. The opera was to be a kind of Lohengrin or Parsifal, with the Holy Ghost as redeemer. This idea of Bruckner's may have been inspired by the moment of "Transubstantiation" in the Catholic service when silence envelops the church, the devout kneel down and the priest raises the chalice.

Being a devout Catholic, educated in a parochial school, playing the organ in churches, he was profoundly stirred by that moment of transubstantation when God descends and the soul of the pious unites with the Divine. In the finales of his symphonies he portrayed the downward sweep of the Divine from Heaven to earth, and the storming of the Holy Ghost; for Bruckner's symphonies are Catholic mass celebrations. Their orchestral lustre is the pomp of Catholic church service; their enhancements are prayers; their much defamed rests, the quiet of the transubstantiation. In their climax, the symphonic themes become chorales,

the greatest and most brilliant form of musical devotion.

Every morning found Bruckner kneeling before a big crucifix in his room, praying the "Pater Noster" and "Gegruesst seist Du". At mass he prayed so loud that the priest had to request him to restrain himself. Bruckner's last symphony was dedicated to the "Good Lord".

This Catholic devoutness was inherent in the Bruckner family. Anton Bruckner's brother, Ignaz, lived in the St. Florian convent and worked as a gardener and bellows blower. When he left the convent he became melancholy; he claimed "he had to worry terribly" and was afraid "he would go to pieces"*. He did not compose himself until he was re-admitted to the convent.

Such traits of religious madness were not foreign to Anton Bruckner. In 1867, suffering from a condition of extreme depression, he went in quest of a hydropathic institution, deeply dejected and filled with thoughts of suicide. Always it was prayer that came to his rescue, and in gratitude for this he adopted the melody: "Benedictus qui venit", from his Mass in F Minor, into the Third Symphony.

He was a creative musician, and music was a means of saving himself from mental agony.

Thoughts of death later inspired Bruckner to the ending of the Fourth Symphony. He called it the "Death Clock", and never played it without a feeling of horror. He said, then, deeply moved: "The death clock . . . strikes inexorably, without abatement, till everything is over." These black thoughts vanished before the radiant lustre of the Holy Ghost.

---

* Bruckner's sister, Sali, too, was mentally deranged in the last years of her life.

As is usually the case, Anton Bruckner's faith—the Catholic faith of his Upper Austrian homeland—goes back to his youth. The boy was never tired of building "altars" and "sacred tombs" and, standing upon all sorts of implements, of "preaching a sermon". Bruckner never forgot the mystic impressions of the Christmas Eve Mass, which he attended at his mother's side. Among his childhood recollections were the ostentatious baroque churches of Upper Austria, where the organ resounded through the wide halls that were adorned with frescoes and marble saints.

Thus symphonies to him had to become prayers and divine services, and the Descent of the Holy Ghost the greatest experience; one that he continued to celebrate in all his music, in the masses and in the "Te Deum", as well as in the finales of his symphonies. This vision, the Glory of Heaven, meant to Bruckner what the choral prayer meant to Bach, the jubilation of festive masses to Beethoven, the radiation of divine love to Mahler: the heavenly radiance that strikes a life of fear, terror and depressions.

In speaking of great artists one can distinguish between two kinds of experiences: "elemental experiences" and "formative experiences." Elemental experiences come from the recesses of their soul and grow out of the roots of their personality. Formative experiences originate in external life.

One of Beethoven's elemental experiences was the realization of how the tempest and the struggles of his inner life resolved into peace. Time and again Beethoven's music portrayed this psychic development of the taming and formation of wild strength that emanated from the unconscious. Subjective artist that Beethoven was, he himself interpreted his creation in the most varying works. All these pictures are merely variations of one and the same experience.

One of the most beautiful scenes in which Beethoven depicted the battle and progressive quieting of his soul was the Adagio of the Piano Concerto in G-Major. Some people tried to visualize Orpheus in this music, who pacifies the Furies with his singing; but it is not necessary to transform such a soul reflection into a theatrical scene. The inflexible unison of the string orchestra, confronted by the mild tones of the pleading, entreating piano, speak for themselves: they are the pictures of a battle between menacing forces of the soul and gentle supplications, between violence and lament.

More and more the stirring song expands in the music. More and more the hard, inexorable, inflexible tones are repressed, until the mood becomes quite peaceful, only the sweet song of the soul is heard and finally the droning—now powerless—sounds only quite shadowy from the depth.

Mozart, too, had composed some music in which impressive laments are confronted by passionate agitation; so, for instance, in the slow movement of the Piano Concerto in D-Minor, which Beethoven loved so well. However, these contrasts of mood are shaped into contrasting pictures that are in harmonic balance. Mozart did not have the slightest intention of portraying a progressing psychic development and the pacification of a mental conflict. He had experienced a change of moods, rather than a psychic struggle of the moods.

That the soul calmed down after a storm, and the black clouds dispersed, was a typical Beethoven experience. And he always portrayed this experience in music anew: the battles from which peace went forth, the origin of beauty, the pacification and calming of the agitated soul.

A symbolic illustration of this calming of the soul is found in Beethoven's Pastoral Symphony. The musical description of the thunderstorm that comes closer and closer, that mounts in intensity and threatens mightily, then gradually decreases until the landscape is all peaceful and the shepherd's flute intones "glad and thankful feelings"—this description is not meant to be only realistic. Nature, which doesn't sound anywhere in Mozart's music, was to Beethoven the reflection of human moods.

Beethoven was the great musician of the Rousseau epoch which, following Rousseau's "New Heloise" considered the high mountains and the lakes, storms and sunshine linked with the human soul; they were no longer just the "back drops" of life, but filled with life, passion and feeling. Thunderstorm and peace in nature symbolized to Beethoven thunderstorm and peace in the soul. That is what he portrayed in the Pastoral Symphony with music; and, as indicated with particular beauty by the pious finale of the Pastoral Symphony, he accepted it as a religious occurrence. After experiencing storms of the soul, Beethoven always sought peace in nature, and he revered this peace as a divine blessing.

Going out from the identical sentiment, Beethoven also composed the "Agnus Dei" in the 'Missa Solemnis'. According to Thayer the supplication for peace no longer fits into the pattern of sacred music, for martial trumpets peal resoundingly into the mass music.

Even when Beethoven was working on the "Credo" fugue—in 1820—he conceived the peculiar, entirely subjective treatment of the "Dona nobis pacem" (supplication for peace) in this part of the Mass: "Agnus Dei like a recitativ". . . (there follow some notes) and: "Dona in D-Minor, only toward the end in major, in the middle again agnus dei."

The "Credo" sketches are interrupted in the middle by the idea of achieving peace only after violent struggles and serious disturbances. As happened so often with Beethoven, he experienced an eruption of massed emotions that had collected in the unconscious and invaded the sacred texts.

"Strength of conviction of inward peace above everything . . . Victory!", one reads in the Beethoven sketches. But: Victory presupposes battle. And the descriptions of these battles are interpolated in the "Dona nobis pacem." First come the martial fanfares with the frightened alto and tenor calls, the soprano cry and the agitated tremolo of the orchestra; then, after some tranquillity, a raging orchestral storm, wild exertion, chaotic masses. One motif of "Dona nobis pacem" struggles in the tumult until the chorus, in long chords, cries: Agnus, the soprano pleads for peace, and an humble prayer for peace brings the work to a close.

In one of Beethoven's sketches one reads: "Dona nobis pacem illustrating inner and outer peace."

At the time Beethoven was composing this battle episode of "Agnus Dei" there reigned a state of peace with no danger of war. Yet four years later, when Beethoven composed the Ninth Symphony, he inserted a very similar battle episode in the final movement; a sign that in both these great works, the same idea penetrated the music forcibly from without.

Just as in the "Missa Solemnis" peace had to be gained by battle, so too, in the Ninth Symphony, joy had to be won. In the Ninth Symphony this takes place after the heroic solo of the tenor: "Laufet Brueder Eure Bahn, Freudig wie ein Held zum Siege," in a tempestuous orchestral phrase that is constructed in the same manner as the battle phrase of the "Missa Solemnis." In the latter, the plea for peace had to fight; in the former, joy. Not until the excitement abates does the joyous melody of the chorus celebrate victory.

Battle and victory, chaos and peace, storm and calm: this development is represented in both compositions. Not because the text demanded it—as a matter of fact, in "Missa Solemnis" the text was contradictory to the sacred purport of the work—but because it was a basic experience of Beethoven's. It was his personal vision, a typical picture of his mental conflicts that surged from the depths of the artist's personality and pervaded works that were in no way connected with these fantasies.

These visions simply had a special power that propelled them into works as foreign to them as, of a certainty, the description of a battle is foreign to a Mass.

In "Missa Solemnis" the word 'Pacem' (peace) stirred up battle pictures in Beethoven's soul because Beethoven knew peace only as the calm after storm and tempest. In the Ninth Symphony the words "Hero" and "Victory" drew Beethoven's heroic forces from the unconscious where they were in readiness to march to battle at any time.

These soul formations that accumulated in the unconscious mind are imbued with something super-personal. They are more powerful than the artist himself, who is overwhelmed by them. They are demons in his soul, forces that can be subdued only by extremely strong artistic fantasy.

Beethoven described the path from formless and elemental eruptions, mental conflicts and tempests to peace and lucid forms in many more passages of his music; for that was the path of his fantasy. Some such passages were in the Piano Fantasy opus 77; in the Largo, out of which—in the "Hammerklaviersonate"—the Fugue emerges; in the piano introduction of the "Choral Fantasy," and in the beginning of the fourth movement of the Ninth Symphony. All of these compositions start off with thunderstorms and end up with tranquillity. The elements are unleashed. The storms rage. Gradually, the agitated masses calm down. Quiet reigns. Unrest and formlessness becomes lovely form, melody that emerges from chaos and begins to sing in a world that has again become serene.

Haydn was the first composer to allow the Allegro of a symphony to originate from a darkly-colored, slow introduction. Occasionally he joined this introduction thematically with the Allegro. Mozart followed his example. He had learned well from Haydn how to prepare a symphonic allegro with a slow introduction. We have a copy that he made of such a "grave" introduction of a Haydn symphony.

In his "Linzer Symphony," composed in 1783, Mozart wrote his first introduction of that type. Beethoven himself, in his first two symphonies, followed the Haydn-Mozart example. But Beethoven created something new and personal, once the Beethovenic storms broke loose in the "Appassionata"; it was not change of moods, as Haydn and Mozart portrayed, nor contrasts of night and light, but the development of moods in mental conflicts. He pictures the brightening and calming of a passionate soul; the moral serenity that generates beauty. In Faustian struggles Beethoven subjected the dark forces of his soul to his fantasy, over and over again, and this, his elemental experience, he portrays in ever new shapes

In order to explain these workings of the soul, and to show clearly what strength is inherent in the complexes of the unconscious among great artists, let me cite an example from another field of art: painting.

No other artist was so much akin to Beethoven as was Michelangelo. He was, like Beethoven, the "Terrible"; subject to fits of fear and terror, with traits of a persecution complex. Sometimes he indulged in melancholy moods—he himself spoke occasionally of his "bizarria" —other times he was in a state of extreme aggressiveness. The Marchese of Massa said that Michelangelo: "sempre aveva voluto combattere uomini." (He always wanted to fight men.)

His work, too, was a veritable battle. When he held the chisel, he attacked the marble with gigantic force, in an "aggressive state akin to destruction," according to Justi in his book on Michelangelo. Watching him work, one expected the marble to be shattered.

His works were created in an interchange of dreamy idleness and melancholy stagnation and an incredible intensity of mental and physical accomplishment.

Among these works, the paintings of the Sistine Chapel have achieved world fame.

Originally Michelangelo was to have adorned the plafond of the narrow church with the Twelve Apostles. The rest was to have been ornamental decoration. Out of this original design grew the painting that covers the ceiling and spreads down to the Lunettes and wall copings. From the originally planned Twelve Apostles there developed the mighty prophets and sybils: statues that had become frescoes, yet had retained the bulk of plastic sculptures.

In a sequence of mighty pictures the story of mankind was depicted: Pilgrims in their travels, resting at night and breaking camp in the morning to continue their search for God. The ancestors of Christ, first Christian era; the story of Creation with God soaring through Cosmos, His nod creating sun and moon, animals and vegetables and the first man; the fall of man, expulsion from Paradise, the Flood, as the close of old history and the inception of a new history. The stories of Judith, David and Goliath, the iron snake, and Esther and Hamann as symbols of salvation through faith. The whole was decorated with amorettes and moldings, and with twenty "Nudi," the beautiful nude youths who, in many poses demonstrating the loveliness of the young body, sit upon the balustrade, bending and bowing, leaning back and bending down.

The artistic imagination that painted the blooming young bodies of boys upon the wall of one of the most sacred chapels of Christianity—where the story of mankind summons humanity to atone for their sins, and the prophets and sybils proclaim the word of God—certainly is remarkable enough to demand an explanation.

The frescoes were a powerful sermon on universe and mankind, sin and salvation. Justifiably, one imagined seeing in the pictures of the prophets the effect of the sermons held by Savanarola on the great square in Florence in front of a crowd that included Michelangelo.

The story of Creation and the Fall of man belongs to the oldest Christian art treasure, and was portrayed before Michelangelo repeatedly on the walls and portals of churches. Neither are the young servants of the prophets and sybils new who bring the scrolls, light the lamps and listen quietly; and amorettes are an old ornament of churches. But never before did one see in churches nude youths exposing their bodies in heathen splendor. This is certainly as much personal invention as Beethoven's fantasies of processions of happy people singing joyous choruses, or his visions of battle and peace of the soul.

It is no conjecture that a coercive artistic enlightenment created these young boys.

In his early Florentine days Michelangelo already portrayed a similar fantasy in a work of art, to wit: the picture of Madonna Doni. In this painting the Madonna, turning backwards, takes the Christ Child from the hands of St. Joseph. Her appearance bears some resemblance to the sybils of the Sistine Chapel, in the powerful stature, the great form, the statue-like aspect.

The Madonna is a sister in spirit to the "Delphica" or "Libica," and a premonition of things to come. Even more so, though, are the five naked youths in the background, sitting atop the rocky rampart or leaning against each other. Here we already have the same linking of Christian doctrine and holy history with the pagan portrayal of beauty in nude boys, that adorns the Sistine Chapel in even grander illustration.

Before Michelangelo painted the plafond of the Sistine Chapel, these same nude boys appear in the designs for the Julius monument side by side with prophets and sybils enthroned on the dais of the tomb. Amorettes and mouldings can be found here too, just as in the Sixtina.

It is quite possible that all these plastic ideas were re-cast onto the ceiling of the Sistine Chapel in changed shape after the plan for the Julius monument retreated into Michelangelo's inner self because of inhibitions. It is a certainty, at any rate, that the pictures of naked boys were vivid in Michelangelo's fantasy.

They had been created by a vision of masculine body beauty that did not disappear until Michelangelo was seized by the religious moods of his old age. Until that time, this vision invaded even spiritual art productions. From "Madonna Doni" to the paintings of the Sistine Chapel, the vision increased consistently in strength and imaginative power. In like manner, Beethoven's vision of storm and peace in the soul that had first appeared in the Choral Fantasy, grew more and more from there to the Ninth Symphony.

No intelligent person will deny that this vision of nude boys was inspired by Eros; nor did any of the art experts who wrote about Michelangelo's "Madonna Doni" and the host of boyish figures on the Sistine plafond deny this. Symonds speaks of "athletic youths, faces of feminine delicacy and poignant fascination."

V. Scheffler declares it to be "an erotic mania that created its ideals here . . . not abstract art formulas, but ideals animated by the warmth of corresponding perception."

Justi, the greatest Michelangelo connoisseur, was reminded by the youths of "Madonna Doni" of "youths in Attica in the Palaestra as portrayed by Plato at the entrance of his dialogue "Charmide."

Hadrian the Sixth, the fanatical pope, called the Chapel a "stufa d'ignudi,"—a bathroom.

That Michelangelo loved women is indicated by his poems. But even the most passionate of these poems express only resignation and grief over unrequited passion.

In this respect, too, Michelangelo reminds one of Beethoven.

"Always Michelangelo speaks of his torments, his consuming fire, of tears; never does he mention the fulfillment of his desires." (Hermann Grimm, Michelangelo).

In verses written in his old age, Michelangelo speaks of the passions of his youth, of the times "when no rein could check blind passion" and in which he, "fatally wounded a thousand times over, nevertheless remained unvanquished." But not until he was an old man did Michelangelo draw the portrait of a woman—that of his platonic friend Vittoria Colonna.

The most beautiful sculpture of a woman was created by Michelangelo at the age of twenty-four. It is the "Pietà," and Michelangelo himself explains why he sculpted the God-Mother as a graceful young woman, younger, even, than the Son that rests on her lap. Michelangelo's mother was nineteen when he was born, and the memory of his young mother is retained in the picture. This explanation is surely more plausible than Michelangelo's religious and philosophical interpretation.

Michelangelo's boyhood friend, Francesco Granacci, is described as a particularly handsome youth, and his last friend, whom he loved devotedly, was a youth of great beauty. His name was Tommaso di Cavalieri, and Vasari tells us that he was able to wheedle anything he wanted out of the old master. Michelangelo dedicated a sonnet to him, in which he says "he feels himself pervaded anew by all the freshness, ardour and hope that his own youth had given him a long time ago"; and in another sonnet he says:

> Gentle light shines in your eyes,
> With my own eyes I am blind.
> With you in even steps I wander
> Light are my burdens, not oppressive.

He continues by saying he, himself, is the moon that "is kindled by the sun's glowing ray." And (in yet another sonnet) : "My only consolation is to intensify with my strength the sun which became yours at birth."

The only portrait that the old Michelangelo drew in addition to that of Vittoria Colonna was the picture of this handsome young man. Infatuation for young masculine beauty was Michelangelo's alter ego. And it was this alter ego that created the twenty young boys on the ceiling of the Sistine Chapel. In the darkness of the soul, this alter ego combined sensuality, appreciation of beauty, enjoyment of nude figures in a concentration of power from which new shapes and artistic forms emanated again and again.

A "complex" of this kind, grown in the subconscious and, with its forces, equally effective in Richard Wagner's life and in great art production, is Wagner's desire for "salvation through love."

Since coming across the motif of the "Fliegender Hollaender" in the works of Heine (the "Flying Dutchman" is redeemed by the love of a woman), Wagner portrayed his longing time and again. It is this longing that creates the tension in the music of "Tristan and Isolde" and finds its release in Isolde's "Liebestod." It inspired Wagner for the ending of "Goetterdaemmerung," where the world is redeemed of the curse as Bruennhilde leaps into the flames. It is the chief motif in Wagner's poetic creation.

It has not been noticed as yet that "Fliegender Hollaender," "Tristan and Isolde" and "Goetterdaemmerung" close with the same harmonies: the turn to the minor subdominant and the retardation over the basic triad—musical expression of yearning that contracts painfully once more before dying away in spiritual peace.

Tristan und Isolde

In all three works of Richard Wagner the "desire for love" is condensed once more in a musical symbol in the final cadence before finding relief. In all three works the final cadence is one and the same thing: proof for the molding power of soul complexes. The harmonies are quasi a formula of emotions: Love—yearning spasm —peace—salvation. They are a musical symbol of Wagner's "love complex."

That which psychiatry terms "complexes" are the oldest and most powerful forms that accumulate in the deep strata of the soul. Among the forces that motivate musical fantasy, they are the strongest. They stamp the personality of the composers with distinctive features, form the types of composers. There is a great difference whether these impacts and radiations from the depth unite harmonically with the other molding forces of the soul, or whether they emerge in eruptions and can only be subdued by extreme exertion.

In the former case the music personalities evolve whose play instincts wrought the mental material without difficulties. Those were the great fabulists, like Haydn or Johann Strauss, who always tell new, fascinating, colorful stories. In the latter case, we have the great spiritual fighters, dramatists, like Beethoven, who battles heroically for mankind; and Bach, who confronts all the struggles of his soul, all his mortal fear, his trespasses, with the strength of the chorale.

There are other composers who are able to formulate the dark forces of their ego only with effort, such as Hector Berlioz, whose fantasy often jumps its bounds, and Gustav Mahler in whom music often becomes an hysterical cry.

Of modern musicians, Richard Strauss is the masterly raconteur of stories, Schoenberg a fighter of great expressionistic power who wrestles with problems.

The longing of romantic individualism to withdraw from music of mood and sensual color, is very much prevalent in all modern musicians. It finally led Schoenberg to abstract music; and Stravinsky, who proves himself a great narrator in the Russian-national manner in such works as "Rites of Spring," "Pulcinella," "Story of the Soldier" and in "Symphony of Psalms," was guided to an ingenious Formalism by it.

However, a new turn toward romanticism is discernible in modern music, and is quite distinct in the music of Russia and the United States. In his last work, "Ode à Napoleon," Arnold Schoenberg anticipated this turn: the music is constructivistic in form, but has extreme agitation of the soul and intensified passion as its substance. Music goes down again into the recesses of the unconscious, from the emotions of which it fled temporarily to abstract formulas.

[154]

CHAPTER VII.

Childhood Memories

THE IMPULSES and forces that push from unconscious soul life into the higher layers of the soul are transformed into musical forms and form combinations in the composer. On their way, they attract other material deposited there by culture and education, by adventure and experience, knowledge of the world and travels, study and thinking.

This ability of organizing and forming is called talent or genius, and it defies all scientific analysis. It is as much a mystery as the life of nature itself. Talent is more the musical formation in higher and more conscious strata of the soul. Talent without spirit is unthinkable. Without emotional power, without riches in the lower layers, without passion, genius is not conceivable.

Of particular import among the experiences of great musicians are the childhood recollections, many of which we have already come across here. What makes these childhood memories so vivid is not just the pictures of by-gone days, but the emotions, adventures and spiritual upheavals that are in back of these pictures and that helped to mold the personality of the composers.

One of the most significant traits in Robert Schumann's creative work was his inclination to revert to childhood. His childhood—contrary to that of Mozart

[155]

—was not a spiritual element that was always alive within him and that was completely present even in the man. In his case, childhood and child sentiment is a quiet corner to which he withdraws. It may have been the latent illness in him (which, incidentally, also caused his sister's melancholia) that drove him to the childhood corner.

Schumann was not a child, as Mozart had been; he reverted back to childhood. It was in such moments of childlike humour that he composed the delightful "Kinderszenen" opus 15; the "Christmas Album", opus 68, the three sonatas for the Young, opus 118, the childish piano pieces opus 85 and "Children's Ball", opus 130.

One of Robert Schumann's childhood recollections is the theme of the horns, trumpets and alto trombones with which the C-Major Symphony begins:

and which weaves through the entire music. It sounds into the finale of the first movement in trumpet tones, and trumpets and horns sound it again in the Scherzo finale. At the close of the fourth movement, the theme first sounds softly in trumpets and trombone, then in a crescendo by all brass instruments. First it is a solemn call, then a festive one.

Schumann did not need any outside impetus to imagine himself back in his childhood days as Moussorgsky did, in whom the death of his mother revived such recollections of days gone by. At that time Moussorgsky composed the berceuse "dors fils de paysan" in memory of the time when his mother had sung the child to sleep; also the two pieces "Souvenirs d'enfant" (Niania et moi, and Premiere punicion).

Neither did Schumann write children's music because he had children of his own, as Debussy did, who composed his "Children's Corner" for his daughter and dedicated it to her with this inscription: "To my little Couchou with many apologies for what she has to listen to". Debussy also composed the ballet "Boite a joujoux" for his daughter. Schumann wrote his children's music for the child within himself.

As a child Robert Schumann heard such brass chorales coming from the church tower every evening, and he admitted that while working on the instrumentation, he felt himself transplanted into his childhood days.

If one pictures the whole situation: the child . . . evening . . . the solemn tone of the trombone from the belfry, one can readily understand that this childish memory was associated with a strange sentimental mood that finds expression in the mysterious accompaniment of the theme by the string orchestra at the start of the symphony. This mood gave strength to the memory which it lifted out of the subconscious.

In Hector Berlioz the memory of the fantastic love of his childhood, Estella, arose again at the time his love for Henriette Smithson aroused his imagination to compose the "Fantastic Symphony". The melody that weaves through the various movements of the symphony as "idée fixe," is the theme of a "Romance" that the infatuated twelve year old Hector Berlioz had composed.

To what extent the agitation of this youthful period affected the composer is proven by the "Overture des Francs-Juges" in which themes reappear which Berlioz had included in a quintet written during the same period. Here, too, it was powerful emotion that revived the old childhood music.

An obscure German poet, von Schack, described in a lovely poem the appearance of such childhood memories:

"Hin durch deine Daemmerhelle
In den Lueften abendfeucht,
Schweben Bilder, die der grelle
Schein des lauten Tags gescheucht.
Traeume und Erinnerungen
Nahen aus der Kinderzeit
Fluestern wie mit Geisterzungen
Von vergangener Seeligkeit."

(Through thine twilight bright, in the dewy evening air, visions hover that were dimmed by the glare of day. *Dreams and memories approach from the days of childhood,* whisper as with ghost-soft tongues of long passed happiness).

Another poet —Matthison—wrote similarly:

Zauberisch erneuen
Sich die *Phantaseyen*
Meiner Kindheit hier so licht!

(Magically renewed again are *the fantasies of my childhood and so light*).

*   *   *

Richard Wagner, too, re-lived by-gone childhood days when, already quite advanced in age, he composed "Parsifal". No work of Wagner's contains so many of his childhood memories as his final opus. As Parsifal stands in front of the Holy Grail, so did thirteen year old Richard stand before the altar of the Kreuzkirche in Dresden while the ceremonial wine and wafers, the body and blood of the Saviour, were offered to the congregation to the accompaniment of the organ and singing.

In his autobiography, Wagner describes the "thrill he experienced at the offering and acceptance of wine and wafer", a thrill that he "remembered to the end of his days". The picture of the Saviour on the cross filled the boy with "painful longing".

Again, like Parsifal, Wagner had lost his father at an early age*, and was brought up by his mother. Parsifal and the flower girls give a replica of the situation described by Wagner in his autobiography, when his sister's friends surround him with playful laughter. Even the Klingsor character, the man who mutilates himself, was known to Wagner in his youth: it was the castrate Sassaroli, who was "ghastly obnoxious" to him.

A musical recollection of this period was the melody of the Gregorian "Amen" which he had heard in the Catholic court chapel. Its memory remained forever in Wagner's soul.

This memory emerged from the unconscious and came to light toward the close of 1854, at the time he was busy with "Tristan and Isolde". Into his fantasy, envisaging Tristan on his death-bed, the figure of Parsifal suddenly entered and, armed, spear in hand, he stood beside Tristan. It was the first vision of the future music drama that was to take shape twenty-three years later.

Likewise in the Tristan period, and simultaneously with the appearance of Parsifal, a melody unfolded that fades out with the "Amen" that Wagner had

---

* This motif is repeated in Wagner's "Siegfried", in "Tristan and Isolde" (Da er mich zeugt' und starb), and in "Parsifal"—proof of how strong it had taken root in Wagner's soul.

heard as a boy, and that emerges from the subconscious with sixth tones:

Then the "Amen" theme vanished. "Walkuere", "Tristan und Isolde", "Meistersinger von Nuernberg", "Siegfried" and "Goetterdaemmerung" were completed; the theatre in Bayreuth was erected and the "Ring of the Nibelungen" performed there.

In 1876 the composition of "Parsifal" was resumed, and in 1878 the solemn music was written. On December 25, 1878—Cosima Wagner's birthday—the "Parsifal" prelude was performed for the first time in the Villa Wahnfried, and again the Dresden "Amen" floated through the room as "faith theme":

CHILDHOOD MEMORIES

The theme that the boy Richard Wagner had heard in Dresden fifty years before, in a period of dreamy piety, and that crossed his memory fleetingly when he was forty, became a conscious recollection in his fantasy in permanent, musical shape.

What gave Wagner's recollection of the "Dresden Amen" such strength that it never left the artist's soul, was the religious sentiment that created the Parsifal epic. The very second that Wagner envisaged the figure of Parsifal, he also heard the Dresden "Amen" again; it associated itself with the person of Parsifal, with services in the Holy Grail, with the offering of the Lord's Supper and with the figure of the youth who revived Wagner's own childhood and all its memories: Catholic church services, administration of the sacrament, the pictures of Christ, and the religious moods of days long past. In this instance, too, childhood memories mean: youthful sentiments stored in the subconscious mind.

*　　*　　*

Johann Sebastian Bach demonstrates an especially beautiful example of a childhood memory that comes to life again in a later work.

It was a custom of the Bach family to get together on a certain day of the year. On this appointed day, all the members of the Bach family—little ones and big ones, the dignified organists and cantors—left their respective homes in Thuringia, in Upper and Lower Saxonia and Franconia and, with their immediate families, gathered either in Erfurt, Eisenach or Arnstadt. Being religious people, they first sang a hymn giving thanks to God. Then they improvised quodlibets and, always ready for some fun, they sang medleys of rough and merry folk tunes, causing much laughter.

Old Bach remembered this custom of his youth when, in 1735, he composed the famous "Variations" on a theme he had written down ten years before. These "Variations" were written for the piano player of Count Kayserling, Goldberg, who had to amuse his master with music during sleepless nights.

The last variation of this great and rather serious work contains a gay laughter as it used to be heard during Bach family gatherings. Two folk tunes make merry in this variation, like in the quodlibets that the members of the Bach family sang at their pow-wows. The memory of such meetings, in which Bach took part as a boy, were awakened in him while he was writing the merry piece. He no doubt had heard and sung the gay rhythms of the folk song: "Kraut und Rueben haben mich vertrieben" and "Ich bin so lang nicht bei dir g'west; Ruck her, Ruck her, Ruck her" in his younger years; and the form of the quodlibet which the musicians in his family enjoyed so much was familiar to him from that time.

Bach was fifty years old when he remembered the pranks of his youth. Perhaps the sight of the children growing up in his house renewed the memories of his own youth.

*   *   *

For no important musician did the musical memories of childhood play such a big part in his work as they did for Josef Haydn. Neither for Mozart nor for Beethoven was the music that they had heard as children of any significance to their work. True, Mozart and Beethoven absorbed everything that belonged to music around them, but only as educational material which they combined with their personalities. The childhood impressions that Mozart and Beethoven gained may well have decided and molded their personalities; but it was not the music they heard as children that was of importance to their artistic development, but rather the spiritual experiences of that period. Mozart was influenced by the happiness and sunshine of his childhood, Beethoven by the sorrow and mental conflicts of the child.

Haydn is an entirely different case. The music that he heard in childhood is of consequence to him.

The most striking feature of Haydn's music is its popularity. Whatever Haydn touched in the way of music instantly became popular music. Even in the greatest forms of music, and in the most erudite technical arts: when Haydn came, grain began to grow, shrubs started blooming and flowers bedecked the meadows. In the taverns the peasants and their girls danced, at the inn tables the peasants drank their wine.

According to Dittersdorf, Emperor Josef did not care for Haydn's "jests and dalliances".

One must compare Haydn's symphonies with the best that were written before him in order to comprehend to what extent Haydn associated symphonic music with earth and nature, landscape and home.

All the lustre of the Italian symphonies that were at home in the opera houses; all the ardour of the Mannheim symphonies and all the wealth of the elaborate symphonies of the North German masters faded when Haydn, combining every one of the symphonic techniques created in Italy, North and South Germany, in addition opened up all the windows to let the scents of the peasant earth and the fresh breath of nature enter the symphony.

Only the Haydn symphony could initiate an historical development that led to the symphony of Schubert in which one heard the rustling of the woods and the brooks, and to Bruckner's symphony with the Upper Austrian countryside as its background.

The Haydn'ish string quartet likewise originates from open-air music, from serenades, divertimenti and cassations; as a matter of fact, Haydn called his first string quartet divertimenti. Many a time young Haydn took part in such serenades in the streets of Vienna, where popular music was played in open air.

Haydn also turned the oratorio into a picture-book showing stream and brook, animals, fish and birds, all the seasons, sunrise and sunset, hunt and vintage. A critique that called the "Jahreszeiten" a 'vulgar imitation of nature in all its details, unworthy of the great artist', was merely proof of the novelty of this Haydn music.

Haydn's Masses are also popular music. Censured because his sacred music was considered too gay, Haydn replied: "Why should I not be gay when I think of the good Lord?" Chuch fanatics would not recognize Haydn's sacred music, and an Archbishop of Vienna—von Hohenwarth—prohibited the performance of Masses by Haydn.

The novelty in Haydn's music was his combination of popularity and musical ingenuity. Proof of how great this ingenuity was is contained in a little-known letter of Rossini's addressed to Leopoldo Cicognani, which reads in part: "Haydn began already to pollute the purity of musical taste by injecting into the music strange chords, artificial modulations and audacious innovations."

Sarti claimed, similarly, that the shocking infractions of rules and the musical ear concocted an unbearable music in the Haydn quartets.

Because of its musical expression, human profundity, contrapuntal intellect, gayness and wittiness, the Haydn symphony was certainly one of the grandest creations of musical fantasy and mental capacity; yet all art therein is so saturated with popular invention that this bold new music appears almost natural. Compared to the music of Haydn, that of Mozart—with its sensitive musical lines, its fine color gradations, its changing moods and sentimentality—seems aristocratic. It has "luminous wings," as though Mozart were akin to Shelley. Haydn's music has its feet firmly on the ground.

Haydn was a man of the people. Even after his London successes had brought him fame, he liked to discuss the news of the day with his neighbors and servants in his house in the suburbs of Vienna, and to play cards with them (according to Griesinger). He had all the virtues of a smalltown burgher: piety, simplicity, thrift, neatness, and was modest in his enjoyment of life. "I have a comfortable home, three or four courses for dinner, and a good glass of wine; I can dress in good cloth and if I feel like driving, a hired carriage is elegant enough for me."

Once he stated: "I associated with emperors, kings and many great gentlemen, and have heard much flattery from them; but I would not care to be familiar with such people, and much prefer to stick to folk of my own class."

Even the family name of Haydn—heathen, in Eng-

lish—is encircled by country air. Haydn is the inhabi-
tant of the heath, and his ancestors were peasant folk.
Even when Haydn's great-grandfather migrated from
a farm village of the Hungarian heath to the city—
Hainburg—he remained the rustic possessor of vineyards and real estate. The same held true of Haydn's
grandfather and father. Haydn's father, a cartwright,
tilled his fields and vineyards, and kept cows and sheep,
pigs, ducks and chickens. At his death, he left cattle
valued at 103 Gulden. Haydn spent his childhood in
rustic surroundings.

As a child Haydn was surrounded by folk music. His
father liked to sing songs, Haydn reported, and accompanied them on the harp. All the children had to join
in the song. As Haydn tells it: "When I was a boy, I
imitated him well in singing his simple, short pieces."

Haydn could not forget these songs even when he
was far advanced in age. A. Chr. Dies reports of
the aged Haydn: "Even now Haydn enjoys remembering those songs," and Griesinger also reports: "The
melodies of those songs had so impressed themselves
upon Josef Haydn's memory that he remembered them
when he was extremely old."

Neither did the old man forget the songs that his
mother had sung. According to Carpani: "Burdened
with age and fame, Haydn still remembered the whole
song treasure of his mother."

Among the popular songs that Haydn heard when
he was a child, there were some church songs. Thus
the aging Haydn tells his friend Griesinger: "Truly, I
am a living piano. For several days now a song is
playing in me, in E-Minor, that I often played in my

CHILDHOOD MEMORIES

youth: It is called 'O Herr, wie lieb ich Dich von Herzen', and I hear it everywhere I go.*

Outside of his parental home, too, Haydn was surrounded by popular music. He heard it at the church-festival and at dances, at harvest frolics and at the vintage. The heath country where Haydn's ancestors had been at home, and where Haydn spent his youth, was filled with singing, dance melodies and love songs since the days of old, and in 1860 more than 600 German church songs were still being sung on the heath.

Such childhood memories came alive in Haydn when he introduced the peasant dance of his homeland into his symphonies. In the trio of the first London Symphony, and in the trio of the sixth London Symphony the peasants dance and stamp. In the trio of the G-Major Symphony of 1786, and in the finale of the symphony "L'Ours", the bag-pipe of Haydn's home plays for the dancers. The melodies contain rustic yodels, and the famous theme of the "Symphony with the kettle-drum roll' is an old children's song. A love song of Haydn's homeland became the Adagio of the Symphony in G-Major, another folk tune the aria of Uriel in the "Creation". Haydn's entire music is pervaded by folk music which he had heard as a child. The music has the same taste of earth as the wine that grows in Haydn's country.

This German folk music is joined by some other national music that Haydn heard in his youth. Not far from Haydn's birthplace, in Rohrau, are some Croatian villages (Parndorf, Neudorf), and Hadow discovered

* The song goes: "Herr ich lieb dich, herr ich lieb dich, herr von Herzen lieb ich dich" and is a processional song. Its beginning is identical with the beginning of the Haydn folk hymn; also, one of the later bars is found in the Haydn melody, but in the major key, not in minor as in the church song.

the influence of Croatian songs in Haydn's music. They are to be found in themes of string quartets (String Quartet in D-Major, opus 17 No. 60) and in symphonies (Symphony in D-Major, in E-flat Major with the kettle-drum roll, in A-Major).

When Haydn came to Eisenstadt as conductor, the influence of Croatian music may have become stronger yet; for Eisenstadt is surrounded by hamlets in which Croats lived. Haydn also became acquainted with gypsy music in his childhood, and this gypsy music whirls in the "Allegretto alla Zingarese" of the String Quartet opus 20, No. 4.

How great was his interest in this type of music, with which he was also surrounded in Eisenstadt, is proved by the collection of gypsy melodies contained in his music library. And finally, Haydn also knew Hungarian music in his youth; for it was at home in the border country between German and Hungarian music, where Haydn was born. He employed it in later works (in the "Rondo all' Ongarese" in the G-Major Piano Trio, and in the finale of the D-Major Piano Concerto).

To all this add the influence of church music. Haydn came from a religious peasant generation. His grandfather's last will contained legacies for the municipal church and the cemetery chapel. If Josef Haydn had acceded to his parents' wishes, he would have turned Catholic clergyman. He stated in later years that he was grateful to his parents for having held him to the fear of God. From his sixth to his fifteenth year Haydn was a chorister; one of his oldest childhood memories goes back to the time when, as a six year old boy, he took part in a procession in Hainburg and beat the drum in the orchestra.

He knew the Gregorian church music as well as the

popular church song. The Antonius chorale which Haydn used in his divertimento for wind instruments in addition to other popular church melodies, was employed by Brahms as the theme of his "Haydn Variations".

Haydn's soulful melody of the "Folk Hymn" originated from many sources, but the richest was the Gregorian chorale; as a boy Haydn heard its "Pater Noster" melody every Sunday in church. Haydn also used a melodic turn of the prayer melody "Gott erhalte" in the Benedictus of his "Mariazeller Messe" and in the second movement of the "Seven Words". (It can also be found in Mozart's motet, Exultate Jubilate).

The melody had its origin in a sacred air, from where it found its way in the course of time into many secular folk tunes. Haydn's melody is indebted to the church for its solemnity; to Haydn's pious soul for its tone of prayer.

The recollections of Haydn's childhood were stored in his soul like heirlooms in the heavy wooden chests in his nursery. This childhood came alive again when he portrayed the rustic room in winter time, in the "Seasons", or the drunken wine chorus with its huzza clamor and bag-pipe accompaniment and, to use Haydn's own words, the "inebriated fugue" of the middle part.

As a child Haydn celebrated church-festival, harvest and vintage festivities in his peasant village, where his father displayed above the front door the green tuft, indicating to the village rustics that here was wine for sale that had grown in his own vineyard. The dance in the vintage celebration of the "Seasons" is a typical folk dance from Lower Austria.

Still another childhood recollection is contained in the description of the hunt in "Jahreszeiten". As a child Haydn had witnessed the hunts on hare, quail and pheasants held by the Counts of Harrach, whose castle was located near Haydn's birthplace. In Eisenstadt, too, the hunt was one of Haydn's favorite pasttimes. The descriptions of the hunts in the "Seasons" are of a realism that can hardly be surpassed. These realistic portrayals are of a popular potency similar to Breughel's illustrations of peasant life, village dances, children's games and roundelays, beggars and the seasons.

Haydn's "Seasons" and "Creation" initiate the history of great realistic modern art in music which, in contrast to sacred or court art, has a completely popular character. Only a person who has spent his childhood in the country, in a village, surrounded by nature, as Haydn did, and descends from a robust family of peasants, can portray in this manner.

One childhood memory of Haydn's shall be mentioned in closing which is not of a general nature but a minute detail in his work.

Haydn liked to remember the incident in his childhood when, six years old, he was to join a procession as drummer because the regular drummer had died and there was no substitute. In order to practice the art of drum beating, little Haydn took a small basket belonging to his mother which the peasants used for baking bread. He took the drumstick and beat upon the basket till the flour flew in all directions. One can imagine with how much pleasure the boy practiced his drumming, and with what pride he marched along in the procession with the rest of the band, cheeks red and, to the great amusement of the onlookers, beating the drum.

Many years later, when Haydn, Europe's most famous composer, gave his concerts in London, he demonstrated to the orchestra his skill in beating the drum which he had learned in Hainburg, and all the musicians of the orchestra were duly astounded.

The recollection of the merry drumming in his childhood gave Haydn the idea of including the kettledrum prank in the G-Major Symphony. This delighted the London audiences greatly and quickly made a favorite of this symphony. The "Symphony with the Kettledrum roll" in E-Flat Major, and the "Kettledrum Mass" also are indications of Haydn's preference for drum effects that dates back to his youth.

* * *

The countryside of Stratford-on-Avon, where Shakespeare spent his boyhood among sloping hills, thickets and orchards, returns repeatedly in Shakespeare's dramas. It forms the background for "A Midsummer Night's Dream" and "Winter Tale". It lends a mood of happiness and peace to the forest of Arden in "As You Like It".

When Goethe wrote "Faust", he saw in his mind's eye the old city of Frankfurt with its narrow lanes and low houses, with its steeples and the river flowing past the city gate, Easter promenade and dance around the linden.

Dating back to his boyhood days, when little Beethoven played on the bank of the Rhine, the longing for free nature still remained in the blood of the composer.

Of the scenic pictures in the "Ring of the Nibelungen", one has completely retained the magic of youthful impressions: the forest scene in "Siegfried" with its rustling of leaves, the bubbling of the light in the woods, the singing of the woodbird and the youth under the linden.

Childhood impressions recreate the feeling of home and native place in man. The environs in which composers grow up as children holds them with magic charm. This childhood landscape becomes music at the hands of great composers, and separation from this landscape evokes the desire to copy its colors and forms in tones.

The national music of two European nations was created by composers who lived abroad and dreamed of the country in which they had spent their childhood. The artists longed for the scenery of their youth, for woods and fields, village and church of their childhood. Thus Glinka becomes the founder of Russian art music while he was in Italy; here, in the sunny landscape of the south, he was seized by nostalgia for the soil of Russia. (1830). "Nostalgia for my homeland", writes Glinka in his memoirs, "gradually led me to the idea of writing Russian music." The folk songs of the Russian peasants began to ring in his mind. The Russian peasant earth began to send forth its fragrance. His childhood called.

Bedrich Smetana, the founder of Czech art music, had the exact same experience. In 1865 Smetana left his country and traveled to Goeteborg, Sweden. Leaving his Czech home, he wrote, deeply moved: "Will I ever see these precious, dear mountains again? And if so, when? And with what emotions? I am always very much afraid when I take leave of these cities. Be happy, my above-all beloved fatherland, my beautiful, one and only fatherland! In your lap I shall gladly rest. Your soil is holy to me." And in 1859 he wrote again from the Nordic country: "Oh our divine Bohemia. Our paradisaic Prague . . . Believe me, if I could, I would serve you forever as your most humble slave, if I might only live with you in our Elysium Bohemia."

One year later Smetana, who until then had written only in German, wrote his first Czech letter, and composed his first chorus to a Czech text. National feeling awoke in him in a foreign country; his childhood called to him. From memories of the Czech village, church festivals and dances in the village inn there originated the first Czech operas. From old sagas in children's books came operas and symphonic poems.

The sojourn in a foreign country had added lustre to the childhood recollections. The fields and forests of Bohemia, the broad river, Hradschin castle, the fables and sagas all appeared more radiant. Nostalgia became creative.

Stravinsky (to name a composer of our age) must have felt similarly when he composed "Petrouchka", "Rites of Spring", "Story of the Soldier". All of these works are music from Russian soil; as Russian as Tolstoi and Dostojewsky; music from the Russian landscape.

The ingenious prattler of "Café Dôme" on Montparnasse in Paris must have felt a strong longing for Russia when he wrote those works; and in the "Symphony of Psalm" he entered the Byzantian church of Russia like a devout child, kneeling before the icons, crossing himself and praying at the tone of the heavy bell. The artful dandy of Boulevard Paris had returned to his childhood.

Even a man as serious as Johannes Brahms was linked to his childhood all his life. Until he was twenty-eight years old, he carefully saved the tin soldiers with which he used to play as a child. He told his friend Dietrich he could not part with them.

From childhood on German folk songs accompanied him on his artistic way, and he always came back to the folk song. In his first piano sonata he uses the folk tune: "Verstohlen geht der Mond auf" (Stealthily the moon rises); and in 1894 he closes his collection "Deutsche Volkslieder" with the same tune, so that the cycle of his creative work is held together by the same folk song.

His love for the folk song first comes to the fore in a Brahms song in opus 7, never again to disappear. "My old, dear songs", one reads in a Brahms letter. Together with Josef Joachim Brahms raved about old folk songs in Goettingen as early as 1852. He called them his "old love", stating: "I see them today with the same eyes, and care for them with the same heart."

Brahms went back furthest to the days of his childhood with the "Volkskinderlieder" (People's childrens' songs) that were published in 1858 without the author's name.

All such childhood memories that emerge from the depth of the unconscious carry with them the remnants of old sentiments. The reminiscent pictures represent a wish, a dream, an emotion of love, a desire or other sentiments for which artists have a particularly vivid memory.

One of Claude Debussy's best known orchestral works is "La Mer" with its wonderful sea moods, the pictures of the waves in the morning light and midday reflection, the play of the waves and the dialogue between wind and water. The music is realistic; it reproduces the sounds and scenes of nature in finely dispersed colors. One hears the sea wind blowing and the roaring of the water. The air is saline.

All this could be the result of keen observation; but

it is more than just observation. Claude Debussy spent his childhood at the coast of Cannes. An excerpt from a letter dated 1908 states: "My recollections of this region go back to my sixth year. I can still see the train tracks that passed our house, and the ocean meeting the horizon, so that at times one thought the train came riding right out of the ocean . . . then there was the street in Antibes that had more roses than I have ever seen in my life, ah, it was a street of intoxicating scents."

This is more than merely recollection of a landscape. All this is steeped in sentiment. It is poetry as well as painting.

In another letter—addressed to Messager—Debussy writes: "You may not know that I was destined to lead the beautiful life of a seaman, and that only a coincidence prevented this from happening. Nevertheless I have always retained a strong passion for the sea. You will say that the ocean doesn't exactly wash the coastline of the Bourgogne (Debussy's country house was located in the Bourgogne), and that my picture is likely to resemble a studio landscape. *But I have innumerable memories.* And that means more to my faculties than a reality."

Debussy's seascapes are not just observations, but a piece of his childhood. They came to the surface while he was in Paris like a colorful vision of his childhood days, the landscape of his southern dreams, a piece of his longing. Like all childhood memories, there is a wish either in, or behind, them.

Upon the oldest layer of juvenile memories are deposited the other memories of later years. They strengthen old sentiments, produce new admixtures; they join cell to cell, until a tree grows, branches spread, leaves unfold. Within a great composer is a centralized spiritual power that joins primitive emotions, soul complexes, childhood memories, juvenile sentiments and later experiences to one single form that holds them all.

Occasionally, temporary compilations are attempted of the materials that have accumulated in the soul. The "Huit scènes de Faust" were composed by Hector Berlioz while he was a very young musician; not until much later do they become the giant tableaux of "The Damnation of Faust."

Beethoven's Choral Fantasy seems like a sketch to the final movement of the Ninth Symphony, composed fifteen years later. In 1843 Richard Wagner composed "Liebesmahl der Apostel" for three male choruses and orchestra, with voices that resounded from the cupola of the church. This was a preliminary study for the choruses in the Holy Grail of "Parsifal", which was written down thirty-five years later.

In 1878 Richard Strauss, then fourteen years old, climbed the Alps in rain and storm. "The next day," he reports, "I portrayed the whole outing on the piano. Of course a huge tone painting and junk." Thirty-seven years later Strauss, at the age of fifty, wrote his "Alpensinfonie", a gigantic panorama that was called "Huge tone painting and junk" by music critics.

In all such cases the identical soul material is molded twice; once prematurely, an attempt at a sketch, and once later with the help of stronger forces, in great style. Between the two formations lies life with new experiences; inner growth of the artist, augmentation of his forces. Deep down, though, are the same old adventures and past sentiments.

CHAPTER VIII.

External and Internal Experiences

EVERY experience that meets the artist on his path of life is attracted by the memories and sentiments stored in the soul, and is combined with them. The treasury of memories increases in size. Soul material accumulates in bulk, experience is piled upon experience, sentiment on sentiment. This reinforcement of old experiences through new ones explains the inner growth of artists.

Great musicians do not repeat themselves, as the lesser ones do who always vary the same formulas. Great musicians are not mechanisms but organisms that grow, expand, digest new material. That which lives in their soul, and is entrenched in the subconscious, attracts new soul material constantly. So it can happen that great musicians, even though they treat the same emotional masses, manage to create new works.

The first three symphonies of Beethoven show this phenomenon quite clearly. All these symphonies form one group. They belong to one another and are variations on one theme. All three symphonies are heroic. Even if the third symphony had not been titled "Eroica" by Beethoven, it would be an heroic epopee; and the first and second symphonies might be called "Eroica" as well, for their music too contains a sublime, stormy rhythm, lustre and energy. The music is animated by the heroic rhythm in the Allegro movements of the first and second symphonies.

[177]

FROM BEETHOVEN TO SHOSTAKOVICH

Young Beethoven may have felt that heroic when, arriving in the imperial city as an unknown composer in November 1792, he disappeared in the multitude, soon to re-emerge in the house of one of Vienna's aristocrats. Here he sat at the piano, storming across the keyboard from bass to treble, surrounded by admiring women. Here he was adored and honored. When he made his first appearance at the National Theatre as pianist, he was met with thundering applause; for instead of singing at the piano, and winding daisy chains, as Mozart had done, he thundered over the keys and, spreading his dark wings, soared into higher regions.

The young musician with the unruly locks of hair falling wildly across his broad forehead had a sensation of power that could be termed Napoleonic. The pale Corsican lieutenant may have felt thus when he watched the people of Paris, or when he ordered his soldiers to storm the Tuileries.

The heroic sensation grows and becomes more intense from the first symphony to the second, and a mighty climax leads from the first two to the third. This latter symphony was dedicated to Napoleon, not because Beethoven wanted to describe Napoleon's victorious march in it, but because in Napoleon's rise to power he visualized his own greatness.

Regardless of how radiant Beethoven's first two symphonies are, there is a powerful gradation between them and his third heroic symphony. The proportions are all much larger. The accents are more pointed, the contrasts more immense. Battle and victory, lament and jubilation unfold in broad surfaces. The emotional masses had grown between the first two symphonies and the third. The heroic soul had waxed greater, more radiant.

The conflicts of the soul, too, had heightened. Powerful chords such as were contained in the Third Symphony had not existed previously, nor such dissonant storms as those in the modulation of the symphony. Unlike the first two symphonies, the hero idea is brightly illuminated from many sides. The gripping funeral march with its laments and transfiguration extols the picture of the hero once more in dismal minor; and the final movement glorifies him for a third time with Beethoven's "Prometheus" music as the creator of new, rich life.

Between the first two symphonies and the third, Beethoven experienced events that stirred up his entire emotional world, and tragedies that challenged his moral strength.

Shortly before Beethoven conceived the idea for his "Eroica", he had become aware of his deafness. In the "Heiligenstaedter Testament" he told posterity of his mental conflicts, his grief and resignation, courage and piety. At the same time he decided to oppose this tragic fate with all his energy: "I shall grab fate by the horns; it shall not get me down entirely."

Also during the same period, he had a passionate love affair—"a lovely, charming girl that loves me and whose love I return"—that stirred up his emotional life. The "Heiligenstaedter Testament" and the three "Love Letters to the Immortal Beloved" indicate how much Beethoven suffered, struggled, wept and exulted in the period preceding his writing of the "Eroica". All the mental conflicts that Beethoven experienced before this time are minor ones compared to these struggles that put Beethoven's highest moral strength and all his heroic disposition to the test. "A hero" to the Beeethoven of the first two symphonies was the equivalent of lustre,

FROM BEETHOVEN TO SHOSTAKOVICH

courage, energy. To the Beethoven of the "Eroica" it meant: Victorious battle with the dark powers of the soul.

Deep down were stored the childhood memories: the oppression of unhappy days, melancholia, solitude; and as relief therefrom: an overbearing feeling of power, longing for joy and happiness, revolt against tyranny. On top of these layers, accumulated in childhood, new layers of similar sentiments were deposited in later years.

As in childhood, they were depressing sentiments alternating with feelings of energy. After Beethoven had been accepted by the aristocratic society of Vienna, he kept his own valet and a horse for a while, (1796) demonstrating by such superficialness that he was every bit as good as the counts and princes. He was always especially sensitive in the company of nobility. He could not stand coercion, blew up and became rough and had fits of rage when he felt depressed, regardless whether it was Fuerst Lichnowsky, or Prince Louis Ferdinand or Archduke Rudolf who was present. Not even Beethoven's friends were safe from such outbursts, and Beethoven's childhood friend from Bonn, Breuning, disappeared from Beethoven's life for a period of ten or twelve years because he had insulted the sensitive man.

Beethoven's self-complacency was always sensitive. In good-natured ridicule, Haydn called Beethoven the "Grand Mogul". The artist knew no limits in his sensation of power. When Napoleon emerged as victor in the battle of Jena, Beethoven remarked: "Too bad that I am not as familiar with the art of warfare as I am with music, I would still vanquish him."

Beethoven's self-conceit was the superstructure above a tottering soul foundation. His moods varied from black melancholia to shining consciousness of power. As late

[180]

as 1818 Beethoven feared he was susceptible to lung disease, as his mother had been.

Such periods of fear and grief were followed by raptures of moral energy. "Courage! No matter what the weaknesses of my body, my spirit shall dominate," an entry in his notebook of 1797 reads, and: "Strength is the morale of people who distinguish themselves above others, and it is mine too," he states in a letter to Zmeskall.

Mental conflicts of this kind expanded Beethoven's soul and created in the Third Symphony new dimensions of music, masses of light and shade, a new monumentality.

This development of heroic moods originated in childhood experiences. No incident out of Beethoven's young days gives such a clear picture of his character as the story, mentioned elsewhere in these pages, about the dirty, neglected boy who, when reprimanded, proudly remarked: "When I will be a gentleman, nobody will notice it any more." To be a gentleman was Beethoven's dream and ideal.

Beethoven's self-conceit, when he first came to Vienna, became apparent in his elegant attire, about which Grillparzer and Czerny commented. Later, isolated because of increasing deafness, Beethoven again began to neglect himself. Kloeber describes him in 1818 as being "very shabby"; in 1813 he had "no good coat and not one whole shirt"; but around 1814, when fame and success gave him back his self-confidence, Czerny reports, he paid attention to his appearance.

The words: "When I will be a gentleman" reflect the ambition of the boy, the Beethovenic feeling of power and the Beethovenic consciousness of the greatness of his personality.

The musical formula for such feeling of lordliness **are** themes that rise with energy. Themes that advance irresistably. Themes that advance like a victorious army, flags raised high. Such themes are musical symbols of Beethoven's power consciousness.

The Allegros of the first and second symphonies have such rising themes:

Beethoven's first piano sonata has the same type of theme:

Later, when Beethoven portrays the tragic fate that threatens to crush man, he uses precipitating themes as symbols for the tragic powers of life:

in the Fifth Symphony

in the Ninth Symphony

Just as a dismal fate invades the world in these symphonies, so does the thunderstorm in the "Pastoral Symphony" penetrate nature. The thunder:

The tempest:

The powers of life that strike man come from above. The elevation of man above his fate makes him proud and courageous. Thus it was on March 27, 1827, when Beethoven died. At five o'clock lightning and thunder crashed down from the skies, and the death chamber was illuminated with a glaring light. But Beethoven opened his eyes for the last time and raised his right hand, clenching his fist. Huettenbrenner, describing these last moments, interpreted this typically Beethovenic gesture to mean: "Courage, soldiers! Advance! Trust me! Our victory is certain!"

The rising and precipitating themes are just as Beethovenic as all other dramatic movements of his emotional world.

Almost all of Haydn's symphonic themes were song-like, harmonically welded of two halves, themes that inhaled and exhaled evenly. Mozart's themes (for instance in the Linz Symphony or the Jupiter Symphony) are often harmonies in three parts. Beethoven's themes are bundles of energy that radiate strength, whether it be that of lightning flashing down, or that of an eagle that soars aloft.

Between the music of the Haydn-Mozart period and the Beethoven era lies the great conversion that was called Rousseau philosophy and that unleashed sentiment and made the moods of nature a picture of human moods. The dirty, unkempt boy who in 1778 dreamed of becoming a "gentleman," was the child of a generation that caused the French Revolution in 1789

The type of the revolutionary is always formed in childhood. Out of the boy who suffers under too much pressure of paternal authority develops the man who hates all authority and tries to destroy the traditional forms of the world.

Schiller, the poet who glorified liberty, had a tyrannical father. Mirabeau, the ardent leader of the French Revolution, was dragged from one prison to another by his father, from Chateau d'If to the Fort de Joux, because the elder Mirabeau considered his tempestuous son a "terrific male as to his physics and to his morals"

Beethoven's revolutionary feeling had the same motivating power. He opposed the authority of tradition with the force of his personality. Ries tells an informative anecdote: he pointed out to Beethoven two fifths in the first Violin Concerto. "Well, who forbade them"? Beethoven asked. Ries answered: "Marpurg, Kirnberger, Fux, et al. All theorists." "Well, then, I permit them!", was Beethoven's retort.

EXTERNAL AND INTERNAL EXPERIENCES

The revolutionary elements in Beethoven's music were the cause of excitement among his conservative contemporaries. The composer Wenzel Tomaschek opined: "He considered oddity and originality to be the essentials of his composition." The pianist Moscheles tells in his memoirs how he heard one day that "a young composer made his appearance in Vienna. He wrote the most peculiar stuff such as nobody could play or understand; crazy music, contrary to all rules. And this composer's name was Beethoven."

Ignaz von Mosel laments that Beethoven "deviated from the path (of a Mozart emulator) originally taken;" "he wanted to break an absolutely new trail and finally landed on the wrong road. And did not his continued deviation from forms that were formerly observed finally lead him to the formless?"

Beethoven was of the conviction that "there is no rule in art that cannot be repealed by a higher one." For this he was considered by a good number of his contemporaries as nothing less than a treasury of classicism, which he was later made by staunch piano and harmonics teachers.

Being a revolutionary himself, Beethoven admired Napoleon. According to Baron de Tremont, who in 1809 came to Vienna to bring Napoleon the resolutions of the state council, and who visited Beethoven at that time, Napoleon was admired by Beethoven because he rose to fame from an obscure position.

Wegeler also described Beethoven's high esteem for Napoleon in 1803, and reported that Beethoven compared him to the greatest Roman consuls. The title page of the "Eroica" is inscribed "Bonaparte" on top and "Beethoven" at the bottom.

FROM BEETHOVEN TO SHOSTAKOVICH

Four years after the insurgents in Paris had stormed the Bastille—the first symbolic act of the French Revolution—Beethoven brought to the operatic stage the liberation of prisoners from their dungeons. Sunlight fell upon the dark prison cell, from the citadel sounded the trumpet signal that heralded freedom, and the crowds exulted in the courtyard of the fortress.

In Beethoven's days all this was realism, one felt the hot breath of life; this was not stylized classicism but the most timely realism.

The theme of the overture to this opera ascends uninterruptedly onwards and upwards within a tone sphere of four octaves. Its impetus is intensified continuously by rhythmic condensation. The rhythmic motif acquires more and more energy, while the tone masses continue in a steady crescendo. The music is that of an attack on the Bastille.

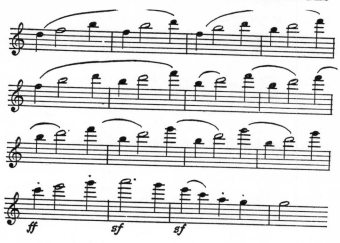

Similar moods of battles for independence and revolutionary action assumed tone and form in Beethoven's "Egmont" music.

The quiet boy who was made an introvert by brutal treatment and who, as such, dreamed of love and liberty, became one of mankind's mightiest fighters for freedom.

An experience that has the power to collect in artistic form all the unconscious sentiments, childhood recollections and moods of by-gone days stored up within the artist, and to create new forms from conscious and unconscious emotions,—that is the experience that produces great works of art. An experience calls. The soul of the artist answers, and the formative forces of the artistic imagination mold the pictures and sensations thus stirred up.

We know more or less definitely of a whole series of Beethoven works which experience of Beethoven's gave the outward impulsion for these particular creations. According to Beethoven, the Adagio of the String Quartet in F-Major was to represent musically the tomb scene in "Romeo and Juliet." Czerny claims that the final movement of the D-Minor Piano Sonata opus 29, No. 2, was inspired by a rider whom Beethoven saw galloping in Heiligenstadt and whose rhythmic motions he reproduced. The Adagio of the Rasumoffsky Quartet in E-Minor was inspired by Beethoven's observation of a starry sky.

Regardless of how well these interpretations are attested to, they nevertheless are somewhat arbitrary and romantic.

On the other hand, one is on safe ground when it comes to the "Dankgesang eines Genesenen" in the A-Minor String Quartet, opus 132. Here an experienced mood that we know quite well turned to music. From the middle of April until early May of 1825 Beethoven suffered from an abdominal ailment. The prescriptions of the attending physician fill Beethoven's diary during that period, so that we are able to follow the entire course of his illness.

The "Dankgesang," of course, was not conceived until after Beethoven was over his illness. Before he took sick he had planned a different Adagio. But in one of the diaries from May or June 1825, there is a pencil notation in Beethoven's handwriting: "Thank-you hymn to God by a sick man on his recovery. Feeling of new strength and re-awakened sensation." In the edition of the Quartet the caption of the Molto Adagio is: "Heiliger Dankgesang eines Genesenen an die Gottheit, in der lyrischen Tonart."

Thus the Beethoven music is directly associated with the event that produced it. The minuet of the String

Quartet also was composed after the illness; before he took sick he had sketched a different minuet. The trio of the present minuet employs a dance tune that Beethoven had composed at the age of twenty for the masquerade halls of Vienna.

It is human to reminisce of happy childhood days in days of old age and illness, as Beethoven did here. Often desires lift recollections from out of the subconscious mind. It doesn't happen just once that we see sentiments and wishes appearing behind memories—images of the imagination against an emotional background.

The short, march-like movement that follows the Adagio and plunges so spiritedly into newly-gained life also was sketched after Beethoven's illness. This, as well as the agitated recitative of the violin, is one of the movements that lead to the disconsolate, passionate finale and are intended as the psychological preparation thereto. The final movement is found among the first sketches of the String Quartet that were written prior to Beethoven's illness; however it is of much earlier date and belongs to the plans for the Ninth Symphony. This was the music that was supposed to have closed the Ninth Symphony when the latter was constructed to end on a dismal note rather than with chorales of rejoicing. Instead, the sombre music that had to retreat before the jubilation of the Ninth Symphony was now incorporated in the A-Minor String Quartet (end of 1823).

It is quite apparent that the music of the String Quartet comes from different sources and that it is first joined to form a unit during the course of artistic work.

A story that reaches far down into the subconscious is also attached to the composition of a movement in the

A-Minor String Quartet that was written in a church mode.

We possess a page from the year 1818 upon which Beethoven sketched the program for a tenth symphony. Here already the Adagio was to be in the "old keys," music of the church in contrast to pagan music. As late as 1825 the idea for such a symphony occupied Beethoven's mind. Plans for a Presto in C Minor, and a short movement in A-flat, both belonging to the tenth symphony, are found in one of Beethoven's sketch books toward the end of 1825, together with sketches for a "Bach" overture.

Holz reports that Beethoven played the complete tenth symphony on the piano; it was ready in all parts in the sketches, and in 1827 Beethoven writes: "I have a completely sketched symphony lying in my desk."

It is probable that Beethoven's interest in ancient church modes, as shown in the plans for the tenth symphony, is also connected with his oratorio projects. The oratorio "Der Sieg des Kreuzes" that Beethoven was to compose for the 'Society of Music Friends' after completion of the Ninth Symphony, ended with "Christian Songs" that extolled the victory of Christendom. In 1827, when Beethoven toyed with the idea of writing an oratorio "Saul," he wanted (according to Holz) "to write choruses in the old keys." In particular he desired a chorus "in the Lydian mode," which can be found in "Dankgesang."

In "Dankgesang eines Genesenen," the Lydian key enhances the ethereal character of the music. It is the key of an exalted sphere. It rids the music of its earthly tone and steeps it in heavenly light.

The form of "Dankgesang" was also pre-existent in Beethoven's imagination. The transfigured movement has the same musical form that Beethoven had invented as early as 1823 for the slow movement of the Ninth Symphony. It is the form of a variation whereby a solemn theme alternates with a lively theme:

NINTH SYMPHONY	A-MINOR STRING QUARTET
1. Adagio molto e cantabile	1. Molto Adagio
2. Andante Moderato	2. Andante
3. Tempo 1 *Variation of* 1	3. Molto Adagio *Variation of* 1
4. Andante *Variation of* 2	4. Andante *Variation of* 2
5. Adagio (Interlude) *Variation of* 1	5. Molto Adagio *Variation of* 1
6. Lo stesso tempo. Variation of 1	

The variation form takes on new meaning here. No longer is it a decorative ornament, a sort of frieze consisting of alternating pictures, a parade of fantasy. The variation sequence is a rising and soaring, a mystic exhibition. The last variation is the top step of this upward path, and the grandest glorification of the sounding phenomena. A profoundly religious mood spreads over this last variation.

The first such mystic variation, ending with religious enhancement, had been written by Beethoven in the C-Minor Piano Sonata, opus 111, simultaneously with sketches for the Missa Solemnis and plans for the Ninth Symphony. Thus part of the religious ecstasy in the Mass and of the mighty visions of the Ninth Symphony infiltrated into these variations.

Considering all this, it becomes clear that the experience which motivated Beethoven's fantasy, viz: his ailment and reconvalescence, set in motion forces of his imagination that were in no way connected with the experience per se. Contrary to the serious illness that inspired Richard Strauss to write the realistic descriptions of "Death and Transfiguration," Beethoven's malady was not a source of artistic inspiration. It merely opened the gates to the subconscious, where art forms and tones awaited liberation. It facilitated inspiration in that various experiences converged.

The chief experience was not his illness, but religious experience which occupied Beethoven so greatly in his declining years.

Never did Beethoven write so many prayer adagios as during the period of the Ninth Symphony and the last string quartets; never did he delve so deeply into mystic regions. At no time did he soar so high above the earth as when, overwhelmed by religious moods while walking in Moedling "evenings among and on the mountains," he wrote, in 1818:

Gott al-lein ist un-ser Herr Er al-lein

In the same summer Beethoven wrote down prayers in his diary, such as: "Sei mein Fels, mein Licht, ewig meine Zuversicht" (Be my rock, my light, eternally my trust).

The new Beethovenic variation form that aspired to the light; the ancient church mode that gave the music an expression of Gothic piety, are the forms of religious moods which, long before Beethoven took sick, accumulated designs and tones in his soul that pressed toward formation.

Such forms, that originated and grew in the unconscious mind, have a vigour all their own. They form automatically. Their generative strength has the force-fulness of proceedings in nature. The musical form that Beethoven employs in "Dankgesang": the form of variation that soars on high, has something of the lustre and the indestructible life of Platonic ideas. It first assumed physical shape in the C-Minor Sonata and in the Adagio of the Ninth Symphony, and in the Adagio of the A-Minor Quartet it again becomes a cathedral.

The greater the composer, the longer the road from experience to art production. Great artists use experiences with merely slight changes only in episodes of compositions, more as an adorning arabesque than as important substance. When Beethoven lets the nightingale, the bob-white and the cuckoo sound their respective calls in the slow movement of the Pastoral Symphony, we of a certainty have a realistic picture in miniature that animates the slow movement charmingly. But this little picture, created by keen observation of nature, could easily be removed from the slow movement without harming the great musical form.

An identical naturalistic detail in the peasant music of the Pastoral Symphony is the bassoon player who sounds his three tones into the dance music where they fit and where they don't fit. This, too, had been a realistic experience of Beethoven's. In the lower Austrian village of Heiligenkreuz a drunken bassoon player was thrown out of the inn, and he was the one Beethoven immortalized in the "Pastorale." No doubt the naturalism of his Dutch homeland came alive in Beethoven when he included this drunken bassoonist in the sublime symphony.

Breughel painted such taverns with the customers sitting before their tall beer steins, smoking long clay pipes, and with drinks. Breughel also pictured the stomping peasant dance which Beethoven portrayed with similar naturalistic force in music in the Pastoral Symphony ('Lustiges Zusammensein der Landleute').

When Richard Strauss composed "Rosenkavalier," he included a like realistic feature in the third act of the opera. When the music at the inn plays waltzes, with many wrong basses in the contrabasses, this detail always reminds me of the walk I took with Strauss in the suburbs of Vienna. From a tavern came the sound of dance music and Strauss stood still a long time, listening to the music. The wrong basses played by the musicians had caught his attention and caused his merriment, and they are now perpetuated in "Rosenkavalier." They are now a small, merry detail. An ornament in the picture, not the picture itself.

Realistic observations can be found quite often in Beethoven's sketch books. They are occasional observations of nature, or of life, such as the song of the postilion* which Beethoven entered in his sketch book in Carlsbad in 1812:

Another such observation occurred at the time that Beethoven had just sketched the first movement of the

---

* Bach wrote such an "Aria di Postiglione" in gay fugue form at the finale of his "Capriccio". Schubert, in his song "Die Post", lets the postilion blow merrily.

Pastoral Symphony; a notation of the rolling thunder (1808):

Such an occasional observation of nature could, when the time was ripe, become part of a musical composition. Thus Beethoven had entered in his sketch book, in 1803:

and

Originally, this was merely the notation of an observation in nature. A realistic memorandum. Not until Beethoven was writing the scene at the brook did he remember this observation, which then swelled with melodic material and began to sing:

This was five years after the first notation of the phenomenon of the babbling brook, in 1808. For five years the rhythmic motif must have led a subterranean life in the abyss of the soul. Between this first notation of the murmuring brook and the work that led to the "scene at the brook" came the Fifth Symphony, wherein Beethoven brought all his tragic conflicts to a victorious decision. Not until he finished the Fifth Symphony with the brilliant, triumphant procession did Beethoven become free inwardly and, thereby, capable of presenting the union of man and nature in symphonic form.

Now he could first derive pleasure from nature; could hear the birds chirping at the brook, the shepherd blowing his pipe. Even the storm, image of mental conflicts in man, resolved itself in peaceful and religious moods and was merely a powerful episode in a universe molded and organized by God.

Beethoven always considered occurrences in nature as a revelation of God. This accounts for the Pastoral Symphony closing with religious strains. The melody of the shepherd changes to a pious chorale intoned by the precentor. It is then repeated by the chorus, and sings the praise of God, creator of the universe.

Additional proof that Beethoven sensed the Spirit of God in nature is found in a sheet of paper upon which he wrote on a day in the autumn of 1815 when he sought peace under the trees of Bald Mountain.

"Allmaechtiger	"O, Gott, welche
im Walde	Herrlichkeit
ich bin selig	in einer
gluecklich im	solchen Waldgegend
Wald jeder	in den Hoehen
Baum spricht	ist Ruhe—
durch dich"	Ruhe ihm zu dienen—"

(Almighty, in the forest I rejoice, happy am I, every tree speaks through you. O, Lord, what glory in such forest environment. In the heights is peace—peace to serve Him.)

Such profound appreciation of nature precludes virtuosity in realistic landscape painting. Descriptions such as those in Strauss' Alpensinfonie—the waterfalls, murmuring of the forest, alpine meadows and the storm, which does not possess the majesty of the Beethovenic tempest but sounds rather like the noise of a wind machine—are not Beethoven's realism. A world without God—and be it ever so masterfully pictured—is not Beethoven's world. His favorite book was Christian Sturm's "Betrachtungen der Werke Gottes in der Natur" (Observations of God's creations in nature.)

Although Beethoven wrote down the murmuring of the brook in his sketchbook and employed its rhythmic motion five years later in the Pastoral Symphony, it cannot be said that he made naturalistic use of the sketch. As carefully as Beethoven marked the tone ranges of the small and the larger brook in his sketch book, the key in the "Pastorale" is nevertheless different. Of importance were the vision of the gently murmuring, singing brook, and the peaceful scenery with the chirping birds.

This scenery had a tone and color all its own, and they were the factors that decided the choice of the key (B Major). The rhythmic movement returns in the symphony; but Beethoven's musical fancy transformed the murmuring of the brook that he had written down, into the charming melody, the color of the atmosphere and the mood of the landscape.

The observation that he had noted in his book had been grasped and re-formed by the formative forces of his fantasy. These formative forces took root in the depth of the subconscious and were nourished by inner

[197]

experiences. It was not until around 1870—when naturalism made scientific studies of universe and mankind; when men like Flaubert and Zola gathered material for their novels like naturalists and accumulated "Documents Humains" in the manner of sociologists and psychologists; and when Claude Monet sat before the same haystack at all hours of the day and year to study the illumination as a scientist—that the external experience assumed significance in music.

With part of his personality Richard Wagner, the romanticist, also belongs to the modern realistic-scientific century.

While working on "Lohengrin" he studied the mediaeval ages like a scientist, and when he wrote the "Meistersinger" he studied the customs of the master singers in the singing school, much as an explorer does. The castle in "Tannhaeuser" is portrayed just as naturalistically as the warriors of King Henry and the tribunal scene in "Lohengrin", and as the narrow streets of Nuernberg with the lilacs and the linden fronting the Gothic houses, with the night watchman and the festival lawn.

Every one admires the realism with which Richard Wagner described the smithy in "Siegfried": the flickering fire in the furnace, the hissing smoke, the hammer strokes and the sound of the anvil. But few people know that Wagner composed this realistic scene while living across the street from a tinsmith in Zuerich who: "deafened my ears all day long with his far-reaching din." Even Siegfried's fit of rage against the "bungling smith", Mime, had been inspired by Wagner's ire against the tinsmith vis-à-vis. Wagner himself admitted as much. Without this external experience of the smithy, the music to the first act of "Siegfried" would not have received its steel timbre.

External experiences of a composer, travels, reading matter and pictures of daily life can impart color, stronger reality and richer details to a work of art. But it takes internal experiences in the composers to produce art that comes from the depth.

When Beethoven's deafness set in, his heroic struggles with fate began; their changing phases are perpetuated in his compositions. The triumphant march at the close of the Fifth Symphony, and the jubilant choruses at the end of the Ninth Symphony were the highest exaltation of his mind and vital energy.

When Bedrich Smetana became deaf, he described quite realistically the incipient deafness, in his string quartet "Aus meinem Leben", with a shrill, high, piercing tone of the violin that sounded in his ears when the malady befell him. There follows touching, submissive, resigned music.

Beethoven's heroic reaction, as well as Smetana's plaintive resignation grow from the basic foundations of their respective personalities.

The whole life of the composers, from childhood to maturity, is contained in the different attitude; and the life of both is also contained in the strong rhythms, the virile power and the monumental harmonics of Beethoven, and in the soft song, the gentle minor harmonies and the popular simplicity of Smetana's music.

External occurrences, fate, travels, studies, books, are of value to the creative composer only when they can change to inner experiences. Traveling played no part at all in the life of classical musicians. Felix Mendelssohn-Bartholdy was the first composer of modern times to derive inspiration for his music from impressions gained while traveling in Scotland and Italy. The peculiar atmosphere of the north and the south suggested tones and tone colors to him. Fog, wind and ocean waves had local coloring. As a man of rich, fine culture, he absorbed the peculiarities of the countries, and the songs of the gondoliers that were sung in Venice, and the Neapolitan tarantella echoed within him.

In a letter of July 30, 1829, written from Edinburgh, Felix Mendelssohn-Bartholdy narrates how, at dusk, he entered the palace where Queen Mary had lived and loved: "One sees a small room, with a winding stair at the door; up these stairs they went, and found Rizzio in the little room and dragged him out; three rooms further there is a dark corner, where they murdered him. In the chapel right next to it there is no roof, much grass and ivy grows on it, and at its broken altar Mary was crowned Queen of Scotland. Everything there is broken, wormeaten, and the clear sky shines through. I believe that today I found there the beginning of my Scotch Symphony."

Almost at the same time that Felix Mendelssohn, the cultured voyager, composed symphonies, Karl Maria von Weber traveled to foreign countries in spirit. He discovered a Turkish dance melody by De la Borde and used it for the dance of the moors in his opera "Oberon", and an Egyptian melody, sketched by Niebuhr, served him as the first finale to "Oberon". In his "Turandot" overture Weber adopted the Chinese melody "Lieu-ye-kin" which he found among works by Pater Amiot.

Weber initiates the period in which local coloring of foreign countries was studied. Two original Egyptian tunes are found in Verdi's "Aida", Spanish melodies in Bizet's "Carmen," and Puccini employs Japanese strains in "Madame Butterfly".

EXTERNAL AND INTERNAL EXPERIENCES

Experiences gained through reading also began to play a part in music only during the 19th century. In 1808 Beethoven started to sketch music for a "Macbeth". Otherwise there is no Shakespearian influence noticeable in his works. But young Felix Mendelssohn starts off a series of musicians who seek inspiration in their literary education, and who transform into tone poetic works together with the whole spiritual atmosphere that surrounds them. Mendelssohn's "Midsummer Night's Dream" is more than just tuneful theatrical music. It is a part of Shakespearian fantasy, set to music by a man of the finest literary education. Later it was Franz Liszt who became the most noble representative of this type of musician. Literary education turns creative in Liszt, and his inspirations are derived from Goethe, Dante, Lamartine and Tasso.

The number of external experiences gained through education has increased tremendously in the modern era. Compared to the culture of a Richard Strauss, Haydn and Mozart have very little education — that is, if education is to be measured by the amount of books an artist has read, rather than by the originality of that which was learned. The education of a genius like Bach consisted almost exclusively of the bible; but what Bach found therein sufficed for a life-time of music. Among the more recent composers Johannes Brahms was the last of these strong Protestant bible readers; he himself compiled the text of his "Deutsches Requiem" from biblical phrases.

The fact remains that outside experiences are able to motivate the inner forces in creative minds, and that only the strength and the wealth of these inner forces are of significance, not the colorful surface of life and not the versatility of spiritual interests.

Bach lived in a very narrow, musty circle. Home, school and church were his world. His knowledge of life, in contrast to Haendel's, was not gleaned from traveling through foreign countries, or by associating with high society, Roman cardinals, Hannoveranian princes and English aristocrats. He learned in the manner of the burgher living in the family circle and attending to his job. But his inner life was so rich that whatever it brought assumed significance, sense and shape, and religion gave Bach's unruffled life the magnificent background and the outlook upon the Eternal.

It was religious life almost exclusively that gave mediaeval musicians spiritual purport. The great musicians were men of the church, employed in cathedrals and other churches. At best they received their education in a monastery school. But we can hardly conceive of the strength and intensity of a faith that erected magnificent cathedrals, that presented biblical stories and figures in innumerable pictures and statues and that digested all ancient culture in the Christian tendency.

In the case of Haydn it was still almost entirely his creed that made up his education; it was the religion of his forebearers which he had learned in village schools, village church services and in the St. Stephan's school in Vienna. Not until Beethoven's time do we come across modern musicians who sought a general education in the works of philosophers and poets and who, in Kant, Goethe and Schiller, found a new religion of ethical humanity, as Beethoven did.

In works of great musicians, a certain instinct tells us where their music was inspired only by outside episodes and educational interests, and where something rushes up from the foundations of their personalities that is stronger than external life.

EXTERNAL AND INTERNAL EXPERIENCES

Like all important composers, Mozart, too, first started to absorb all the music forms that had been created by the composers of his era. The symphony of his time was the Italian opera overture with its rustling, festive gleam; the symphony of the Mannheimer symphonic composers and of Josef Haydn, and the North German symphony of Philipp Emmanuel Bach. All this Mozart first had to digest and then to give it the expression of his own personality.

We know that Mozart's artistic impressionability equalled his human pliability. . . . When Mozart became acquainted in Mannheim with the then new form of the melodrama (1778), he was so enthusiastic that he immediately considered treating the opera recitative in this manner, and started to experiment with this form. The same thing happened when Mozart heard Bach and Haendel music at the house of Baron Swieten (1782) and began to write fugues.

In 1789 Mozart came to Leipsic where Doles, the precentor at St. Thomas, taught him the Bach motets. The Bach form of the choral fugue made such a deep impression on him that he wrote the singing of the armour-clad men in "Magic Flute" in that style, with the chorale as cantus firmus over a fugue. For the cantus firmus he chose a Protestant chorale: "Es woll' uns Gott gnaedig sein."

With the same susceptible fantasy Mozart gathered in the symphony all the symphonic forms that had grown in Italy, France, Austria and Germany. All this music was festive, rustling; it was ideal for society and entertainment.

All this lovely, lively music is intent on decorating a gay moment in life; it is the typical music for the candle-lit rococo salons of the 18th century where men in embroidered coats court women in crinolines. But in 1773, among all this music one suddenly comes upon a symphony that is dismal and passionate, the first symphony that Mozart wrote in the minor key.

In the agitated orchestra, in the syncopes of the beginning, in the sharp accents and the tremoli there is such a strong personal expression that, of a sudden, one feels quite close to the Mozart who later wrote the symphony in G-Minor, the G-Minor String Quartet and the Piano Concerto in D-Minor. One has the same sensation as when one encounters "Hamlet" among Shakespeare's works: here is something entirely personal, something that only he could feel, his innermost thoughts. This work is not just a piece of art, it is a confession. The character of Hamlet is the true, most intimate Shakespeare. The G-Minor Symphony of seventeen-year old Mozart is the true and most intimate Mozart: the Mozart behind the gleaming, ornamental rococo facade.

This work, although composed a year before Goethe's "Werther" was published, nevertheless is Werther-like in character. Mozart, who wrote down symphonies as social music with a light hand, followed up the G-Minor Symphony with formal symphonies again: in 1771 he composed seven symphonies, in 1772, eight; and so on. Then in 1786 came the Linzer Symphony which starts off the series of Mozart's most magnificent symphonies. The G-Minor Symphony of the year 1788 brings the fulfillment of that which was heralded in the G-Minor Symphony of 1773. It is the classical work of Mozart, the tragedian, whose tear-stained face was first visible in 1773.

We do not know what occurrence gave Mozartian symphonic music its moving personal expression, but we do know, from other instances, that intimate, personal experiences influenced great Mozart music and displaced formal balance there.

Whoever witnessed a performance of Mozart's "Don Giovanni" will have come to the conclusion that the tragic parts of this opera were too momentous in proportion to the buffo parts. The tragic shadows thrown by the events of this opera are so dark that they weigh heavily upon the gay performance. This is why, soon after creation of the work, the conventional finale that closes "Don Giovanni" in old buffo tradition began to be abbreviated or omitted altogether. An attempt at abbreviation was already included in the original score, and at the first performance of "Don Giovanni" in Vienna, the opera ended with the infernal ride and in a doleful D-Minor, which later became general practice in the theatre.

The restoration of the merry finale ensemble began only with the modern Mozart renaissance. The modern Mozartians who went forth from the Wagner school (Hermann Levi in Munich, Richard Strauss and Gustav Mahler) and sought divine gaiety and graceful play in Mozart works, would not miss the cheerful ending. The address to the audience that delineates the moral of the play gives the Mozartian performance an unreal character. This disturbs the tragic and lets reality appear as an image of the imagination. For the naturalistic theatre era that had dawned, the abrogation of seriousness and the irony of the ending was something that was artistically fine and unusual.

Stylistically, too, the retention of the merry finale was proper. Mozart's "Don Giovanni" had been called "dramma giocoso" by the composer. In the 17th century, at the opera house of Venice buffo operas, fantastic operas and burlesques were called thus. The word

[205]

signified a cheerful world without stylization, a theatre of playful fantasy. In our time Richard Strauss composed such music in "Ariadne on Naxos", and Feruccio Busoni in "Arlecchino".

The buffo principle of "Don Giovanni" is indisputable. In the Mozart opera, Don Juan goes from one embarrassing situation to another. He is conceived as a comical, rather than as a romantic-tragic figure and, as a buffo character, he is thrown into the inferno at the end. A scene as dismal as the cemetery scene, with all the terror and nocturnal mood, is composed in a gay E-Major as an Allegro con brio.

However, although the buffo character of Mozart's Don Juan is clear, the disproportionate heaviness of the tragic parts is equally clear. Already the first scene with the death of the Comthur is permeated with an awe of the Beyond. In the small trio in which the dying Comthur sings with choking voice, Don Juan is nobly moved and Leporello's legs tremble, there is a black color that is quite unusual. The orchestral postlude describes death and dying with an emotion that sings in deep feeling.

Toward the end of the opera the tragic moods mount. In the cemetery scene ghostly voices are heard; horror trickles through the music; the voice of the Comthur sounds majestically; even Don Juan is perplexed; and the cemetery scene fades out, depressed.

The final scene reaches the climax of tragedy with the appearance of the statue. With the first terrible beats of the orchestra one is transplanted to the realm of the supernatural. The majestic voice of morality resounds powerfully. The voices of the Beyond become audible. Across the stage blows a wind that is not of this world. Declamation, together with the chromatic tone figures, the rhythmic accents and the orchestral timbre describe the celestial world, while the choral voices of infernal spirits resound from the depth, into which Don Juan sinks.

Never before and never after did a composer portray with such magnitude the terror, majesty and destruction of the Beyond, as Mozart did in "Don Giovanni." It was shortly before his death, when he was already pale and ailing, that Mozart returned to these moods. In the "Dies Irae" of his Requiem he let the trombone of perdition resound equally great and powerful and solemn before entering the "great Beyond" whence he had captured the tones of the "Don Giovanni" finale.

The thought of death, the Beyond and perdition, of moral justice and judgment excited Mozart to such an extent that he imparted to the tragic scenes of "Don Giovanni" a tragic power great enough to almost burst the frame of a gay opera.

Such music is entirely personal; just as personal as Bach's emotion when a text makes mention of death. Whether it is a great mystic work such as the cantata "Gottes Zeit ist die allerbeste Zeit", composed in his youth, in which the theme of death and resurrection was first treated by Bach, or whether it is a small song like "Komm suesser Tod", or a choral prelude such as "Vor Deinen Thron tret ich allhier", or the description of the Saviour's death in a Bach Passion: whenever the word "death" or "dying" appears, one seems to see Bach in closer proximity and to hear his strong, agitated voice louder. Mozart's duel, the cemetery and banquet scenes in "Don Giovanni" give the same effect.

In the period during which Mozart wrote the music for "Don Giovanni", there was nothing that occupied his mind as much as the thought of death.

[207]

This meditation it was that had attracted Mozart to Free-Masonry, where he received enlightenment that afforded him consolation. Under date of April 4, 1787, having heard of his father's illness, he wrote to him: "Since death (to be exact) is the main purpose of our life, I have, for the past few years, so acquainted myself with this true, best friend of man that its picture not only does not frighten me, but actually comforts and consoles me!"

One of the most moving compositions written by Mozart for purposes of free masonry is "Maurerische Trauermusik", composed in 1785, the year of "Nozze di Figaro". It is a wonderful work, very personal already in the veiled tone blends of the oboes, clarinets, three bassett horns, one horn in E-flat, one horn in C and the contrabassoon, in addition to the string orchestra. It is rich in expression of profound grief, with the serious admonition of a chorale that is reminiscent of a Catholic penitential psalm. This is music which, with its glorification, resembles the music of "Magic Flute", and, with its dark color, the music of "Requiem".

The solemnity of this music shows how deeply Mozart was affected by the death of the two free masons for whose funeral the music was written; it also shows that there was gentle pain as well as passionate storm in his soul, which he pacified with the solemn exhortation of the Cantus Firmus.

Such moods were further intensified by personal events; just as Mozart started working on "Don Giovanni", he was informed of his father's death (May 28, 1787).

Certainly this news was capable of twisting Mozart's soul in its very depths. Since Mozart had been a child, his father appeared to him to be the representative of

God on earth. "Papa comes right after God", Mozart used to say. His father was the wise leader, the strict, but just, teacher; he was the clever impresario on concert tours, and his authority was always equally strong. When Mozart, enroute to Paris in 1778, stopped off at Mannheim, fell in love with Aloysia Weber and made fantastic plans to go to Italy with the young, unknown singer, the elder Mozart had merely to write a severe letter to lead Wolfgang back to the right path: "Get to Paris, and get there soon", the father commanded, "sit down with big people—aut Caesar aut nihil" (either Caesar or nothing). And Mozart obeyed; he went to Paris and left Aloysia.

Wolfgang got himself into the same dilemma in Vienna in 1781. He fell in love with Constanze Weber and was coerced into a promise of marriage by her intriguing mother and shrewd guardian. It took all of Leopold Mozart's paternal authority to convince his son not to leave the service of the Archbishop, not to construct his life on an uncertain existence and not to marry a girl of dubious reputation. Leopold Mozart warned, threatened, reminded his son of his obligations. This time, however, his authority availed him nothing. Mozart, ordinarily easily persuaded, remained adamant. "I must confess that not in one line of your letter do I recognize my father! A father, yes; but not the best, most loving father who was always solicitous of his and his children's honor; in a word, not—my father."

Mozart had to marry without his father's consent, which he had requested, reaching him on time. Not even the success of "Abduction from the Seraglio" pacified his father; and although there was a reconciliation later on, the break was there and remained in the soul of both Leopold Mozart and his son.

The conflict with his father gave Mozart his human self-reliance. He had withdrawn from the authority of the prudent man who, though dry, nevertheless was superior, and had guided his every step till then. Mozart advanced toward life in the manner of one who lives his own life and even though, as his father had feared, he foundered, still we have the great masterpieces that originated only after Mozart had liberated himself.

Still and all, Mozart's conflict with his father—a human conflict of eternal significance as long as there are fathers and sons—was a wound in Mozart's soul, and when the news of Leopold Mozart's death came to Vienna, this wound started to bleed again. "I wish to inform you", Mozart wrote to his friend Jacquin, "that today, on coming home, I received the news of the sad passing of my best father. You can imagine my condition."

The libretto of the opera "Don Giovanni" which Mozart began to compose at that time reminded him of things out of his own life.

He had been something of a Don Giovanni himself: many was the time he had played with girls, fallen in love quickly and, just as quickly, fallen out of love again; a smiling boy, a youth always ready for fun, a butterfly flitting through life. In "Marriage of Figaro", Cherubin described the erotic sentiments of Mozart's own youth. But Cherubin, grown up, becomes Don Juan.

Don Giovanni was Mozart, or at least a piece of Mozart. The demonic Don Juan, the Byronic Don Juan, the romantic eroticist as Richard Strauss portrayed him, are all alien to Mozart. Mozart's Don Giovanni is a buffo, and the single scene in "Don Giovanni" in which Don Juan wins a woman—the scene with Zerline—is completely light, charming and comic; in short, Mozartian.

Into the life of this Don Giovanni the grave voice of the Comthur rings, just as it so often resounded in Mozart's life; a noble voice of warning, dignified admonition, a voice with ethical power, the voice of his father.

Mozart inserted this contrast between gay, playful enjoyment of life and strict admonition in the overture to "Don Giovanni" in an Allegro. The overture (after the ghostly apparition in the Andante) does not describe Don Giovanni alone, but Don Giovanni and the warning voice:

For Mozart the Comthur assumed the features of his father who had predicted in one of his letters: "In your mature years, after my death, you will love me more than ever."

If, however, Mozart envisaged the Comthur with the features of his own father, then it was only natural that all emotions stirred up by the news of his death should attach themselves to this image.

The father had gone to the great Beyond that had come to Mozart's mind the very minute he had learned of Leopold Mozart's illness. His voice had become a voice from the Beyond; his image was embraced by the air from the Beyond. Now, all this was gathered in the "Don Giovanni" music and swelled it with tones from the world to come, with sublime, solemn, majestic harmonies. In the score to the final scene one notices how Mozart increased the expression of supermundane paroxysm.

Originally, when the marble statue appears onstage, the score was missing the rising and descending scales of the violins and flutes that "like an eerie rushing wind, evoke a chilling terror" (O. Jahn, Mozart, Vol. 2, page 409). Not until Mozart saw the statue on the stage in his fantasy did that passage begin to sound within him, and he subsequently inserted the tones of the Beyond in the score in small notes (since there was lack of space). Now the music first sounded as coming from a higher sphere.

Shakespeare gives us a similar example. His father died in 1661, and in the same year he wrote "Hamlet". The relations between father and son came to the foreground of his psychical life. He began to brood over filial love and respect. The father strode across the stage as a ghost, letting his spectral voice be heard, as later Mozart was to have the Comthur do. Neither in "Hamlet" nor in "Don Giovanni" is the cemetery scene missing with thoughts of death and transitoriness.

Even much later, in "Zauberfloete", Mozart still hears the monitorial, warning, grave, voice of his father. Mozart, accustomed to guidance and authority, saw in free-masonry a substitute for his father. The master of the lodge, whose directions free-mason Mozart followed, replaced his father. He was the wise authority who, in Mozart's Viennese period, "came right after God". Thus it could happen easily that Mozart poured sentiments into the character of Sarastro that were linked with recollections of his father, and that Mozart, in the Sarastro arias, idealized his father's voice.

In this way the personal experience and sentiment

that converges in the most grandiose moments of both "Don Giovanni" and "Magic Flute" was actually the creative medium. Whatever the news of his father's death stirred up in Mozart's heart gave the Comthur scenes of "Don Giovanni" the grandeur and mightiness that burdens the buffo style of the opera so heavily.

The figure of the Comthur was exalted. It was set against a background of moods from Beyond, the atmosphere of a loftier world by which it is surrounded, supermundane solemnity and magnitude. The contrast between Don Giovanni—Comthur, was intensified by moral ethics.

In "Magic Flute" the figure of Sarastro was ennobled. When Mozart composed the music for "Don Giovanni" he was so agitated by the news of his father's death that all his emotions were of the strongest dramatic energy and gave the music tragic profundity. By the time he was writing "Zauberfloete", all this agitation had paled to a noble memory and had become pure solemnity. Mozart himself was personified by the fanciful youth, Tamino; Constanze had become Papagena. The fabulous mood of Mozart's childhood had returned, in which the figure of his father no longer threatened; instead, like a prince out of a fairy tale, it spoke words of wisdom and gave good advice.

When Mozart began to compose the "Don Giovanni" music, the news of his father's passing thus was the stone that fell to the bottom of his soul and disturbed all the waters there. The external event touched off inner experiences. The voices of childhood began to resound. Old sentiments rose from the depth.

However, the outside occurrence is always only the occasion that sets off vibration of soul motions. Important is the wealth of the musician's soul in internal experiences. The creative musician is richer in childhood impressions than other people; he is richer in past sentiments and mental conflicts, in dreams and desires, in woes and joys that have gone by. He has a retentive memory; he preserves past moods and feelings as though they were today's. Soul life of the creative musician is so flexible that it is easy for him to adopt himself to any mood. Thus it was possible for Haendel to imagine the moods of whole nations in the hour of victory and defeat. Thus did Bach experience the suffering of the Lord. Thus did Haydn laugh and weep, dance and pray in his symphonies.

In this way Mozart was Cherubin and Don Juan; ecstatic lover as Belmonte and Tamino; jesting servant as Leporello; a mobile Figaro, a solemn priest. He could transform his soul into a woman's psyche; he could be nobly suffering women like Elvira and the countess, tragic women like Donna Anna and the Queen of the Night; or graceful as Zerline or Papagena.

By the same token Beethoven was the lonely suffering hero, or the exulting population, a dreamer at an abyss or a praying man in a cathedral. And Richard Wagner could be a pagan sinner at the Venusberg, a solemn saint in the Holy Grail, a malicious dwarf in the person of Alberich, and a radiant young hero as Siegfried.

The souls of great musicians contain all moods, all sentiments and all struggles; and even that which only passed through the soul fleetingly could swell and become powerful. Shakespeare, the actor who had only a small part and who found another actor obstructing his path, could feel like Macbeth. Mozart, leading a bourgeois life, nevertheless was able to experience rage, vindictiveness and noble passion which grew from small impulses to the proportion of the Donna Anna aria.

Beethoven's hatred of oppression and submission was capable of swelling to a love of freedom of gigantic proportions.

Whenever an occurrence begins to affect the creative artist, it is grasped by the artistic imagination, transformed, enlarged, embellished and steeped in a bright light. An adagio melody by Haydn or Beethoven is just an idealizing re-molding of a human sentiment by artistic fantasy which purifies the sentiment, enhances it, organizes it and shapes it into a sounding arch.

A particularly instructive instance for the spiritualization of outside events by artistic fantasy is given by the story about the origin of Richard Wagner's "Meistersinger von Nuernberg".

At the age of twenty Richard Wagner had gone to Nuremberg for the first time, visiting his sister who was working in the theatre there. Wagner had just completed his youthful opera "Die Feen" and was enroute to Leipsic.

The following year he returned to Nuremberg (1834). On this occasion he experienced an episode which he describes in great detail in his autobiography, probably because a heavy emotional accent lay upon this recollection.

Wagner tells about a comical singer, the master cabinet-maker Lauermann. He was an eccentric who imagined himself a good singer and for this reason was the butt of many a joke. Wagner describes his singing in many details: "The lips quivered, his teeth gnashed, the eye twisted convulsively and finally, in a hoarse, fat voice he broke into a totally trivial street song. . . . Enormous laughter broke out among all the listeners, which immediately infuriated the unhappy master."

Wagner further narrates how one of these railleries

resulted in a street brawl: "a confusion which, due to the screaming and tumult, and the inexplicable increase in the number of combatants, soon assumed a truly demoniac character." "Then, suddenly, I heard a fall—and as if by magic the entire mob dispersed in all directions. Hardly one minute after the most violent turmoil of several hundred persons, I was able to walk home through the lonely, moon-lit streets."

From this external event originated the second act of "Meistersinger of Nuernberg".

All the elements are given in this occurrence: the comical singer . . . the laughter of the audience . . . the extreme rage of the singer . . . the street riot and ensuing fight . . . the dispersing of the crowd . . . the moonlit street . . . the quietness . . . the deserted street. Nothing is missing to make the second act of "Meistersinger" vigorous, merry and poetic.

Eleven years later, when Wagner was sketching a comic opera in Marienbad that was to be the gay counterpart of the singing contest in "Tannhaeuser"—a satyric play after the serious play—he recalled the street scene in Nuremberg. He saw Hans Sachs sitting on his cobbler stool in front of his shop, hammering the shoes; he saw the anger of Beckmesser, plucking at his lute; he saw the masters and apprentices and journeymen converging from the street corners and starting to fight. He saw the yelling mob scatter, and the moon rise above the gables of Nuremberg's houses.

What had been an outside experience in Nuremberg had been glorified by artistic fancy eleven years later. It had been linked with the "Meistersinger" material that followed "Tannhaeuser" as its comic counterpart. It became an important scene of the "Meistersinger" fable which Wagner sketched in 1845, and from this

scene the invention of the "Meistersinger" action emanated.

Then the memory of the occurrence and the composition disappeared for another sixteen years.

In August 1861 Wagner again came to Nuremberg.
On the occasion of this visit (according to his autobiography) he had a little hotel episode from which he
took the name 'Magdalena' for the housekeeper of
Pogner's house. (Magdalena was the name of the cham-
bermaid in the hotel who showed Wagner to his room).

During the same year Wagner wrote: "I decided to
complete 'Meistersinger' ".

We can state with some certainty the external occurrence that took place in Venice in 1861 and that stirred
up the inner experiences around which the "Meistersinger" now grouped themselves: it was the visit in
Venice of Otto and Mathilde Wesendonck.

Three years had passed since Richard Wagner had
left the house in Zurich where his love to Mathilde
Wesendonck had inspired the composition of "Tristan"
and filled the music of the first act with passionate emotional storm. He had fled to Venice when the great
crisis had driven him from Zurich. In the peace of
Venice, when night lay upon the canals and the calls
of the gondoliers sounded from the distance—like Bran-
gaene's call in the night—the love music of the second
act took shape. The third act was composed in Lucerne.
In this opus the experience of his great love for Mathilde
Wesendonck became a work of art.

For Wagner this was a period gone by. In the letters
which he wrote to Mathilde after this episode, he repeatedly addressed her as "child". This is no longer
written by passion, but by remote feeling. Wagner often
signed his letters to Mathilde: "The Master". He had

become aware of his strength and magnitude. Tristan, to whom love meant fate and death, had become Hans Sachs who is above passion and who conquers and masters his love for Evchen. Out of this changed attitude the "Meistersinger" originated, which was first supposed to be called "Hans Sachs". (Letter to Minna Wagner, December 13, 1861).

Contrary to the sketch from the year 1845, young Walter Stolzing was no longer the main hero, nor was Stolzing's contest against the master singers the chief action. At that time the contest was to have been a humorous reflection of Tannhaeuser's battle against the knightly singers. Now it was Hans Sachs who became the center of action; the old master, the great poet who had learned to accept resignation. In Hans Sachs, Richard Wagner visualized himself. He was then nearing his fiftieth birthday.

At no other time in Wagner's life was he so aware of his genius. "It is quite clear to me that this work will be my most perfect masterpiece," he wrote to Mathilde Wesendonck. "Since today, since the first morning hour of my birthday, I know that the Meistersinger will be my masterpiece," he wrote to Weissheimer. And to Peter Cornelius: "This will be my most ingenious production." And in a letter to Minna Wagner he says: "I am working at my composition with incredible zeal: it gives me so much pleasure and amusement that I am always sorry when I finally have to stop at the end of the day. Sometimes laughter, sometimes tears prevented me from continuing my work."

Wagner was fully aware that this gaiety and feeling of strength was a sensation of relief based on the suppression of his infatuation for Mathilde Wesendonck.

It was a feeling of health after having overcome tragedy. That is why he wrote to Mathilde: "The old sketch offered little or nothing. Why, *one must have been in paradise* in order to know what lies hidden therein." Paradise was the house in Zurich where he had loved Mathilde and which he had to leave. This letter, which echoes in the song of Hans Sachs: "Als Evchen aus dem Paradies von Gott dem Herrn verstossen" (*When Eva was driven from Paradise* by the Lord God) is signed: "Farewell! Child! The Master."

Quite in character with Hans Sachs, he writes Mathilde for her birthday:

Viel Glueck, und dass es blueh und wachs
das wuenscht von Herzen Euch Hans Sachs.

(Much luck, and may it bloom and grow, my heartfelt wish, Hans Sachs, your beau).

Already while Wagner was changing the composition of Meistersinger in accordance with the new sentiment of his personality and life, the music sounded in his soul. He conceived the overture in the train from Venice to Vienna, and on his fiftieth birthday he heard in his soul the prelude to the third act in which the renounced Hans Sachs is comforted by the choral jubilation of the people. "Once you hear the introduction to the third act, and, following that, the chorus," Wagner wrote to Mathilde, "and the enthusiasm with which the population receives Hans Sachs, you will no doubt remember how I felt today, on my birthday."

New pictures continued to settle around the core of the street scene in Nuremberg. In this growth the internal experiences are the tools that mold the piece of art and gather the material necessary for such growth. It is life that presents the artist with material: the street scene in Nuremberg, the comical singer, the brawl, the name of "Magdalena". Additional material is found in books; for instance all the information that Wagner found in Wagensail's Nuremberg Chronicle on "Customs and art of the master singers." Other ideas are inspired by people; for example, Wagner fashioned Pogner after the model of Otto Wesendonck, while Beckmesser assumed some of the traits of Hanslick.

However, all this would remain a dead substance if the inner experiences of the artist did not impart some of his own life to the material. Stolzing was Wagner in his youth; Hans Sachs, Wagner at the age of fifty. And finally, outside events and internal experiences must join hands at a focal point. This focal point, whence the forces of fantasy radiated, was Wagner's affair with Mathilde Wesendonck; but at a time when it was no longer acute, when Wagner, resigned, could contemplate it with humour. This central experience was reinforced by all the unconscious sentiments and emotions in Wagner's soul.

Richard Wagner was twenty-one years old when, on a moonlit night in Nuremberg, he had experienced an event that set his artistic fantasy in motion. He was forty-eight when he wrote down the sketch for the Meistersinger as we now know the opera. In between lies a big stretch of Wagner's life: his battle against the conservative forces of his era; his evolution to mastership; his love of Mathilde Wesendonck; his wisdom in art that formed the dialogue in the third act of "Meistersinger," his faith in his greatness, and his popularity.

In all great works of art the inner experiences motivate the formative forces. The external experiences call. From out of the depth of soul life comes the answer.

CHAPTER IX.

Retrospect: The Origin of
Beethoven's Ninth Symphony

AMONG MUSICAL compositions there are some outstanding, powerful works of art that people view
with the same admiration and awe with which they
contemplate the dome of St. Peter jutting forth among
the rooftops of Rome, or the great Gothic cathedrals
of the moyen age towering above the houses of old
cities. Some of these masterpieces of music are the
Dutch masses, the "Matthaeus Passion" and "Johannis
Passion" of Johann Sebastian Bach; the magnificent
Haendel oratorios, Beethoven's Ninth Symphony, and,
in opera, Mozart's "Magic Flute", Beethoven's "Fidelio"
and Richard Wagner's "Tristan and Isolde". The noblest utterances expressed by man in music are contained
in such works, and the magnitude of the musical construction corresponds to the profundity of the music.

To describe the origin of such great works will always remain a vain effort; but from time to time it is
possible to glance into the darkness where these huge
formations take place. One should not be surprised,
then, to find that the forces of the soul that create such
works are merely enhancements of abilities inherent in
all men, and that the relation of fantasy and intelligence,
unconscious impulses and mental lucidity, suppressed
emotions and organizing faculties, recollections and pat-

terns is exactly the same as in other productive achievements of mankind. To be sure, the proportions between such abilities are enormously augmented.

The measure of humanity, sentiment, passion, sense of beauty; the ability to remember and to experience and the plastic power are gigantic, not human.

The fundamental talents and forces are the same in all men; it is just that the creative artist possesses these faculties in incomparably larger proportions. Not only that his fantasy is much more sensuous, colorful and plastic than that of the ordinary person, and his critical mind keener. He experiences the world—the external as well as the internal world—with more intensity. In addition, the collaboration of his unconscious and conscious mental forces is much more mobile. Still, the artistic world is but an enhancement of talents found in embryonic form in every human soul.

I.

The analysis of the origin of Beethoven's Ninth Symphony will show clearly that the same forces are effective in such a gigantic tone construction as those we have met previously. The foundations of the tonal structure are imbedded in the subconscious. In the depth of music are all the human sentiments, desires and recollections found in every subconscious. Forms that were molded in the subconscious take possession of the soul, force their way through. A great part of the creative work takes place as though automatically. It seems as though an alter ego were creative within the artist, although this second ego is merely our collective self; just as mediaeval mystics already stated: "Omnis homo unus homo" (all men, the same man.)

In the work of the Ninth Symphony lies Beethoven's

whole life. The artistic idea of the Ninth Symphony accompanied Beethoven over a period of thirty years in various forms in all his artistic works. Whatever he writes has a bearing on the Ninth Symphony. In his life the Ninth Symphony is like a mighty mountain range that is visible in the background of a landscape. From this landscape all paths lead to the mountain passes; all brooks flow from the mountains into the valley.

From 1790 on, when the twenty year old composer wrote the cantata at the death of Josef II and the "Cantata on the occasion of Leopold II becoming Emperor," Beethoven is very close to Schiller's "Ode of Joy". The latter cantata ends with a powerful chorus of jubilation that became music to the words: "Stuerzet nieder, Millionen" in the following manner:

Ihr stürzt   nie - der   Mil- li -   o -   nen

Who wouldn't think, hearing these words and tones, of the choral phrase in the Ninth Symphony where the basses sing in trumpet tones: "Ihr stuerzt nieder, Millionen"? This resemblance becomes more striking when the basses in the cantata, just as in the "Ode of Joy," start in to imitate. There is the same mood, the same type of hymnic melody, the same musical form. Like the lyricist, the composer at that time already had been standing in front of Schiller's temple of joy. Three years later his foot touched the shining marble steps of this temple.

In 1793 Beethoven conceived the idea of setting Schiller's "Ode of Joy" to music. We learn this from a letter written by Fischenich, from Bonn, to Charlotte von Schiller, the poet's widow. (January 26, 1793.) "I

am inclosing a composition of the poem 'Feuerfarbe'*
and want to hear your opinion. It is by a young man in
Bonn whose musical talents are being praised by everybody and whom the Elector has sent to Vienna to
Haydn. *He will also compose Schiller's Freude, every
stanza separately.* I expect something accomplished, for
as I know him, he has been created wholly for the great
and sublime."

Of course, this is not yet the Ninth Symphony itself.
But an idea flashes up that later was to become a glow-
ing flame: the "Ode of Joy" by Schiller, composed by
Beethoven.

The Ninth Symphony would not be the Ninth Symphony without the crowning finale of the joyous choruses. These jubilation choruses make the symphony
what it is: a secular mass; a divine service of humanity.

In 1817 Beethoven began his uninterrupted work on
the score of the Ninth Symphony. The work was completed 1823-24. Schindler marks the manuscript February 1824.

I I .

In the history of art there is but one single work that,
like the Ninth Symphony, would accompany the entire
life of a great artist and take nourishment from all the
forces of this life: Goethe's "Faust" epos. As a young
poet Goethe wrote down the first "Faust" scenes in
Strassburg, and fifty-six years later, an old man, he
completed the whole drama of "Faust." The work that
was begun in Strassburg was continued in Italy.

In 1790 the first "Faust" fragment was published.
In 1806 "Faust" Part I was published. In 1824 Goethe

---

* Poetry of Sofie v. Mereau, the wife of Clemens Brentano.
The composition by Beethoven later was published in the 8 songs,
opus 52, 1805.

started work on Part II, and by 1831 the entire poem was completed. During all these years the "Faust" epos absorbed everything that Goethe had experienced; the storm and stress of his youth, his love of Friedericke von Sesenheim; court life at Weimar; and his enthusiasm for the ancient world. In the work was contained the whole development of Goethe, from titanic youth to active man who had learned self-control. "Faust" was Goethe in toto; not just the poet at a certain stage of his life, as "Werther" and "Tasso" had represented him.

The case of Beethoven's Ninth Symphony is quite similar. It is Beethoven at his peak. The first movement repeats once again the tragic battles that Beethoven had described in the Fifth Symphony; but viewed from a higher outlook, as though in profound retrospect upon all the tragedy he had experienced.

In the Fifth Symphony Beethoven was in the midst of battle; here, in the Ninth, he is somewhat removed therefrom. The Fifth Symphony was a drama; the Ninth Symphony is a descriptive epos. The Scherzo again unleashes the rhythmic powers that Beethoven set free in the Seventh and Eighth Symphonies. Again the Adagio aspires with prayers to the heights which Beethoven had reached shortly before in the "Hammerklaviersonate." And the final movement recapitulates the combined choral jubilation of "Chorfantasie," of the "Fidelio" finale and the "Missa Solemnis."

Thus the Ninth Symphony became a monument to the life and personality of Beethoven. Whatever Beethoven experienced, felt or struggled for was given supreme expression in this work. Beethoven's entire life and production twines itself around this work, upon which the vital forces from all his other works converge. Compared to the music of the Ninth Symphony, all his other music was either a preparation, or a partial form of his personality, a basic design or a single mood. Even a work as powerful as the "Missa Solemnis," which occupied Beethoven's fantasy over a period of five years side by side with his labor at the Ninth Symphony, had to make its contribution to the choruses of that symphony.

When young Beethoven first conceived the idea of setting Schiller's "Ode of Joy" to music, it was just a fleeting vision that came and went. But it never disappeared completely. Again and again it emerges from the subconscious. Repeatedly it seeks materialization.

In the years following Fischenich's letter, Beethoven's sketch books show plans dealing with the "Ode of Joy." In a sketch book of the year 1798 we find among sketches to the String Quartet in D-Major—the first of the string quartets opus 18—the following:

In other words, a sketch to the religious climax of "Ode of Joy."

I I I .

It is quite clear, and easily comprehensible, and requires no conjectures as to what made the "Ode of Joy" so dear to Beethoven's heart that he repeatedly reverted to the idea of setting it to music. Melancholy moods accompanied Beethoven from childhood on. A heavy pressure lay upon his soul early in life that separated him from other people and made him the lonely companion of his troubles. A "misanthrope" . . . "in-

trovert and serious minded" . . . "shy and taciturn"
. . . a "softspoken man" . . . "morose among people," are some of the opinions expressed about the boy
by his contemporaries.

The moods of the melancholy boy alternated between
reveries and fits of rage, between gentleness and ob-
stinacy. As mentioned elsewhere in this book, Caecilia
Fischer describes him, leaning at the window, his head
cupped in his hands, gravely looking out. When called,
he did not reply. Frau von Breuning spoke of the boy's
"Raptus."

To spend a day of happiness and joy and rejoicing
with people, was a dream that young Beethoven had
over and over again.

Such a dream was already glorified by Beethoven
when, at the age of twenty, he composed "Josefskan-
tate"; it is a vision of happy, liberated people who ascend to the light, and rejoice. The same dream appeared before his fantasy when, in a sad hour, as the
leaves fell from the trees and the world seemed autumnal to the musician who was growing deaf, Beethoven
wrote the "Heiligenstaedter Testament" in 1802. The
stirring document ends with a prayer: "O Vorsehung
—lass einmal einen reinen *Tag der Freude* mir erchei-
nen—so lange schon ist der wahren Freude inniger
Widerhall mir fremd—o—wann—o wann o Gottheit
—kann ich im Tempel der Natur und der Menschen
ihn wieder fuehlen—Nie? Nein—es waere zu hart."
(O Providence, let me see one pure day of joy, so long
already I have not known the sweet echo of true joy.
When, oh when, Oh Almighty, can I feel it again in
the temple of nature and man—never?—No that would
be too hard).

The "pure day of joy" came to Beethoven much

later. And he set foot in the "temple of nature and man" exultantly when he composed the joyous hymns of the Ninth Symphony.

How strong was the desire in Beethoven's soul for such a day of joy and happiness, brotherhood of man and general adoration of God is indicated in ever new attempts to let people's choruses jubilate happily.

Three years after Beethoven had written down the Heiligenstaedter Testament (1805) he caused the "Fidelio" choruses to ascend to heaven ecstatically with hymns of happiness and liberty. Just like in the "Ode of Joy," this is a simple, almost popular melody in plain chords which is sung first by the soloists, then by the whole chorus; there is no end to the jubilation.*

As the final chorus of an opera this choral piece is certainly much too long. At this point the opera becomes an oratorio, or, better yet, a symphonic finale such as that of the Ninth Symphony. The noble, moving "Fidelio" chorus that is so rich musically, expands instead of accelerating the motion of the opera toward the end.

What Beethoven set to music here was an inner experience, a vision, a dream of his fancy rather than an opera finale. What he heard in his fantasy was happy jubilation, the jubilation of all mankind, exultation without ending.

Again three years later (1808) Beethoven attempted to mold a similar vision in a form that appears like a sketch to the final movement of the Ninth Symphony, in the Fantasy for Pianoforte, Chorus and Orchestra, opus 80. This work is the first design for the joyous

---

* Even the text of these jubilation hymns in "Fidelio" is identical to the "Ode of Joy" with the words: "Wer ein holdes Weib errungen, stimm in unsern Jubel ein".

choruses of the Ninth Symphony. The musical structure is the same. With this music the final movement of the Ninth appears like a Fata Morgana in the distance.

The orchestral recitatives, the variations on a folk-song theme, and the large choruses: everything that helps build the final movement of the Ninth Symphony, is already present here in form and shape, precipitated out of the composer's soul by forces that were stronger than conscious will.

On the road leading from the sketches to "Ode of Joy" written down in 1793, to the final movement of the Ninth Symphony of the year 1822, one of the most important stations is the Fantasy for Piano, Chorus and Orchestra, opus 80. The cupola that arches over the Ninth Symphony is discernible from here.

Like the melody of "Freude schoener Goetterfunken," that of the Piano Fantasy is one of those simple, naive themes that always come to Beethoven when he lets the masses exult. The theme goes back to Beethoven's youth. The melody is that of the song "Gegenliebe," composed by Beethoven at the age of twenty-five (1795). When he sketched the Piano Fantasy—during the second half of 1808—the song received a new text that glorifies the might of music. Verses such as: "Wenn der Toene Zauber walten—und des Wortes Weihe spricht—muss sich Herrliches gestalten—Nacht und Stuerme werden Licht" must have stirred Beethoven deeply, for often enough he had experienced how night and storms turn to light when the charm of tones reigned.

The orchestral variations on this theme recall quite distinctly those of the Ninth Symphony, especially at the point where the melody resounds as "marcia assai vivace" with trumpet fanfares and chords played by the strings. The grouping and arrangement of the choral movements is the same as in the Ninth Symphony. At first the soloists call to the choir with the first words of the melody, then the chorus joins in.

The most surprising moment in the chorus of "Piano Fantasy" is the great gradation that is brought about with an unusually harmonic deflection. It is identical in "Piano Fantasy" and in the Ninth Symphony. In the Piano Fantasy the choir sings with ecstatic force:

In the Ninth Symphony the chorus, standing before God, sings:

RETROSPECT: BEETHOVEN'S SYMPHONY

In 1809 Baron Tremont came to Vienna to bring Napoleon the resolutions of the state council. Beethoven presented him with a leaf from his sketchbook dating to the time when the Piano Fantasy had its first performance. This leaf indicates how close to the Ninth Symphony one is at that time, for on it appears the beginning of the first movement of the Ninth Symphony; sheet-lightning that precedes the eruption of the symphonic thunderstorm in 1817.

I V.

In the following years the clouds gathered from all sides, clouds from which the lightning and thunder of the Ninth Symphony were to erupt. Higher powers gathered these clouds. The idea of setting Schiller's "Ode of Joy" to music never eased its hold on Beethoven. Repeatedly, it escaped from the unconscious; again and again it pressed toward artistic formation.

In 1809 Beethoven had sketched an overture, "for any occasion—or for use in a concert." This was the overture that was later called—without any justification—"Overture for the Name Festival." Beethoven himself christened it: "Grand Overture in C invented for large orchestra." After the first sketching the work was put aside, to be resumed two years later—1811. There exist fragments of a started score from that period.

In 1812 the idea of the hymn of joy penetrates this overture. In the midst of sketches of the Seventh and Eighth Symphonies that Beethoven wrote down in the summer of 1812, when he was taking the baths in Bohemia, one comes across the remark: "Freude schoener Goetterfunken Tochter Overture ausarbeiten." Two pages further is a sketch to the hymn of joy:

[231]

Freu - de schö - ner Göt -

ter Fun - ken

and a combination of the jubilant melody together with the incidental movement of the overture*:

Freu - de schö - ner Göt - ter - fun - ken

Beethoven's idea was to combine Schiller's Ode of Joy with the overture opus 115, and to give the whole work the form of a choral overture. Then overture and hymn of joy diverged. The overture was resumed in September 1814 as an independent orchestral work that was to help celebrate the Vienna Congress; it was completed and performed for the first time on December 25, 1815 as an "Overture." And the Ode of Joy reappears in 1822 among the sketches to Beethoven's Ninth Symphony.

---

* The incidental movement of the overture also plays a part in the sketches to the Scherzo of the Ninth Symphony. Bars 74 to 77 of the Scherzo: originated therefrom. Everywhere in the overture one is close to the Ninth Symphony.

RETROSPECT: BEETHOVEN'S SYMPHONY

The dark clouds of the D-Minor in the Ninth Symphony loomed increasingly black on the horizon. They were already in existence when Beethoven was still working on the gay symphonies in A-Major (Seventh Symphony and in F-Major (Eighth Symphony). It is peculiar that it was first a key mood alone that was associated with the idea of a ninth symphony. Before even themes took shape, the key was there, the tragic D-Minor: among the sketches for the second movement of the Seventh Symphony is a notation: "Second symphony in D-Minor," and in the plans for the Eighth Symphony a note: "Sinfonia in D-Minor—third symphony."

A theme from the Ninth Symphony flashes up for the first time in 1815. It is the start of a fugue that later became the Scherzo of the Ninth Symphony.

At about the same time, the idea for the beginning of the Ninth Symphony was sketched in the same book with these words: *"Symphony, first beginning in only 4 voices, 2 violins, viola and bass.* Inbetween Forte with other voices *and, if possible, every other instrument to join by and by."*

In 1817 the fugue theme reappears, like a lonely, errant soul looking for a body. At that time the body was to have been a string quintet. But the soul was not redeemed until the fugue theme found its place in the sketches of the Ninth Symphony. To be sure, it had to wander around in these sketches for quite a while before it found a niche in the Scherzo: in 1822 it was

[233]

even supposed to form the final movement of the Symphony.

All the foregoing details show what goes on within the composer. The appearance of ideas in various surroundings, the emergence of forms and thoughts from the unconscious, and the forces of the unconscious that propel them; the wanderings of such ideas without definite plan, the many attempts at formation: all this gives the impression of being automatic. The composer's fantasy is the scene of such proceedings rather than the source. It is passively subject to the building and forming, and is not an active force. The motivating and molding powers are something over which the composer has no jurisdiction in the early stage of creative work. Not his "ego," but an "it," something super-personal, sets the whole play of sounding forms in motion.

V.

The first sketches for the first movement of the Ninth Symphony are to be found on various loose pages from the year 1817. Toward the end of 1817, or early in 1818, various motifs from the first movement pass like ragged clouds. Bars 63 and 64, with the agitated accompaniment in the second violins and violas, seem to be separated from their context, as though illuminated by lightning:

These are followed by the peaceful horn motif as it sounds at the end of the movement, in D-Major, with the accompaniment of the second horn; ergo, a phrase of the movement's finale:

After this motif there follow the stormy 1/32 violin runs from the finale of the exposition, and then bars 11 to 20 of the beginning. One has the feeling that for a long time motifs and combinations had accumulated in the subconscious mind of the composer, and that now an explosion had blown them to the surface.

After this eruption a preliminary arranging begins. Four movements appear; the Allegro with its sextolet accompaniment (although, somewhat undecided, Beethoven wrote: "at first perhaps triolets also") and a precipitant beginning and drum beats; a second piece for four horns and the kettledrums that are now found at the end of the Adagio; the Scherzo into which an Allegro maestoso was to have been inserted. A new scherzo is also sketched. But there is no trace of the final movement. Beethoven had not yet considered composing Schiller's hymn of joy.

However, we are in possession of a page from 1818 which shows that Beethoven was thinking of another symphony. The adagio was to be a "cantique ecclesiastic"; a "pious song in a symphony in the old keys. . . . Herr Gott dich loben wir—alleluja—entweder fuer sich allein oder als einleitung in eine Fuge" (Dear Lord, we praise Thee—hallelujah—either by itself or as introduction to a fugue.) The allegro was to be a Bacchus festival. Either in the last piece, or even in the adagio of this symphony, voices were to be interpolated.* The adagio was to be repeated in the last piece**, *whereby "then the singing voices were to come in gradually."*

At this point Beethoven, who at that time was considering writing an oratorio, conceived the idea of a choral symphony. He was then altogether imbued by choral timbre. It was also in the fall of 1818 that he started working at "Missa Solemnis", and at the same time he wanted to study the Gregorian chants; therefore the idea of writing music in the ancient modes was foremost in his mind just around 1818. Yet in connection with this choral symphony Beethoven did not think about the composition of Schiller's Ode of Joy.

Then work on the Ninth Symphony stopped for quite some time and receded behind the work on the last three piano sonatas, on the overture opus 124 and "Missa Solemnis". It was resumed in the summer or fall of 1822.

Now the idea of placing the "Freude schoener Gotterfunken" at the end of the symphony first makes its appearance.

The melody is sketched in D major, ergo in the key that it was to retain.

But Beethoven had to wrestle for a long time with the idea of giving the symphony a choral finale. As late

---

* In the Ninth Symphony, too, Beethoven once considered interposing the chorus in the adagio. In front of the sketches for the adagio he remarks once: "Perhaps it is more suitable to insert the chorus here already".

** This thought is realized in the final movement of the "Ninth".

as June or July of 1823 he was considering an instrumental finale, and in the fall of the same year he reverted to the passionate theme that he had decided upon for the finale:

Had Beethoven carried out this plan, the Ninth Symphony would have had a dismal, stormy, passionate ending like the String Quartet in A minor, opus 132, which, three years later, received the same music for its final movement.

From the sketch books of the Ninth Symphony from the years 1822 and 1823 one can see quite plainly how the idea of the hymn of joy thrusts itself out of the subconscious, is repressed and pushes itself through. On pages from June or July of 1823 a note is to be found: "Maybe the chorus of Freude Schoener after all."

The joyful melody assumed various shapes. Even after Beethoven had found the present melody, he sketched an entirely different melody in 3/8 time during the last months of 1822:

It was finally the accumulated strength of the unconscious that helped the melody of joy to emerge. Here, in the subconscious, the old plans of a choral arrangement of the joy melody—from the years 1793, 1798, 1805, 1808 and 1812—had been thrown together and had finally achieved such strength that they raised the dome of the great choral finale to the summit.

Once before Beethoven had experienced such an eruption when he composed the Fifth Symphony. Who, today, could imagine this symphony as anything but a music that battles its way from tragic night to heroic victory? The festive march of the final movement belongs to the idea of the work. Before its radiance the shadows of the sombre "fate motif" disappear. This "fate motif" had knocked menacingly at the gates in all the movements of the symphony. Now it becomes a spectral memory that is dispelled by the jubilation of the victory march.

And yet, in the first plans for the Fifth Symphony is found not the heroic victory march, but a dismal closing movement (end of 1807 or 1808):

The march of victory, which is associated with the whole idea of the Fifth Symphony, does not appear until later, after the victorious jubilation of the "Fidelio" music had carried it along.

It was exactly the same with the choral exultation of the Ninth Symphony.

[238]

RETROSPECT : BEETHOVEN'S SYMPHONY

In the instrumental introduction to the finale of the Ninth Symphony Beethoven describes the chaos out of which the joyous melody arises, then the growth of the melody and the expansion of tones; the soul filled with music that assumes the cadence of words.

The forms of the choral fantasy from 1808 expanded mightily. Whatever Beethoven experienced between 1808 and 1822 joined this music. A part of these experiences were his plans to set Goethe's "Faust" to music, which were especially vivid around 1822, and his reading of "Kritik der praktischen Vernunft". The words with which Kant ended "Kritik der praktischen Vernunft": "The star-spangled heaven above me, and the moral law within me" made a particularly strong impression on Beethoven. He entered them in his conversation book of 1820, and they echo mysteriously in the chorus of the Ninth Symphony: "Ahnest Du den Schoepfer Welt, Such ihn ueberm Sternenzelt, Ueber Sternen muss er wohnen."

However, the prayers of "Missa Solemnis" and the ecstasies of this divine vision accompanied the choral music of the "Ninth" from 1818 to 1822. All the choruses and festive processions of happy people whom Beethoven had heard exulting in his fantasy—from his youthful cantatas to Fidelio—were enhanced to hymnic timbre.

V I .

The germ from which the Ninth Symphony grew consisted of dreams of happiness that came to an unhappy child; the wishes and visions that brighten a hard childhood, the reveries of a suffering soul. Such childhood desires can produce dreams, or world religions, great deeds or great works of art such as the Ninth Symphony. On the road from childhood to maturity these childish desires and reveries are nourished with the whole life of the artist. They digest all vitality, all emotions, all thoughts. They draw artistic material from all occurrences that are deposited, preserved and re-molded in the subconscious.

It is not conscious artistic intention that creates such works, but an inner necessity and a must. Art works of this type contain vital and spiritual forces that grow in the soul. These are constantly in action, they construct forms and unite to build artistic shapes. The history of the Ninth Symphony shows very clearly how such fantasies of the unconscious mind take shape at various stages in the artists' development, until at the highest and most mature step they become gigantic forms beside which earlier formations appear small and sketchy.

We know that Beethoven, while composing his greatest masterpieces, was in a condition of excitement that was terrifying to his friends. During 1823, when he was working at the Ninth Symphony, Beethoven often returned from walks around Hetzendorf without his hat; and while writing the Missa Solemnis he resembled a maniac, howling absentmindedly and lashing about with his hands.

If one considers that Beethoven worked on the Ninth Symphony for a period of six and a half years, and that during this time (1817/18—1824) additional works such as the Hammerklaviersonate, the Diabelli Variations, the C minor Sonata and the Missa Solemnis were created and that Beethoven often worked on several movements of each work simultaneously*, one gets an

---

* In the sketchbook of 1819, for instance, we find plans for the Credo (Descendid, Et incarnatus est, Crucifixus and closing fugue), for Sanctus, Pleni sunt coeli, Benedictur and Agnus Dei side by side

idea of the upheaval within him and of the tumultuous forces in his soul that had to be organized.

Beethoven must surely have had the feeling that he was a tool of higher powers whose voices spoke in him; or, to quote Coleridge: that his artistic work was "a repetition in the finite mind of the eternal act of creation in the infinite I am."

He did not know that these powers were the products of his innermost soul, and that impulses, desires, images and visions which set the artistic forms in motion construct the contents of his unconscious soul life; nor that they are the past and the history of man. Artistic fantasy to Beethoven was something divine, not human. The romantic type of great musician who belongs more to religious faith than to science, has no greater cham pion among the composers than Beethoven.

PART II

The Work of Musical Fantasy

CHAPTER X.

Organizing the Musical Fantasy

So far we have spoken only of the activity of the subconscious, and of the instinctive impulses that set
the musical imagination in motion.

However, this is just the beginning of the artistic process of creation. The moment the subconscious releases
the forms that were constructed there, these formations
are grasped by the conscious forces of the soul. Artistic
work sets in, and further formation takes place in an
interchange of unconscious and conscious forces. Like
a team of good tennis players, unconscious and conscious forces volley the ball. They display extreme activity, tension of mind and energy in handling the ball,
which flies to and fro and is always hit on the right
spot by correctly adjusted nerves.

In great art production the correct relation between
unconscious and conscious soul forces is the result of a
complicated organization. Great composers have man-
aged this collaboration of various intellectual talents
so perfectly that the transformation of unconscious impulses into conscious work takes place without interruption. Only in this way can we explain the bulk of
compositions that were laid down in many volumes
by such composers as Palestrina, Bach, Haendel, Haydn,
Mozart, Beethoven, Wagner, Richard Strauss and Igor
Stravinsky. Every musician stands astounded before

[245]

the many volumes of the great classic editions; volumes that prove a creative ability so perfectly organized that all forces are converted into artistic form without waste or loss. A factory that organizes the work of many hundreds of laborers on the production line so that all activity is accomplished in the shortest time and with the most economical exploitation of all hands, is child's play compared to the disposition of the talents necessary to artistic creation.

Without most perfect collaboration of all talents, all unconscious and conscious forces, the whole imagination and all critical faculties, compositorial work as achieved by the great musicians would be inconceivable. If there were a defect anywhere in the distribution of the compositorial forces, artistic work would be interrupted time and again by inhibitions. The work of the imagination would cool off repeatedly, and the finished product would turn out irregular. It would be necessary to start all over again.

If one bears in mind how many years of inspiration and work go into compositions such as the Ninth Symphony, the Missa Solemnis, the score to "Ring of the Nibelungen"; and if one further considers that in all the time that was necessary to produce such music, work had to continue in a steady flux and in even strength, one attains the proper measure with which to admire the organization of labor contained in such works.

It took just such perfect play and counter-play of all creative forces to enable classical musicians to produce a large part of their compositions as performance of their office, in commission or as an ordinary day's work.

Bach's cantatas, most of them pensive, mystic, musical sermons on the Sunday gospels, were written for every Sunday and holiday of the year. In addition, Bach wrote organ music for the church services; rustling preludes, fugues for the closing of the services, imaginative choral preludes, choral variations and choral fugues. For funerals Bach wrote glorious motets that to this day are the greatest wonders of contrapuntal art.

For instruction purposes the preludes and fugues of the "Wohltemperiertes Klavier" were written; for social entertainment, suites and concertos. And all this work was accomplished without interruption, in greatest uniformity; it was always masterly, the technique always nourished by many sources, and always universal. Bach's inspiration may have been stronger or weaker, according to whether the text of a cantata or motet coincided with a group of unconscious emotions or not; but the mastery of formation was always the same.

As conductor for the Prince Estherhazy, Haydn waited every morning and every afternoon in the ante-room of the Prince in company of other court servants. Dressed in light-blue dress-coat embellished with silver braids and buttons, light-blue vest with silver trimmings, white cravat and sword at his side, Haydn had to wait attendance in case "music was commanded".

Haydn wrote symphonies, cantatas, sacred music and operatic music on commission. On the occasion of visits by noblemen, and for religious services, concerts in the palace and music in the castle gardens, Haydn had to write music on command; and in 1765 he was ordered "to work more diligently at composing." Only a thoroughly studied, smooth technique made it possible to write so much good, new and genuinely Haydnish music.*

All Mozart's operatic works were written in commission; Mozart's concertos for his concerts: technique obeyed him easily and surely.

Not until we come to Beethoven do we find a composer who was driven to work by his personality, and who wrote music to relax his soul, or to give his personality artistic expression. Still, there was plenty that Beethoven wrote on commission or on order; profound music such as the "Diabelli Variations", ingenious music like that of the "Rasumoffsky Quartets," and the magnificent music of "Fidelio".

The free, modern composer smiles compassionately at Haydn waiting in uniform for the orders of his Prince, or at Mozart eating at the servants' table of the Archbishop of Salzburg together with the cook, the valet and the pastry chef. Yet this same modern composer gladly sells himself to a film company and, stopwatch in hand, composes the requested film music on command.

To keep the clockwork of artistic fantasy going in increasing perfection over a period of many years is a task that can be accomplished only by some one in whose innermost being the sources of fantasy rustle continuously, and in whom the wheels and machineries that keep such sources in constant flow work without friction.

There are numerous artistic half-natures in whom either the sources of imagination dry up rapidly, or in

---

* Haydn's employment contract contains this clause: "By order of His Serene Highness, the Vice Conductor shall be bound to compose such music as His Highness might command, such compositions not to be communicated to anybody, much less to be copied; they are to be reserved solely for His Highness. Without specific knowledge and gracious permission he is not to compose for any one else."

whom the technical wheels do not function properly. Many young musicians whose fancy is incited by youth are exhausted when they become older. As young musicians they feel themselves in a creative mood; inspiration is not lacking; their sketchbooks are crowded with themes, and when they sit at the piano they are hardly distinguishable from true artists. Often they possess rich, musical souls. But they do not possess the faculty of keeping the fantasy fresh and alive over a long period and in enlarged forms by means of work.

The sources which, in artistic setting, would irrigate the land and nourish a blooming vegetation, gush forth their water, which evaporates quickly. In such composers the transformation of fantasy into work does not function. The transition stagnates between unconscious and conscious soul forces. After several revolutions the wheels of imagination stand still.

There are many half-natures who can produce large works only in their youth, when the imagination has not yet been cooled off by life. Actually, youth itself is talent and originality. It is freshly planted in life. It has lustre because it is not used up, and because its talent often has the magic of a spring morning.

How wonderful is the radiant talent of a Pergolesi, who died at the age of twenty-six, with a last glance toward the Bay of Naples, toward Capri and Sorrento, the serene blue ocean and the vineyards that sparkle in his melodies. How beautiful is the lustre in the songs of a Stephen Foster, and how dazzling the youthfulness of George Gershwin's music! Music of this kind is the true music of youth.

The question as to whether this music could have expanded and be brought into greater form by work can perhaps be answered in the affirmative in the case of

Pergolesi. In the case of Gershwin it is doubtful. For even while "An American in Paris" is brilliantly ingenious, vivacious and witty, it is, nonetheless, a brilliant inspiration rather than great form. "Rhapsody in Blue" is a scintillating potpourri, hastily sketched, but not elaborated upon. "Porgy and Bess" is another ingenious sketch.

An expansion of Foster's talents was entirely out of the question. His nature was that of a popular singer and improviser; as such he was a genius who, in an hour of inspiration, sang songs to the people which they repeated.

It is freshness, originality and intellect that is creative in youth; but it is not until these talents are strengthened by life, enriched by experience, and ennobled by technical work—when they undergo a chemical change like old wine, and when they grow in unison with man—that great art forms are produced. Brilliant, radiant youthful imagination alone has no permanency. It is a flame that flares up but quickly dies down because it lacks new fuel. Life furnishes this fuel, and fate and experience, as well as the technique that distributes the fuel properly. In every true artist the fantasy is strengthened by technique; only the dilettante, the semi-artist and the spurious talents are hampered by it.

When great artists created masterworks at an age in which artistic fancy begins to cool—as for instance Beethoven in the last string quartets, Verdi in the wonder opus "Falstaff" and Wagner in "Parsifal"—they owe thanks to their grand technical ability for auxiliary forces that gave impetus to the imagination of their old age.

Beethoven amplified his technique by studying Bach's polyphonous music, thus making it possible for him to create the last string quartets. The agile technical hand of Verdi created the witty, humorous, sketchy style of

"Falstaff"; Wagner's technique that had expanded immeasurably in the "Nibelungenring", in "Tristan and Isolde" and in "Meistersinger of Nuernberg", produced "Parsifal". Technical mastery allows artistic fancy—which, at an advanced age loses strength and sensuality—to work with complete freedom, and substitutes technical wisdom for the natural freshness missing in the imagination.

The total sum of fantasy and technique remains the same in older years as it was during youth. In later years fantasy is weaker, but technique stronger. In youth, technique is weaker, the imagination greater. Thus the sum of artistic forces remains unchanged.

The very great composers show an harmonic balance in the relation between fantasy and technique, between the strength of latent resources and the strength of organizing forces. The penetration of unconscious and conscious creative forces in such masters as Mozart or Haendel is so perfect that it is hard to distinguish where invention ends and execution begins.

Mozart's work is described in a letter which, although not authentic, is nonetheless Mozartian in its trend of thought: "When I am all by myself, and in a pleasant mood, for instance while traveling in a coach, or after a good meal, or while taking a walk, or at night, when I cannot fall asleep, then ideas come streaming toward me most easily. From where, and how, I do not know, nor can I do anything about it. Those ideas that I like, I keep in my mind, probably hum them to myself; at least that is what others have told me.

"If I hold on to these, I get a notion here and there as to where I could use such a fragment in making a pie, according to counterpoint, timbre of the various instruments, etc. This sets my soul afire—that is, if

I am not disturbed—and grows more and more. I enlarge upon it yet, and make it brighter, and the thing is truly almost complete in my head, even though it is long. After that, I can take it in at a glance in my mind, like a beautiful picture or a handsome person, and in my imagination I do not hear it piece by piece, but as a whole, altogether. Now that is a feast! All that finding and making works in me as in a lovely realistic dream: but to listen to the whole thing together is the best of all."

This description of Mozartian work illustrates particularly well the natural growth of musical ideas, the expansion of thoughts, the creation of great forms. One gets an impression, not of work, but of development. The ideas come "as in a stream". They become "larger"; all forms grow "broader and brighter". The finding and making takes place "like in a beautifully realistic dream". And, finally, the composer can visualize the forms as a unity; not "one after the other, but simultaneously." The growth of a tree, the broadening of its trunk, the appearance of leaves and blossoms can be described similarly.

In a conversation with Schloesser (1823), Beethoven also described his creative work, and Schloesser, who later became court conductor at Darmstadt, wrote it down: "I carry my thoughts with me a long time, often very long, before writing them down. My memory is so faithful that I am sure, once I have conceived a theme, I will not forget it, even years later. I change quite a bit, discard some, and try again until I am finally satisfied; then, in my head, begins the refinement in all directions; broadwise, upwards, into the depth, into the narrow. Since I am aware of what I want, the fundamental idea never leaves me; it mounts, it grows; I hear and see the picture in its whole expansion as in a mold. There remains only the labor of writing it down, which is done rapidly according to the time I have left over; for occasionally I work on several things simultaneously, although I am sure of not confusing one with the other."

This description puts more stress on artistic work ("I change quite a bit, discard," etc.) than does Mozart's. One has more the impression of conscious formation than of growing and blooming.

Almost the entire fantasy process of Mozart takes place in the protective envelopment of the subconscious. Mozart postpones parting from his inner fancies as long as possible. He lets the compositions mature in his mind, and dislikes separating from them. Unconscious growth and maturing, and conscious arranging can meet undisturbed within the composer and influence one another. Thus Mozart escapes the danger of having critical sifting cool off the creative procedure. Fantasy and technique can be fused in the warmth of inner life without invention and sensible thinking giving off dross.

Only when the music is absolutely form ripe, when the imagination is evenly distributed and artistic critique has smoothed the musical forms to an even polish —then Mozart sketches the score. His wonderful tone memory holds fast to the music, and he copies it from there.

Not even Mozart's father could understand why his son postponed writing down a completed composition and waited until the last moment to do so. Solid, dry musician that he was, he could not grasp the fact that a fanciful artist like his son was linked with human ties to the music that had grown in him, and that he disliked tearing himself away from the new, blood-warm life that had formed within him.

Ever so often the elder Mozart—who, as a composer was an educated, but unimaginative artisan—scolded his son for deferring his matters (December 11, 1777). When Mozart finished "Nozze di Figaro," his father wrote: "It (you) has always procrastinated, and taken its own sweet time as per its usual nice habit" (November 11, 1875). And even in Vienna Mozart had to defend himself against his father: "Please believe me that I do not like idleness, but work." (May 26, 1781).

Mozart's mind was always occupied with trying to combine his easy-flowing, radiant fantasy with work. In 1778 he wrote to his father from Paris: "You know that I live in music, as it were, that I am busy with it all day long; that I like to speculate, study and mull over it."

His fantasy with all its auxiliary forces was perpetually in motion. When he washed his hands in the morning—forenoon was Mozart's time for composing —he walked to and fro, according to his sister-in-law, and "never stood still, clicked one heel against the other, and was always pensive."

At other times, too, his hands and feet were always in motion. "He was forever playing with something, for instance his hat, pockets, watch-chain, tables or chairs, as though they were a piano." His wife, Constanze, reports that when she and Mozart were traveling by coach, "he would look at the environments quietly and attentively; his face, which was inclined to be more introspect and sober than gay and free, began to brighten gradually until, finally, he would start to sing, or rather to rumble, and would burst out: 'If only I had this theme down on paper'."

ORGANIZING THE MUSICAL FANTASY

When the barber came to shave Mozart, Mozart jumped up every minute and went to the piano; he could not sit still because music was overflowing in him as in a boiling cauldron. While playing billiards and skittles, Mozart indulged in musical thoughts. The Duet for Two Violins of the year 1786 bears the title: "Untern Kegelscheiben" (When playing Skittles). The first quintet in "Magic Flute" was composed while Mozart played billiards in a cafe.

When riding in the Prater, he was uneasy on the horse, for he was more occupied with music than with the animal. Sitting in his box at the opera, his hands were always in restless motion, and his lips pursed for singing or whistling. "He was always more or less composing," Nissen reports.

Wherever Mozart came across a new technique, he immediately utilized it in his music. When Mozart became acquainted with the then new form of melodrama in Mannheim (1778)—Benda's "Medea" and "Ariadne"—he carried it around with him in order to study it, and he wrote to his father: "One should treat most of the recitatives in an opera in this manner."

When he heard the Bach and Haendel fugues in the house of Baron van Swieten in Vienna, in 1782, he did nothing but improvise fugues at home, compose fugues for piano, and arrange fugues for strings, among them five fugues from Bach's "Wohltemperiertes Klavier." A whole series of fugue sketches from this period indicate Mozart's impulsive urge to expand his technique.

No composer of the 18th century absorbed as much in music forms and music technique as did Mozart. He learned from the total European music. His faculty of absorbing music forms was tremendous. Traveling in Italy, France and Germany, he listened everywhere to music, studies new operas, new symphonies, new string quartets, new arias. The letters which the boy wrote from Italy, and later from Paris, show clearly how much his attention was kept on the stretch when hearing operas or singers.

When Mozart studied musical techniques, he did so in the most universal sense. Only Bach can compare with Mozart's universality, which tried all the possibilities of a form or a technique. Not even Beethoven can equal Mozart's technical wealth. Mozart's technical mind was not only broad, but lithe; he was susceptible to every impression, and even the most difficult technical problems became play of his intellect, as proven by the finale of the Jupiter Symphony.

In opera, Mozart masters all the opera forms of the important European countries: the Italian opera seria, the Italian opera buffo, the great French court opera and the German operetta. He masters all styles, fashions all forms. "There is not easily a famous master to be found whom I have not studied diligently, often several times," Mozart himself claimed.

A wonderful tone memory and a uniquely keen eye for the essentials in old as well as new music are always alert in Mozart. His ability to take in a score at a glance was seldom equalled. As a boy he already aroused admiration when he played by sight, and once, in 1782, when he played an opera by Umlauf at sight, the astonished composer remarked: "One thing is certain, Mozart has the devil in his head, in his body and in his fingers. He played my opera (which is written so miserably that I myself can hardly read it) as though he had composed it himself."

Mozart's glance must have taken in such scores the way one sees a landscape from the mountain top, with woods, fields, houses and river forming one clear, distinct picture. Even Bach fugues, Haendel choruses and Bach's motets for eight voices were immediately a brightly illuminated landscape of music in which Mozart knew every path.

Just as unfailing was his music memory. Any music that Mozart had completed in his mind was as good as written down. When lack of time prevented him from writing the score of the Linzer Symphony in C major (1783), Mozart wrote it directly into the instruments. The score stood out in his memory as bright and as clear as a score lying on the conductor's desk. In 1782, while composing a prelude with fugue, Mozart wrote the fugue on music-paper, at the same time composing the prelude as though he had divided himself into a composer and a note writer who were working simultaneously.

Mozart had worked out in his mind the new sonata for the concert of the violinist, Regina Strinasacchi (Vienna, April 29, 1784). Shortly before the concert, Mozart sent the artist the violin part which he had quickly jotted down. There was no time to write the piano part, and Mozart played his part from memory.

The trumpet and drum parts in the second "Don Giovanni" finale were also completed mentally by Mozart, who then brought the manuscript to the orchestra himself. He was uncertain about only one spot, as to whether there were four bars too many or too few. The overture to the opera had been written down during the night before the performance. It was certainly all finished in his memory when he wrote it. Writing was a cumbersome, mechanical business for Mozart. Living reality was the singing and sounding in his soul, the play of tones and the blooming of tone forms.

Mozart's enjoyment of this inward singing was so great that he never continued compositions which, for one reason or another, he did not complete. He preferred to start afresh with something new. We are in possession of over a hundred such fragments that Mozart left undone. Mozart sketches are among the greatest rarities, for music ripened in Mozart's fantasy without outside help. He had no oppressive emotional inhibitions to overcome as did Beethoven who, with the help of sketches, had to snatch his idea from the subconscious. Occasionally, Mozart would sketch contrapuntal combinations; but such sketches referred only to contrapuntal details, never to invention or form.

Mozart's artistic organism is the most perfect. Everything that is embraced by the conception of artistic work: expansion of ideas, form condensation, lucid formation and complete transformation of the mental vision into tones—all this transpires with greatest ease and naturalness in Mozart's work. There are no inhibitions and no stoppages. The wheels of the conscious and the unconscious are so perfectly geared that the machinery of musical creation requires only a slight nudge to set it a-going and to keep it moving.

There are also composers who do not succeed at all in organizing all the forces necessary to creative work, or only under great difficulties. There are various reasons for this. It can happen that the subconscious forces are too strong and too eruptive, and cannot be balanced by the conscious forces. Then we have the fantastic, baroque artists who are not able to mold their inner abundance.

A composer as great as Hector Berlioz, whose fantasy most certainly belongs to the most magnificent that music has to offer, did not always succeed in shaping his romantic inner world. This is the fantasy that performed so grandly in matters adventurous and fantastic, and that created the gloomy "Gang zum Hochgericht," the exciting "Hoellenritt," the eerie pictures of "Walpurgisnacht," as well as delicate play of colors such as "Irrlichtertanz." But a composition like the "Romeo and Juliet" music of Berlioz still is an unformed lump and, despite some beautiful spots, a monstrosity of form.

Among modern composers, Max Reger often gives the impression of being overwhelmed by music; as though conscious forming force were unable to cope with all the elemental quaintness in his subconscious. No matter how much Reger sought the assistance of Bach or classical forms; no matter how tightly he grasped the variation or fugue forms in order to save himself from the deluge within him, many is the time he founders in the raging flood.

Gustav Mahler is another composer who creates the impression of being overcome by the impulses and visions of his subconscious. The moments of hysterical terror and panicky fear that show up so often in his symphonies prove best that Mahler frequently was obsessed, and not always master of the forms.

There is yet another manner in which the balance of unconscious and conscious soul particles—upon which all compositorial work is based—can be destroyed. It is possible that the conscious forces are too strong in proportion to the unconscious powers. This results in the rational composers, who often may have an excellent understanding for the essence of musical forms, and a magnificent mastery of musical techniques, but lack the corresponding instinctive talents of fantasy. Among them are the often so highly esteemed academicians who occupy high positions in all music countries; one such—despite fine taste, French technique and esprit—is Saint Saens. And, to go to the top of the ladder, even a composer like Brahms shows dry passages where (for example, in "Triumphlied") the knowledge of musical technique, the art of imitating old masters and knowledge of form secrets were far superior to inspiration.

To come back to modern composers: Without a doubt Igor Stravinsky went through an evolution that changed the perfect balance of unconscious fantasy and keen logic that existed in his great masterworks, beginning with "Fire Bird" and continuing with "Symphony of Psalms" and "Oedipus Rex." Conscious thinking tore loose from the musing of his fantasy; intellect, ingenuity and wit predominate.

This preference of intellectualism is in agreement with what Stravinsky says in "Chronicle of my Life".

The magnificent conjuration of prehistoric Russia in "Rites of Spring," the puppet play in "Petrouchka," the folklore-like ballad of "Story of a Soldier," the Russian village and Russian townspeople in "Wedding," and the Byzantine cathedral in "Symphony of Psalms"— all this is created by inspiration that was as strong, as elementary and as forceful as every other great artistic inspiration and that was to be expected like any great artistic vision.

Being capable of having inspirations that produced the roundelays of the youths and virgins in "Rites of Spring," the solemn incantations of the priests, the spring sacrifice, the pounding of the seeds into the soil; and, in addition, being able to mold in music myths and barbarism, prehistoric times and the magic of the bloody rites, and to link in masterly fashion unconscious fantasy and conscious form—that is what made Stravinsky great; not the ingenious plays of his later years, however clearsighted they may be.

Harmonizing of unconscious and conscious forces, and the complicated machinery of musical creation can also be disturbed by processes that border on the pathological. Productive moods and soul forces may fail to function temporarily. The re-formation of visionary life into musical shape may be disturbed for a longer or shorter period. The wheels of the great factory suddenly stand still. The powers and their auxiliaries strike.

In 1891 Hugo Wolf experienced a complete stoppage of his composing activity that lasted for four years. The great song cycles, Moericke, Goethe, Eichendorff, the Spanish cycle, and the first volume of the Italian Song Book had been published in almost uninterrupted succession. The second volume of the Italian Song Book was already announced, when Hugo Wolf seemed to stand before a vacuum, an abyss. Movingly he voices his laments: "I would almost believe that I have reached the end of my life. Impossible that I can write songs or music to Ibsen dramas over a period of thirty years, and yet I will never get to that much desired opera. I simply have reached the end. May it soon be a total end—there is nothing I would wish more."—(June 1891).

"I am afraid that my mood will not clear up. But I carry my misfortune in me, and, thus, with me. You will understand when I confess that during my entire stay here I did not write down one note; indeed, that I do nothing, absolutely nothing. Anyhow, have pity with me, who is lost to art—Hugo Wolf." (June 1891).

In August of 1891 one reads: "You ask me about my opera. Dear Lord, I would be satisfied if I could write even the smallest song—not to speak of an opera! I am certain that I am through, entirely through—and a fool he who gives more than he has. Recently I read a phrase in a novel by Ludwig which I consider well worth pondering about: 'The highest to which he could aspire was, to die in fame for something; now he aspires to something greater, to live for something without fame'. And this, I think, is something too. Always, your from now on ingloriously living Hugo Wolf."

This feeling of impotency increased constantly, and was given gripping expression in a letter dated April 26, 1893. "I cannot express what I suffer under this continuing idleness. I would like nothing better than to hang myself from the next best branch of the cherry trees that are now in full bloom. This wonderful Spring with its secretive living and moving teases me unutterably. This eternally blue sky, this continuous sprouting and blossoming in nature, the caressing fragrances pregnant with spring sun and flower scent, this 'I yearn, and don't rightly know what for' are driving me crazy. Everywhere this confusing urge for life, birth and formation—and only I who, like the most insignificant grass plot, am also a creature of God, may not partake of this feast of resurrection except as a spectator consumed by envy and grief. Everything within me is as though dead. Not even the softest tone sounds in me, it has become quiet and bleak inside me like on a snow covered cemetery. God knows how and when this will end."

During this period of artistic sterility Hugo Wolf found it impossible to play piano because the sound of the instrument reminded him reproachfully of his muteness. Opera librettos that were sent to him were criticized with particular irritability, probably because they failed to arouse the sleeping music. The chirping of the sparrows irks him; of course, the birds sing their songs incessantly, without a sign of exhaustion. "That my sleep should be ended at three o'clock in the morning is not yet the worst; but to have to listen to that accursed tirili the whole day long and to be powerless, because the birds here are considered inviolable like the swans in the territory of the Holy Grail—that is asking too much altogether." (July 10, 1893).

"You inquire about the reasons for my ill humour," Hugo Wolf wrote to his friend Faisst, "and want to put balm on my wounds. Ah, if you only could! No earthly herb can soothe my suffering. Only God is able to help me. Give me ideas, shake the sleeping demon within me awake that makes me obsessed, and I will adore you as my god, and will build you altars. But this is an appeal to gods, not to men. Let the former be the judges of my fate. Whichever way it may turn out, even if it be the very worst, I will bear it, though no sunlight may brighten my sad life. And with this let us end—once and for all—this melancholy chapter of my life . . . If the so painfully desired productiveness would just reappear, my happiness would be complete. However, I was unfortunately not yet able to find the proper magic formula to arouse this mysterious power from its sleep." (January 7, 1895).

Suddenly, after four years of barrenness and impotency, the full flow of music again begins to rustle. The machinery that regulates the resources of the subconscious and the distribution of the driving forces begins to move its wheels. "I cannot tell you how much I look forward to spring this year," Wolf writes in March of 1895, "for it is beginning to bloom and exult in me too, although for the time being only in the embryonic stage.

But everything urges outwards and demands shape and formation. This time, however, I do not intend to direct my 'melodic thread of water'* toward the flower beds of lyricism, nor let it run out in the sands of absolute music; no matter how thin and sparse it may flow, I will show it the way over crags and rocks whence it may discharge itself head foremost into the great ocean of the most exalted passions, into the drama."

Now, almost intoxicated by re-awakened musical power, he is glad of spring, the spring that had bothered him so much during the period of exhaustion. He, himself, is so filled with music that the libretto of the opera "Corregidor," which he once spurned, now seems full of music too. Within three weeks of almost incessant exaltation, the piano score of the opera was completed. "I work . . . like a maniac from six in the morning uninterruptedly until dusk. Imagine my bliss!," he writes to a friend, still steaming from the heat of work.

Practically at the same time, Wolf writes to another friend: "From six in the morning until late at night I work without cessation like a madman. Ideas and notions rush toward me in such abundance that I am hardly able to catch up with holding them. In short, it's going marvelously! Come to me as quickly as you can! No excuses! No evasions! You have to come! How are you? If you are as well as I am, you are to be envied."

At that time Hugo Wolf was in a frenzy of music, and inflamed by the text of the opera which made the music within him boil. Supplements to the text which his librettist, Frau Mayreder-Obermayer, sent him,

---

* The word is found in a dogmatic critique about Wolf's songs that appeared in Vienna.

could not reach him fast enough, as the music "haunts him in all his bones." "Only quick, quick, quick, for God's sake—or, as the Corregidor says: 'for the sake of Christ's nails!' Hurry!!!" Or: "For heaven's sake, you are not going to let the holidays keep you from working and bring me to despair? You can't be so cruel!"

If a supplementary piece to be sent in by the librettist takes too long in arriving, he writes the music quasi into the vacuum. "The verses are wonderful, even if they do not correspond with the music that I wrote down in anticipation. But that doesn't matter. The anticipated music can be used for the transition, and your verses will give me inspiration for new ideas."

The superabundance after years of sterility, and exultation after many hours of despair made Wolf see the characters of the libretto grand and magnificent. And it may have been a fear that lurked in the depths of his soul—fear that this sudden eruption of creative forces might dry up again—that drove him to finish his opera as rapidly as possible with all his might. He was inflamed, enthusiastic, inebriated.

Every dramatist experiences a moment when he plucks the figures of his fantasy out of his soul, as it were, gives them a cool glance and looks at them as though they were strangers. In that respect the dramatist is akin to the actor who watches the passions being played onstage and sees them as something foreign. Hugo Wolf rarely reached that stage during his ecstasy. He was forever living in the delirium of his music; when he played the monologue of his Tio for Lucas, he was so gripped that "he had to break off in dread and awe."

In similar manner, the German poet Friedrich Hebbel suffered a complete stoppage of his productiveness from 1844 to 1846, according to his diaries. The Austrian poet Grillparzer also knew many hours of impotency (diaries of 1826): "My condition in the last few months was really terrible. Never had I experienced such a conviction—not to be allayed—that all mental production was at an end; never did I experience such a drying up of all inner resources."

In 1902-3 Claude Debussy lived through such a period of exhaustion. "I am not writing a single note any more," he informs his friend André Messager. "Too long I have been like a squeezed lemon, and my brains will no longer produce . . . " On September 7, 1903, he complains further: "Same condition. Music is the most unbearable of all Megaeras. You cannot imagine all the things I have done in order to get back in her good graces." In 1907 Debussy again experienced a lengthy period of sterility. He suffered from phobias and feared he would rot "in the employment of nothingness."

Debussy's sensitive nerves produced inhibitions. He lived in dreams, surrounded himself with precious, fragile objects. As a boy he already adorned his room with butterflies; later he collected Japanese woodcuts, valuable canes, and was able to work only in a light green room with green carpet and green walls. Nerves of this sort are easily irritated, and this nervous irritation becomes fear, depression, hyper-refinement, and continual dissatisfaction with accomplished work.

"Don't forget," Debussy reminded Gatti-Casazza, "that I sometimes need weeks before deciding upon one chord as substitute for another."

While Debussy was writing the score to "Pelleas and Melisande," he was forever changing what he had completed; the nervous doubt was always prevalent as to whether the music he had written was correct. He discarded the "Fountain Scene" right after he finished the plan for the score (12 pages with sketches for the instrumentation). Even during rehearsals Debussy made alterations incessantly, and after the performance he still retouched the score.

In between periods of artistic activity, Debussy knew intervals of daydreaming; he would stand on one of the Seine bridges at sunset, staring into the water, or would take refuge in primitive psychic conditions. For instance, during the Paris Exposition of 1889, he would listen dreamily to Javanese and Siamese orchestras, to the foreign scales, drums, gongs and rattles. Often the sensitive musician reverted to the primitivity of childish talk and, like a child, said: "bav—bav" instead of "brave—brave," or "soi soi" instead of soignée."

Life must have appeared brutal, shrill and rough to Debussy, whose nerves were so sensitive that the world seemed to evaporate in mood, colored mist, in plays of lights and specks. Such nerves could easily be intimidated, and fail to function.

Hugo Wolf's exhaustion was of a different type. As a young man Wolf was always constantly worrying that his productiveness might come to a sudden end. "It is a terrible thought that often gives me grave hours and is liable to bring me to the brink of insanity."

Hugo Wolf's psychic life always moved in cycles of depression and exaltation. I read the diary kept by the doctors of the insane asylum in which Hugo Wolf spent the last years of his life, and noted with shock that even in his psychopathy, Wolf lived in such regular cycles of depression and euphoria.

The four years of Hugo Wolf's aridity were an enlargement of the depressive cycle. They were a pathological phenomenon; a dark shadow cast onto the artist's path by his mental illness, premonition of the night that devoured his genius.

Unlike Baudelaire, or W. Blake, Hugo Wolf was not one of those pathological artists who transform their augmented agitation, or even hallucinations or morbid dreams, into works of art, while their procedure of work remains free of morbidity. In Wolf's case the healthy root of creation—which, according to Edgar A. Poe, can also produce eccentric art—was affected by his illness. Incipient insanity furnished Poe with hallucinations and frightful phantoms which he used as material in his art works. Insanity made Hugo Wolf altogether incapable of producing; it attacked the artistic organism itself, just as it first weakened Robert Schumann before destroying him.

A distinction must be made between periods of apparent stagnation and such instances of stoppage of artistic working forces, as given in the foregoing, whereby collaboration of the various soul particles actively engaged in work is disturbed. Michelangelo, for example, experienced times—sometimes of longer duration, sometimes only a short while—when he lapsed into melancholia, brooding morosely like his Jeremiah, and did no work.

One such period happened in the years 1521-1523. During these intervals powerful figures and images accumulated in Michelangelo's mind that surged and heaved like thunderclouds. Such intervals belong to the picture of his creation. In contrast to Rubens or Raphael, Michelangelo was never in constant activity of inventing and completing, living in the midst of a workshop where young artists executed all artistic ideas quickly and cleverly. He was alone with his gigantic designs; they piled up within him and forced their way from dark soul moods to the light.

Michelangelo's plans were always of overwhelming magnitude. In Carrara he once wanted to shape a Colossus from a marble block. For the tomb of Julius he planned over 40 statues. The ceiling of the Sistine Chapel was populated by a host of figures; Judgment Day was a deluge of rising and falling figures. Such masses of pictures and statues overwhelmed his fantasy, which had to arrange all these visions. Beethoven was similarly overwhelmed by the tone masses of "Missa Solemnis".

What seemed to be a working pause for Michelangelo was, in reality, a period of intense mental work; and the intense sense of fear that often broke out in Michelangelo in such times and that on several occasions drove him to flee, was a fear of the masses of ideas and forms that had not yet been artistically mastered.

Richard Wagner also knew such fits of fear to accompany his work. When he had completed "Tannhaeuser", he felt as though he had escaped some mortal danger, and he wrote to Uhlig: "When I am finished with some work such as 'Walkuere', I always feel as though I had sweated some terrible anguish out of my life."

Great artists also show periods of apparent unproductiveness that are associated with spiritual and artistic development. Of famous composers who became increasingly great in their work, and who continued to grow, only Bach, Haendel, the classicists and, in modern time, Verdi, give the picture of uninterrupted development, in which the working forces expand more and more.

Beginning with his first opera, "Oberto, Conte di S. Bonifazio" (1839) all the way through to "Falstaff" (1893) Verdi goes through an evolution that is never checked. The musical forms become ever greater and purer; artistic energy, originally wild and raw, becomes increasingly subdued; melodies arch broader; the dramatic forces are more evenly distributed. Out of the young composer Verdi who jumps at the opera audience like a wildcat, there develops the great master of "Aida" and "Othello" who composes grand musical dramas of passion and who, in "Falstaff", wisely balances the passions: love and jealousy, and considers life as a merry game. In short, Verdi grows like a tree whose trunk becomes stronger and stronger, whose branches spread wider and wider and whose foliage crown grows increasingly taller.

Richard Wagner experienced a similar growth; but between the completion of "Lohengrin" and the inception of work on the "Ring of the Nibelungen" is a pause of five years duration in which Wagner does no compositorial work. In this time he writes theoretical essays with which he explains his ideas on the position of art in modern life, and on the relation between opera and drama. He conducts concerts in order to demonstrate his style of interpreting classical compositions. He writes "Ring of the Nibelungen" and plans a Wagner theatre until, finally, the music-producing forces, enhanced and enriched, show themselves again and in 1853, in Spezia, the motifs for the "Rheingold" music resound in his fantasy. In reality, the five music-less years were a period of preparation and inner development during which Wagner clarified his goals and ideas.

A similar period is found in the life of Johannes Brahms, between the Piano Concerto in D-minor (com-

[270]

pleted in 1854 as a sonata for two pianos) and the Serenade in A-major (1860). The pause in Brahms' work—his sojourn in peaceful Detmold falls in that time—separates Brahms the romanticist from Brahms the classicist. The fantastic period of Brahms' youth is over. Now begins the time of classical severity. Between the D-minor Concerto and the Serenade in A-major lies the quiet period of clarification and musing over the artistic problems of the age. The great composer Brahms who conceals his romantic sentiment behind a classic façade, acquires his form of life and art in the six years between opus 15 and opus 16, six years in which he did not publish anything.

It is not musical fantasy that grows in great composers with a rich development, but the organization of all the partial forces of fantasy and technique; the faculty of the composer to turn all impulses and experiences to artistic forms.

In Bach, who wrote his great organ works, passions and motets while in Leipsic, it was not the fantasy that had grown greater; for in the romantic organ works of his youth, and in youthful motets such as "Actus Tragicus", this fantasy was probably more passionate and more imaginative than in the master's later years. Rather, in addition to fullness of life, it was the technical perfection of musical fantasy that had grown.

Beethoven's great creative period reached its peak with the five large piano sonatas, the Ninth Symphony, Missa Solemnis and the last string quartets; yet it was not the fantasy that had become greater, for in works such as "Appassionata", the Fifth Symphony and the String Quartet in F-minor it unfolded its greatest energy and power and displayed a tragic force that is unequalled. No, again it was expansion of technique through promulgation of polyphony, and adoption of the forms of free fantasy into the sonata form.

The new technical media and the combination of this new technique with the augmented life value of the aging composer created Beethoven's masterpieces.

Works of old age, such as Wagner's "Parsifal" or Verdi's "Falstaff" were superior to operas written in their best years of manhood such as "Meistersinger" or "Aida", not by virtue of musical fantasy but by mature wisdom, be it religious mysticism like in "Parsifal", or super-mundane humour as shown in "Falstaff", and by technical wisdom. Growth of great composers is not a growing of fantasy forces which must needs decrease with age; for they are a form of human sensuality, and with sensuality they must lose strength, lustre and color. Growth of composers is a growing of artistic organization and its perfection by life, experience and mastery.

CHAPTER XI.

Productive Moods

A LL ARTISTIC creation is preceded by a condition that can be termed: productive mood.

Productive mood is a condition of expectation. Everything that had accumulated in the subconscious in the way of tone forms presses toward the borders of unconsciousness and conscious soul life. Up to this moment of agitation and tension, the entire musical work had taken place in the darkness of the subconscious. So far nothing was controlled by conscious thinking. The creative instinct did its work of forming undisturbed. But now the internal bulk of tones and tonal forms that had accumulated, had gathered so much strength that it drove toward the light of consciousness that was to brighten subsequent work.

The foregoing applies to larger musical forms. Smaller compositions, short poems, can be ejected from the soul of the artists totally finished. Goethe often wrote down poems as in a dream. It happened often that he woke up in the night with a new poem in his head. In such instances, he reports, he would jump out of bed, run to his desk and, without taking time to place a sheet of paper in horizontal position, he "wrote down the poem from beginning to end diagonally across."

In similar manner Mozart often wrote down compositions as though improvising. Once Mozart had promised the wife of Privy Councillor Bernhard von Keess, in whose house there were concerts twice a week, to compose a new song. However, Mozart forgot his promise, and also forgot to attend the concert at the Keess home. He was sitting in a tavern when a lackey was sent to fetch him. Then Mozart remembered concert and song. He sat down in the coffee-room and wrote the song then and there, and brought it to the Keess home. Frau von Keess sang it immediately while Mozart accompanied her at the piano.

When Mozart was in Prague in 1787, he promised to compose several dances for Count Pachta, but again forgot his promise. When he came to the Count's house, Pachta handed him paper and ink; Mozart sat down and immediately wrote the orchestra score for nine dances. Mozart also improvised canons, and even double canons, as did Beethoven too.

Many a song emerged from the fantasy of Franz Schubert completely formed.

One day Schubert and his friends were sitting in the beer garden "Zum Biersack" in Poetzleinsdorf. Schubert was reading the drinking song from Shakespeare's "Anthony and Cleopatra." Suddenly he exclaimed: "I just got an idea for a beautiful melody. If only I had some music-paper with me!" One of Schubert's friends drew the staff on the back of the menu, and Schubert immediately wrote down the song. The Morning Serenade from Shakespeare's "Cymbeline" originated in similar manner. One day Schubert called for his friend, the painter Schwind, to take a walk with him. Inasmuch as Schwind had to finish a portrait, he gave Schubert the poem and a sheet of paper. Within a very short time Schubert had the composition down on the paper.

PRODUCTIVE MOODS

The first setting of "Erlkoenig" was written equally fast. As Spaun tells it: "One afternoon I went with Mayrhofer to visit Schubert who, at that time, lived with his father at Himmelpfortgrund. We found Schubert, all aglow, reading 'Erlkoenig' aloud from the book. Several times he walked back and forth with the book in his hands; suddenly he sat down, and in the shortest possible time, as quickly as anybody is able to write, the glorious ballad was down on paper. Since Schubert had no piano, we ran over to the convent and there, that very evening, 'Erlkoenig' was sung for the first time and enthusiastically received."

Mozart, too, experienced moments when productive moods came upon him suddenly. The Trio in E flat is called "Kegelstatt-Trio" because Mozart wrote it while playing at nine-pins. The Minuet and Trio of the String Quartet in D-minor was composed by Mozart in 1783 in his wife's room while she was giving birth to her first child.

Schindler reports that "Beethoven was occasionally surprised by moments of sudden inspiration while in the midst of gay company, or sometimes in the street, and usually evoked the curious attention of passersby."

Mahler's song "Tambourgesell" was born between door and hinge, in the very second the composer left the dining room. He sketched it right away in the dark foyer, and ran with the sketch to his favorite spot, a spring near the country-house, where he completed it. One evening in Leipsic Mahler conceived the second stanza of the song "Ringelreihn," both lyrics and music. During the night he suddenly wakened, and the first and third stanzas of the song stood before him in tones and words so clearly that he noted them down instantly.

FROM BEETHOVEN TO SHOSTAKOVICH

The violin theme in the last movement of the First Symphony came to Gustav Mahler while he was spending an evening with company. He went to the next room to write it down and, when it was completed, he walked away with it, to the astonishment of the company.

Debussy often put himself in productive moods by staring at the flowing water from one of the Seine bridges, and watching the golden reflections cast by the setting sun.

However, productive mood and total conception of music work can only coincide in small music forms. Inspirations that cause a composition to emerge to the light of day completely formed, are the exception.

The rule is that only beginnings, first sketches, first attempts at shaping, enter conscious life. Quite often one sees in Beethoven's sketch books how these original conceptions disappear again in the underworld of artistic imagination. Having turned up in the sphere of conscious thinking, they return to the dark of the underworld where they lead a second shadowy existence until, years later, they again come to light.

We find, for instance, among plans for the second and third movement of the Beethoven String Quartet in C-major, opus 59 No 3, the graceful A-minor theme noted down that now is one of the most precious parts of the Seventh Symphony. At that time it probably was to have been included in the C-major Quartet. But it vanished, and went back to where it had come from. Six years later it is rediscovered among the sketches for the Seventh Symphony. For six years the theme was carried back and forth by the underground streams of dark visions and emotions, together with

[276]

other tone forms. Then it was first returned to the banks of the upper world.

The Scherzo melody of the Ninth Symphony had a similar fate. Three years before the Ninth was conceived, one finds notations for the Scherzo (1815). The melody was not inactive in the subconscious during these three years. It lived in the subconscious mind, had a history and destinies. Two years after first coming across this melody, it makes a second attempt at reaching the light. In vain. The creative force is as yet too weak. The melody sinks to the ground where it continues to live in a knot of sounding forms. Then, a year later, it makes a third, and permanent attempt to come to light.

The exact same observation can be made in regard to the Overture opus 115. The motifs of the middle part were sketched three years prior to the composition of the work. For three years these motifs vanish in Hades; they are limp shadows like the souls that hover around the pit that Odysseus dug, and which he holds at bay with his sword.

The vitality of the motifs that are thrown back to the depth of the subconscious is often astounding. The chief theme of the Piano Sonata in C-minor, opus 111, can be found twenty years earlier among notations for the Violin Sonata opus 36, No. 1:

Here, it appears in F-sharp minor. *Twenty years later* it re-emerges in the thundercloud of C-minor.

Thus, a great part of musical formation takes place in the subconscious mind; automatically, as it were. It is a generative process of musical thoughts that has rules all its own. This unconscious work proceeds without interruption deep in the subconscious of great musicians. Normal, everyday life takes its course. The composers may be in company, or in the street, or may be busy with trivial matters. In the meantime, though, the subconscious mind is·at work.

In the "Parsifal" period, Richard Wagner liked to spend the evening in the midst of his family and intimate friends, with some one reading aloud to him out of a book. One evening, Schopenhauer's biography was being read. Suddenly, Wagner called out: "an interrupted cadence, it's going to be A-flat major." Just at that moment he had become aware of the work of the subconscious, which had been proceeding undisturbed by the lecture.

A man as astute as Johannes Brahms was well aware of the autonomy of unconscious work when he told Georg Henschel: "That which is called invention, i.e. a real thought, is more or less a higher presentation, an inspiration; in other words, I cannot take credit for it. From that moment on, I cannot despise this 'gift' nearly enough; by incessant work I must strive to make it my lawful, well-earned property. And that does not necessarily happen soon. An idea is like a seedling; it germinates unaware within. When I have thus found, or invented, the beginning of a song such as (he sang the first half-stanza of 'Mainacht') 'Wann der silberne Mond,' then I close the book, go for a walk or start something different, and *sometimes don't think of it for half a year.* However, nothing gets lost. And when I come back to it after a while, it has unexpectedly assumed shape already, and I can begin to work on it."

Richard Strauss claims similarly: "Musical ideas, like young wine, should be put in storage and taken up again only after they have been allowed to ferment and to ripen. I often jot down a motif or a melody and then tuck it away for a year. *Then when I take it up again I find that quite unconsciously something within me—the imagination—has been at work on it.*"

The productive mood indicates to the composer that the door leading from the unconscious to consciousness —which is usually well guarded—is ready to be opened. Behind this door is an accumulation of music forms and larger musical formations; their emotional power has grown so strong that all these tones, themes, figures and tone visions press against the door. The door can then be opened with one jolt, and the tone figures are pushed into the brighter chambers of consciousness, or the door can close again immediately.

Unconscious and conscious soul particles are separated by a zone of inhibitions resembling those that force dream desires to change to images and figures. It is the work of fantasy to deprive these inhibitions of their power through artistic visions and play of the imagination. The creative power of the artist draws forms and figures from the subconscious and overcomes inhibitions that oppose liberation of the artistic world.

These inhibitions that try to thrust artistic fantasies back into the subconscious and obstruct their path to lighter intellectual regions, are the same forces of the soul that plunge our recollections into the night of oblivion. Goethe once mentioned to Boisseree that he had to write down poems at once, *else he would not find them any more.* When Hebbel wrote his poem "Mutter und Kind," he happened to be leafing through an old diary written ten years previously. In this diary he found the outline of the poem that he composed ten years later, and was very surprised. He had completely forgotten about it.

It was the philosopher W. James who claimed that blanks in consciousness are by no means empty spaces; that they are filled with activity, ("an active gap"). That which we call forgetting is prevented from emerging to consciousness by active forces; it is precipitated, repressed. The gap into which the forgotten is sunk, is full of intensive life: we may forget verses, but the rhythm of these verses tortures us and dances a ghostly dance in the gap. Or we may be bothered by the first letter of a word that wants to take shape; but it remains only a sound, and the word won't form.

Beethoven, more than any other composer, made immediate sketches of his ideas; he wanted to save them from submerging in the "active gap." He considered this sketching to be a weakness and spoke of his "bad habit, dating back to childhood, of instantly writing down the first notions."

Beethoven's sketches were a medium to bring to the surface the ideas that had formed in the unconscious. All the counterforces of the subconscious clung to these musical ideas, as did everything that had been repelled to the subconscious; all the forces of forgetting, all the shadows and demons of the underworld that would draw the musical figures back into the night. On the side of light, consciousness struggled to win these ideas over.

The productive mood is a pendulous condition of

unconscious and conscious forces, of darkness and light. The musical formation that took place in the subconscious has gained so much strength that it urges toward the light. Conscious work has already mobilized all its laboring forces to begin treatment of the raw material.

This condition of "productive mood" often makes itself known to poets as a sounding and singing. A spectral music seems to ring. So far the poets see no figures, but often only colors, undulating fogs. Their fantasy is veiled in twilight in which the forms and figures of the world have dissolved. "My perception," wrote Schiller to Goethe, "is at first without definite and clear object. This does not form until later. A certain musical frame of mind precedes the poetic thought."

The poet Otto Ludwig makes a similar statement. Says he: "I first feel a mood, a musical mood, which becomes color."

This may explain why artists often evoke and enhance productive moods by listening to music. Goethe, for instance, while composing "Iphigenia," wrote to Frau von Stein: "Good night, dearest. I have ordered music to bind my soul and to release the spirits" (February 14, 1799); and, one week later: "With the help of the delightful tones, my soul is gradually freeing itself from the bonds of records and documents. I sit in the green room, a Quattro by my side, and call softly to the distant figures."

It is a known fact that Leonardo da Vinci had music performed while painting the Mona Lisa, not just to conjure the wonderful smile upon the face of his Florentine model, but in order to set his own soul vibrating as well; for it has long been noticed that Mona Lisa's smile was Leonardo's own smile.

FROM BEETHOVEN TO SHOSTAKOVICH

The mysterious, indefinite ringing with which the productive mood frequently announces itself has occasionally been used by poetic musicians for the introduction of their works. Beethoven was probably the first, when he reproduced in tones such a productive mood at the beginning of the Ninth Symphony as introduction to the opus: a rustling and ringing out of which a motif emerges; harmonic expansion, the growth of tones and, as the climax, the lightning and thunder of the great theme that follows the sheet-lightning of the musical mood.

The first theme of Anton Bruckner's "Romantic Symphony" also ascends from an indefinite humming and buzzing. In works of Chopin and Schumann one frequently finds the productive mood entwined in the composition proper. And around 1890 some abstract painters (Leger, Kandinsky, et al) transformed the productive moods of graphic fantasy into colors and forms which, however, were not yet reality, but merely mood and, therefore, dreamlike vision.

I.

The productive mood of artists is dependent upon many factors. Often it is linked in mysterious fashion to nature, as though the creative forces of the artists were but a part of the general creative powers of nature. Many musicians experience an enhancement of productive moods with the approach of spring and summer. Of the musicians whose productive strength decreased in winter and increased again in spring, Beethoven is the greatest. Summertime was Beethoven's period for composing. With the beginning of the warmer season, when the trees spread their foliage and the meadows became verdant, when the songbirds returned

[282]

from the south and the spring seed started to shoot up out of the ground, Beethoven moved from town to the country, as though to be closer to nature. Here, his sketch books filled with notes. In the fall and winter Beethoven then completed what he had designed in spring and summer. "In winter I work but little," Beethoven told Rellstab. "I only write down what I did during the summer, and compose the score." In the fall the fully loaded wagons were driven into the barn.

Mozart also liked to spend the summer in the country or in a garden. He composed "Don Giovanni" in Prague in a summer-house (Bertramka's), and wrote "Zauberfloete" in a small wooden hut that stood in the yard of the "Freihaus" (Baronial house). The duet between Papageno and Papagena in the "Magic Flute" was composed by Mozart under the oaks and beech-trees of Kahlenberg.

In the summer of 1788, after Mozart had moved into a garden flat, he wrote to Puchberg: "In the ten days that I have been living here, I have worked more than in the two months during which I lived in the other dwelling." Mozart had spent his childhood in Salzburg, where the mountains look down upon the old city; he knew, therefore, that nature tends to intensify productive moods. "It is very silly," said Mozart, "that we have to hatch our work in the room."

Among modern musicians, Richard Strauss is one who has his productive mood in summer only. Says he: "Cherries do not blossom in the winter, nor do musical ideas come readily when nature is bleak and cold. I am a great lover of nature. Hence it is natural I do my best creative work in the Bavarian highlands during the spring and summer. In fact, I usually compose from spring to autumn and then write out and polish the detailed scores in the winter."

Igor Stravinsky is another who composes only in spring and summer. During these seasons he spends three hours every morning at his bureaucratically neat desk. As a young composer, he wrote the scores here in many colors, so that they looked like the choral books of Byzantine churches. Later he wrote in black and white.

There were great poets, too, who were dependent on the seasons. Goethe believed he could not compose during the winter as the low barometer depressed him. It is an exception when a poet as sombre as the drama-tist Friedrich Hebbel wrote only in the autumn and in winter, and belongs to the pathological traits of his personality.

The spring season oppressed Hebbel, and he con-fessed in his diary: "I have never really felt smaller than in spring. The sprouting infinity presses around my breast and strangles me. Not until summer do I feel easier, and the inner Vesuvius erupts with its old fire." On another page he writes: "Fall is starting in, the leaves are falling, the spirit of destruction weaves through the air, the world is getting stern and gray. The season usually made a deep impression on my soul, I was refreshed and lively."

However, that autumn should enhance the pro-ductive mood is not a normal reaction; healthy artistic natures find their creative power augmented by light, warmth, sun and the blooming of nature.

Schiller clearly recognized dependence of productive mood upon light and sun when he wrote to Goethe under date of February 27, 1795: *"With all our boasted independence, how greatly are we tied to the*

forces of nature, and what is our will if nature fails us.
For five weeks I have been brooding over something
without results, and within three days a *single mild
ray of sunshine* released it in me. To be sure, my perseverance so far may have prepared this development,
*but the development itself was brought to me by the
warming sun.*"

Goethe's reply was this: "We can do nothing but
build the woodpile and let it dry well; it catches fire
at the right moment, and we ourselves are surprised
by it."

The difference between day and night is likewise important to the productive mood. Normally, the productive mood is animated by the light of day. Dependency of the productive mood upon night may be considered a pathological variant. Haydn, Mozart, Beethoven, Richard Wagner were all day workers.

The one night worker among modern musicians was
Claude Debussy. He needed the quiet and solitude.
The world had to vanish in shadows if he was to hear
his subtle, melting harmonies. Nothing loud and shrill
was allowed to disturb him.

Similarly, Balzac only worked at night, by candle-
light, garbed in the cowl of a Dominican monk. Romantic fantasy seems to depend on the night; classic
fantasy on daytime.

It may come as a surprise to many to find the waltz
king, Johann Strauss, among the night workers; but
the singer of the joy of life considered the night hour
not so much the hour of romanticism as the hour of
eroticism. In the adjoining room, his wife lay in bed,
and when Strauss sat at his work table and composed
his waltzes—with pencil—he needed the erotic atmos-

phere. He wrote waltzes and, in the midst of his work, he would send amorous notes into his wife's room.

One of these billet doux reads:

"Monday night, 1 A.M. You whispered so much into my ear today that made me happy—you must not blame me if I sip from the cup of joy, longing and bliss. Let us be merry—on ne vit qu'une fois."

There follow on the slip of paper the opening measures to "Cagliostro" that had just occurred to Johann Strauss:

and were later changed to the whirling

The sensuous waltz melodies of Johann Strauss originated in sensual night hour. They are caresses and kisses.

Peculiar were Mozart's relations to the times of day. He employed the early morning hours for composing. Even when he had spent the previous evening in company, he would start to write at six or seven in the morning. In later years he did this lying in bed, like Rossini and Donizetti. Very rarely, and unwillingly, did Mozart compose at times other than early morning. Only when there was pressing work, as for instance when he had to complete "Marriage of Figaro," did he use the entire forenoon for writing. He had to be very hard-pressed when he made use of the night, as he did in writing the overture to "Don Giovanni." And then he had to drink punch, and his wife had to tell him fairy tales, to keep him awake.

If Mozart's composing is bound to the day, the night belongs to free fantasy. From childhood on he prefers to play at night. If he sat down to the piano at nine in the evening, he could not be separated from it before midnight, according to Schlichtegroll, or he would have improvised all through the night. "In his adult years, too," Niemetschek reports, "he spent half the night at the piano. Only having heard Mozart in such hours could one comprehend the profundity, the full extent of his musical genius; free and independent of every consideration, his spirit was able to soar in gallant flight to the highest regions of art."

Improvising and composing were two different matters for Mozart. They were different processes.

In nocturnal improvisations, Mozart abandoned himself to free play of his invention. The world of his fantasy was stirred up. His emotional agitation found direct expression in melodies and passages that were manifold and colorful. The musical ideas did not unfold from a center, as they did in a composition. But while composing, Mozart never came to the piano. Not until he had the composition completed did he play it for his wife or for friends. "I have just finished a small duet for Figaro that I want you to hear," Mozart said to Kelly when he had written down the charming duet: 'Condel perche finora,' and he sat down at the instrument which thus far he had not needed. Then they both sang the duet.

Improvising, to Mozart, meant submerging in the

stream of his musical ideas. Composing meant: to divert waters from this stream into canals so they would move mills. Free fantasy is a matter of wealth, colors, variety of musical ideas. Composing means order, measure, form. Free fantasy unfolds for Mozart in the quiet of night because it strings pictures together like a dream. Composing preferred the day because it arranged musical ideas, made them lucid and organized them in distinct forms.

Beethoven likewise experienced improvising and composing as separate functions. When he sat down at the piano in the presence of company, he almost never played his own compositions, but began to improvise freely. While improvising he gave himself up to the full wealth of his ideas. He tried his powers in free invention and caused a turmoil in the realm of tones. In improvising he was animated by the sense of power of his personality.

When Beethoven starts his Piano Concerto in E-flat major with the tempestuous piano passages that roll and hammer all over the instrument, every listener hears Beethoven's sense of power and the titanism of his personality. It was this personality that distinguished Beethoven's free improvising from Mozart's harmonic piano playing. Yet this imaginative power of Beethoven's that broke through in the improvisation, has nothing to do with his composing faculty. Very rarely did such free improvising—no matter how bold and great it may have been—result in composition.

Of Beethoven, only one case is known where the composing process began with free fantasy. Ferdinand Ries reports how he once visited Beethoven in Baden. "As I entered the house, I heard him improvising in his room. In order not to disturb him at it, I stood listening at the door and noticed that he rhapsodically flung down individual passages which he then seemed to be trying out first one way, then another." Then Beethoven and Ries went for a walk in the surrounding woods of Baden. "I noticed that Beethoven was preoccupied and was humming to himself; experience had taught me that in such moments he was in the best humour for work, and I was careful not to disturb him, but walked mutely at his side.

"In the individual phrases that he was humming, I thought to detect some resemblance with the passages he had been playing in his room." During the entire promenade Beethoven continued "to hum various incomprehensible phrases and tones and to sing them out loud." As soon as he reached home, he sat down to the piano full of impatience, and exclaimed: "Now I'll play something for you!" The music he created this way was the first movement of the great F-minor Sonata.

Of the musical classicists, Josef Haydn was the only one who improvised at the piano in order to find themes and musical ideas for his compositions. Unlike Mozart and Beethoven, Haydn did not consider improvising so much a separate sphere of musical activity as a preparation for creative work. Noting down the ideas found at the piano was already the second step in the working process of Haydn and not, as in the case of Beethoven, the vestibule of musical creation.

We are in possession of a manuscript (at present in the Mozarteum in Salzburg) that was presumably written by Haydn's servant and copyist Elssler, father of the famous dancer Fanny Elssler. This manuscript gives us a good idea about Haydn's daily schedule and his work. It is entitled: "Tagesordnung des Sel. Herrn

[289]

von Haydn" (Daily plan of the late Herr von Haydn),
and reads as follows:

"In the summer time it was ordered to get up at
half-past six. The first task was shaving, which he did
himself until he was seventy-three years old. After shaving he dressed completely. If a pupil was present while
he was dressing, the pupil had to play his lesson for
Haydn. The mistakes were corrected immediately, the
pupil instructed accordingly, and then a new example
was given. This took an hour and a half. Promptly at
eight o'clock breakfast had to be on the table, and
right after breakfast Haydn sat down to the piano
and improvised, at the same time sketching the plan
of the composition. The hours from eight until half-
past eleven daily were destined for that. At half-past
eleven calls were either made or accepted, or a walk
was taken until half-past one. From two to three was
the dinner hour. After dinner Haydn always undertook
some little domestic chore. Then he took the sketch
that was designed in the morning and scored it, for
which he needed three to four hours. At eight Haydn
usually went out, but returned home again at nine; he
then either sat down to writing scores, or he took a
book and read until ten o'clock. Ten o'clock in the
evening was the appointed hour for supper, which consisted of bread and wine. Haydn had made a rule of
eating only bread and wine in the evening, but he
broke the rule here and there when he was invited out
to supper. At the table Haydn liked a jocular conversation, and gay entertainment in general. At half-past
eleven Haydn went to bed; when he was older, even
later."

The sketches of "Creation" that we have give a good
idea of the thoroughness and deliberation of Haydn's

planning. Being the son of an artisan, Haydn knew the blessing of careful work. He rejected obscurity, artificialness and unnaturalness. In the manuscript of the second movement of Symphony No. 41, Haydn corrected several measures that sounded too unnatural, and he wrote next to it: "This was for much too learned ears." And inbetween sketches for "Creation" it says in Haydn's handwriting: "And I told him it is not good to be interesting."

The composer Schultz visited Haydn in Eisenstadt in 1770. Haydn showed him some works, and when Schultz expressed surprise at Haydn's diligence, the latter remarked: "Well, you see, I arise early, and as soon as I am dressed I fall upon my knees and pray to God and the Holy Virgin that I may succeed again today. Following a bite for breakfast, I sit down at the piano and begin searching. If I find something soon, then without much trouble I can continue. If I cannot go ahead, then I realize that through some offense I have forfeited grace, and then I pray again for grace until I feel that I have been forgiven."

Schultz, traveling in the company of a Polish countess whom he was teaching piano, was completely overwhelmed by Haydn's naivité, modesty and purity.

Haydn always sat down to the piano fully dressed. He stayed there till he found the ideas suitable to his purpose, which he then immediately set down on paper. During the afternoon Haydn let the sketches run through his mind until he saw the whole musical development clearly before his eyes. Then he first wrote down the work clearly and distinctly, and it needed no further corrections. "That is possible," claimed Haydn, "because I did not write until I was quite certain of my matter."

Somehow Haydn's inventive talent was dependent upon the tone of the piano. When Haydn composed three piano sonatas in 1788, he wrote to his publisher, Artaria: "In order to do a particularly good job of composing your three piano sonatas, I found it necessary to buy a new piano." It was an instrument of the piano maker Wenzel Schanz which he liked especially well.

In 1790 Haydn recommended Schanz to his friend, Frau Genzinger, "as the best master in his profession; his pianos are of special lightness and pleasant treatment." And on another occasion he regrets that his friend still does not use a Schanz piano. It is quite likely that the tone of these pianos, described as being especially soft, animated Haydn's fantasy. Mozart preferred pianos by Anton Walter, which Haydn found too heavy. "One can not play everything with suitable daintiness," he wrote to Frau von Genzinger.

"Once I caught hold of an idea, I made every effort to adjust it to the rules of art, and to sustain it. Thus I tried to help myself, and that is what so many of our new composers lack; they string one piece next to the other, break off when they have barely begun. But even after hearing it, nothing remains in the heart."

With Haydn, the process of elaboration that develops themes, re-forms them and bares their intrinsic value, took place inwardly. Improvising at the piano had brought forth themes from the unconscious mind. The actual working procedure: the selection and examination of the themes, the formation of larger pattern associations; the maturing and growing of musical thoughts took place in the fantasy of the composer Haydn, within the inner world in which critical thinking controls the working procedure.

This elaboration of thoughts required time if one did not wish to forcibly accelerate the forming process. When a certain symphony, promised by Haydn to Frau von Genzinger for her anniversary, had not been completed on that day, Haydn assured her: "This poor promised symphony, since its preparation, has hovered continuously before my fantasy; it is only due (unfortunately) to some hitherto urgent events that the symphony could not be brought into the world."

Haydn needed time to work on his ideas. He says of himself that "he had never been a speedwriter" and that he always "composed with deliberation and diligence." He laid the greatest stress on invention of melody: "It's the melody that gives music its charm (said Haydn to Kelly); and to produce it is extremely difficult. The mechanism of music can be learned by perseverance and study; but the invention of a pretty melody is the work of the genius, and such a melody requires no further adornment in order to please. If you would know whether it is really beautiful, sing it without accompaniment."

Nothing was further from Haydn's mind than a convenient conservatism. "What does that mean? Art is free, and should not be confined by the chains of handicraft. The ear—that is, the educated ear—must decide, and I consider myself as much authorized as the next one to make laws in that respect."

And on another occasion: "If I considered something nice so that, in my opinion, my ear and my heart might well be satisfied; and if I would have had to sacrifice such beauty to dry pedantry, then I would much rather let a small grammatical blunder remain."

As did every truly creative nature, so, too, did Haydn consider the labour of his fancy as the work of super-human forces and as something that overwhelmed him. For a man as pious as Haydn it was a blessing of God, and he himself a weak receptacle for such divine inspirations. Like so many other great artists, Haydn at the peak of his life had the feeling that he was just at the beginning. "Oh God," Haydn wrote when he was in his late sixties, "how much is left undone in this magnificent art, even by a man as I have been." He says to Kalkbrenner: "In my advanced age I first learned to use the wind instruments; now that I understand them, I have to go and can not make use of them."

His pious prayer of thanks for divine blessing was the melody of the "folk hymn." When he was far advanced in years he was in the habit of playing this choral melody three times daily. He always played it with the greatest emotion, and himself called the melody "My Prayer."

Five days prior to his death, Haydn played the melody for the last time, and played it three times in succession, "with expression and taste" according to a report by Griesinger, and happy and proud, for "he had not played the song so well for a long while."

Just as religious people, after saying prayers, enjoy a particularly strong mood of happiness, so did Haydn experience similar moods when he played the melody of the folk hymn. When Nuekomm visited Haydn in 1808, Haydn "advanced toward him quite gayly" and remarked triumphantly: "Do you know that today I played my prayer very cleverly, yes quite cleverly."

As the sketches handed down to us show, Haydn worked more intensively at this simple, intimate melody than at any of his other melodies.

Johann Sebastian Bach had a special way of evoking productive moods. He too required the piano to warm up his fantasy. At the introduction to an improvisation he usually played some strange composition at random from the notes. Like a pilot, he first let his machine warm up a bit before soaring into the air. "You know," Magistrate Pitschel in Leipsic reports, "the famous man in our city who has the greatest praise of music and the admiration of the connoisseurs is not capable of charming others by mixing his tones until he has played something from notes and set his imagination in motion."

Often Bach took a single bass part from some other composer when he was in the humour for improvising, and improvised a trio or quartet with it.

Bach was a big bird who flew off slowly. Foreign music set his composing faculty in motion. Thus Bach took a theme by Legrenzi and worked it into an organ fugue. The B-minor organ fugue begins its flight with a theme by Legrenzi; two piano fugues start with themes by Albinoni. The magnificent theme of the great G-minor Fugue for Organ originates in an orchestral piece by Muffat, the "Italian Concerto" in a symphony by the same master. Mozart shows a similar trait. He is stimulated by foreign masters and uses their themes to soar skywards.

It is known that sixteen piano concertos, four organ concertos and a violin concerto arranged for four pianos are Bach's transcriptions of music by other composers, namely: Vivaldi, Benedetto Marcello, Telemann and the young Duke Johann Ernst von Weimar. These Bach arrangements are free. He does not use these works just to clarify his fantasy; his imagination is activated by alien music. In other words, foreign music is a stimulus for his fantasy.

Richard Wagner never used the piano for his work. While Wagner was writing the score of "Meistersinger von Nuernberg" in the second story of his villa in Triebschen, Hans Richter—who was copying the completed score on the first floor of the house—never heard a tone out of the piano.

Neither did Richard Strauss use the piano to get in the mood. The study of his house in Vienna did not even have a piano. The high raftered Renaissance ceiling that Strauss had brought from Italy and that adorned his study, the Greek statuettes and expensive paintings were sufficient to stimulate the fantasy of "Ricardo il Magnifico."

II.

One little explored problem is the dependence of productive moods upon psychic cycles.

We have already pointed out the regular rotation of depressive and manic moods with which Hugo Wolf was afflicted and which influenced his composing faculty. No less an artist than Goethe noticed the dependency of his work upon regular soul activity. What he wrote in his diary is significant: "I must take closer notice of the circle of good and bad things that revolves within me. Passions, devotion, impulses to do this or that, invention, execution, organization—everything alternates in a regular cycle. Likewise gaiety, sorrow, strength, elasticity, weakness, calmness, greed. Inasmuch as I live on a diet, the procedure is not disturbed and I must find out yet in what time and order I revolve around myself."

It is quite possible that the appearance and disappearance of musical works by Beethoven is associated with such cyclic movements of the soul. For instance, the sketch of "Opferlied" which later was published as opus 121* ("Die Flamme lodert," by Matthison) was first written down by Beethoven in 1794. In 1801 or 1802 the song was taken up for the second time; a third time in 1805 or 1807. The last sketches date back to the years 1822 and 1823, and resulted in the final form. When Beethoven wrote the first sketch, he was twenty-four years old; when he wrote the final sketches, he was fifty-three. In the interim period the work is twice rolled out of the unconscious.

Similarly, cyclic movements withdraw the overture "Zur Namensfeier" from the subconscious four different times. The history of this overture begins in 1809 when the French occupied Vienna. The sketches are plentiful. Gradually the main theme emerges to join them. The key of the overture was to be E-flat major. In 1811 work is resumed. Now the key becomes G major, then reverts back to E-flat major, with the incidental movement in G-major. In 1812 the overture arises from the subconscious for a third time and is joined to the "Ode of Joy" that was inserted in the overture. It is now in the key of C major. In sketchbooks from the years 1814 and 1815 the music appears for the fourth time, in this instance in 6/8 time.

---

* Arrangement for voice, chorus and orchestra. Another arrangement for voice and pianoforte has no opus number.

Between the first and the last note of the overture lies a period of six years. The intervals between the revolutions are almost all alike.

Similarly the idea of composing "Ode of Joy" emerges from Beethoven's subconscious repeatedly in cyclic motion from 1792 on.

The dependence of productive moods from seasons, from day and night and from cyclic movements of the soul indicates to what extent artists are linked to nature, and how much artistic work is a part of general forces of nature. When great musicians, like Beethoven, again and again went in search of nature, it was because they felt very strongly the connection between their spiritual labor and life in nature. The moods that sounded to Beethoven out of woods and fields, from the song of the birds and thunderstorms, were the same as his own moods. "Like a child I look forward to it; how glad I am to be able to walk among the bushes and woods, under trees, herbs and rocks. No man can love the country as much as I do; for the forest, trees and rocks furnish the echo that man desires," Beethoven wrote to Therese Malfatti.

The majesty of the Swiss Alps gave Wagner's musical descriptions of nature in "Ring des Nibelungen" their grand style. Wagner was surrounded by the high peaks of the Alps, upon which the sun gleamed down, when he described the moods of solitude "on blissful heights" in the third act of 'Siegfried.'

The landscape of the central mountains, with brooks and mills, crows, doves, trout, the rustling and falling of leaves, with little villages in which the dogs bark at night—that is the landscape of Franz Schubert's bourgeois romanticist soul. The desolate heath enveloped in mist is the landscape of Johannes Brahms.

PRODUCTIVE MOODS

All musicians who portrayed landscapes and nature
—Schubert, Schumann, Hugo Wolf, Debussy and
Russian composers—described them as pictures of
their own soul. Nature awakened music in great musicians such as Gade, Sibelius, Borodin, Moussorgsky,
Dvorak and Smetana because her moods reflected the
emotional life of man. Nature was man himself, in
whose innermost being it was bright or dark, in whom
storms raged, fog expanded, colorful meadows gleamed and birds sang.

When Mozart traveled by coach and looked out
upon the landscape, he immediately felt music forming within him. Haydn had a little house in his garden in Eisenstadt; here he sat under trees and wrote.
"Jahreszeiten" and "Schoepfung" are replete with descriptions of nature; all of nature becomes music in
these works. How deeply Bach sensed the moods of
nature is demonstrated most touchingly in the recitative "Am Abend, da es kuehle ward," of the St. Mat-
thews Passion. The peace of dusk, the tranquillity of
nature was never felt more profoundly than in this
music.

From Bach to Debussy, music is filled with grandiose descriptions of nature and her moods; the music
of trees and brooks, of birds and animals, the sounds
of day and night, spring, summer, fall and winter
have inspired more music than all other experiences
of great musicians.

III.

All great musicians have their particular knack of
evoking and augmenting productive moods.

Haydn dressed carefully before sitting down to his

desk. Richard Wagner had to be surrounded by luxury to put himself in productive mood. When Wagner started composition of "Ring des Nibelungen," he wrote to Liszt: "You will find it quite nice here. The luxury devil has taken hold of me, and I have furnished my house as pleasantly as possible." And he wrote to Frau Ritter at about the same time: "For some time now I am a fool for luxury."

"Luxury" and "voluptuousness" to Wagner meant velvet curtains and silk covers in his study. The armchairs had to be covered with silk materials which Wagner liked to touch and stroke when he was working, thus enhancing his productive mood by an erotic stimulus. His working room had to be filled with the scent of perfume. Wagner himself donned the costume of the Old German painters in such hours, including the skull-cap of silk and velvet such as his step-father Geyer had worn when standing at the easel.*

As proven by Balzac, Th. A. Hoffman and D'Annunzio, romantic artists like to transform the real world into a dream world.

Debussy, too, surrounded himself with precious objects while working: Japanese lacquered work, Greek statuettes, handsome bookbindings, bibelots, vases, rare canes; he worked in a green room, liked emerald-colored ties and had to have a lot of flowers around him if he was to hear music. Even as a boy he decorated his room with butterflies.

Richard Wagner admitted that he required "a costly cradle" for his work: "If I have to jump into the waves of the imagination in order to satisfy my-

---

* That Wagner wore silk underwear—as we know from 'Letters to a Modiste'—has nothing to do with his passion for silk material. Wagner suffered from shingles, and rough materials irritated the inflammation.

self in an imaginary world, then at least my fantasy has to have some help and my faculty of imagination some support. I cannot live like a dog; I can't lie down on a bed of straw and relish bad liquor. I have to feel flattered somehow if my mind is to succeed with the bloody hard work of building a non-existant world," Wagner wrote. And when he outfitted his apartment in Vienna with luxurious furnishings— this was the apartment in which he composed "Meistersinger".—he declared: "When I am not working, I am oppressed by everything that seems unnecessary; only when I wish to lure and hold the Muse do I seriously consider furnishing my room with calm and coziness."

It appears as though the fantasy of romantic artists requires splendor, luxury and furnishing of their studies with rare objects. Goethe, who was the prototype of the classic poet, could only work in very simple surroundings. And the rooms that first heard the music of Haydn, Mozart, Beethoven and Schubert, as well as the studies of Brahms and Bruckner, were simple bourgeois rooms.

Richard Wagner, who donned a special costume when he was in a productive mood, or when he wished to attain this mood, forms the transition to those artists who employ pathological means in order to overcome their inhibitions. E. T. A. Hoffman, Edgar A. Poe, Musset and others required alcohol to enhance their mood. Of Schiller, Goethe remarked: "Schiller never drank much, he was quite moderate; but in those moments of physical weakness he sought to augment his forces by partaking of some liquor or similar spirits. However, this was harmful to his health and detrimental to production itself."

FROM BEETHOVEN TO SHOSTAKOVICH

Among the composers only Moussorgsky was a pathological drunkard, like Poe. Beethoven drank wine and beer, but only after work, not in order to stimulate his fantasy. Haydn was a wine drinker; for years he lived in a famous wine country (Eisenstadt) and gave a realistic portrayal of the vintage and wine intoxication in the "Seasons." Franz Schubert also enjoyed the wine from Vienna's environments. Max Reger was an avid beer drinker, and a heavier smoker. Balzac was a passionate imbiber of coffee. Debussy loved a delicate tea, which he prepared himself.

Friedrich Schiller kept rotting apples in the drawers of the desk at which he wrote. The strong perfumes in Richard Wagner's study, and the many flowers in Debussy's room had the same function. They were supposed to stimulate the productive mood with strong fragrances.

Richard Wagner's indulgence in snuff is also such a medium. Once Wagner attempted to relinquish this ugly habit. In August of 1853 he suffered heavy mental depressions, and the doctor forbade him to take snuff: "In order to cure my ailing brain nerve, my physician prevailed upon me to give up snuff once and for all," Wagner wrote at that time. "Since six weeks I have not taken a sniff; what that means, only a passionate snuff-taker like myself can understand. Now I first realize that snuff was the only real 'occasionally' refreshing enjoyment; and now I even have to relinquish that. My torment at present is indescribable—but I will go through with it, that's definite. Well, no more snuff-boxes: I will accept only medals."

Several years later Wagner again succumbed to the stimulation of snuff. In 1855 Wagner was at the piano, in London, playing compositions by Weber. As

PRODUCTIVE MOODS

Praeger tells it: "Suddenly he stopped playing and took out his snuff-box, which he found to be empty. To our request to continue with the rehearsals of 'Euryanthe,' he replied in childishly bad humour, half in earnest, half jokingly: 'No more snuff—no more music.' It was morning already, and although I knew that the 'pinch' of snuff had become second habit with him, this time there was no help for it."

We find it just as difficult to picture Wagner with the snuff-box as with a Saxonian dialect.

IV.

The most natural means of animating the forces of fantasy seems to be physical motion. Stimulation of breathing and blood circulation augments the mental powers. The strong emotional agitation of work transfers itself to the body proper, and the physical movement in turn increases the spiritual activity.

During his Strassbourg sojourn, Goethe composed his hymns while wandering, and from Italy he wrote: "The day is long, thinking is undisturbed, and the most glorious pictures of the environment, far from repelling the poetic mood, produce it, in conjunction with motion and fresh air, all the faster." While wandering on the high mountains of Sils Maria, the grand rhythms of Zarathustra's speeches first rang in Nietzsche's soul.

Karl Maria von Weber liked to compose best on lonely walks, and the same holds true of Richard Wagner. Hector Berlioz wrote to him in 1855: "So you want to melt the glaciers with the composition of your 'Nibelungen'! It must be glorious to be able to work in the midst of magnificent scenery in nature."

From Zuerich Wagner often undertook outings into the mountains; he loved the high peaks where there was room for big thoughts and large pictures. In a letter to Liszt he describes the "terribly majestic view on the mountain-ice-snow and glacier world" which he enjoyed from the Faulhorn in the Berner Oberland. In another letter to Liszt he describes his two-day picnic from Wallis through the Formazza Valley to Domodossola. Wagner's music to "Ring des Nibelungen" always has the Swiss Alpine world as its background.

Among the famous musicians, Beethoven was the greatest wanderer. We always visualize him storming through the woods near Vienna, his hair exposed to the wind, his face clouded, howling, humming, singing, or standing still at the brook, listening to the song of the birds and then storming on, his sketchbook in his pocket. Charles Neate, an English pianist who visited Beethoven in Baden near Vienna in 1815, says: "Nature was so to say his nourishment. He seemed to live in nature." And in the autumn of 1817, he wrote to Frau Streicher, in Bonn: "If you are strolling through the forests of our homeland, remember that Beethoven has made poetry there or, as one says now: he has composed."

Stumpff, who made a pilgrimage to Beethoven in 1824, reports what Beethoven told him: "I have to relax in the unspoiled nature and clean my mind . . . Will you go with me to visit my unchanging friends: green thickets, and high trees, green hedges and recesses with rippling brooks? Yes, and the vinetrees which look from the hills to the sun that fecundates them that they may bear grapes? Yes my friend, there is no envy. Come along. What a wonderful morning which promises a beautiful day!"

[304]

And Beethoven says something similar to Stumpff during a walk in the same year, and Stumpff reports it in his Memoirs: "Here I am sitting for hours and my mind is revelling looking at the conceiving and producing children of nature. Here the majestic sun is not covered by a dirty roof made by hands of men. The blue heaven is my sublime roof. Looking to the heaven at night with awe, and staring at the shining stars revolving in eternal circles, at the suns or globes, my spirit is rising beyond the stars which are that many million miles distant to the primeval source, out of which all created things have been flowing and from where new created things will flow eternally."

It was during such an evening promenade that Beethoven entered in his sketchbook:

"Wandering through the woods and over the fields, Beethoven felt himself one with nature and her creator. Here he felt his soul elevated, his fantasy forces strengthened by the association with the divine".

Brahms was another walker and wanderer who sought inspiration in the Vienna woods.

Hugo Wolf's loveliest songs originated during walks on the Poetzleinsdorfer Heide or at the bank of Gmundner Lake. What Hugo Wolf invented during his walks was written down in pencil in the evening and often sung to friends right from the pencil sketches.

Gustav Mahler liked to motivate his fantasy with walks, while Richard Strauss preferred automobile riding to walking. After such rides he liked to stretch out on a sofa next to which there stood a music desk with the score of one of Mozart's string quartets, the study of which animated the imagination. Claude Debussy liked to stroll leisurely, dreamily, through the streets of Paris and watch the reflections of the lights in the water of the Seine. Impressionistic color play, as painted by Claude Monet and Pisarro, fascinated his fantasy. He also loved the ocean as an inspiring phenomenon of nature.

The various means employed by composers to promote productive moods all have the same purpose: either they are supposed to augment the forces of the composer's personality, as Haydn's or Wagner's dress did; or stimulate the imagination, as alcohol or other stimulants do; or, they should lead out of the everyday world, as the room decorations of Richard Wagner and Claude Debussy did.

All these media have in common the ability to overcome inhibitions. They demonstrate that unconscious soul life is separated by barriers from the territory of consciousness. The musical forms that have developed in the realm of the subconscious are interlaced with the emotional impulses of the subconscious. Musical ideas, tone figures, coherent tone masses are set in motion by repressed sentiments and emotions, suppressed recollections and experiences. Sentiments and instincts, and memories of sentiments and instincts transform themselves continuously into tone forms in the subconscious. This entire subconscious working process—like all emotional work of the unconscious—is forced into the deep recesses and forcibly held there. Suppression increases the energy of the unconscious until the moment comes when the forms that have developed in the subconscious break through all inhibitions.

PRODUCTIVE MOODS

The productive mood announces to the composers that the moment is close at hand when the inner music accumulates before the gates of the subconscious and the gates are ready to open up under the pressure of the music bulk.

Chapter XII.

Musical Conception

THE MOMENT in which unconscious music figures break through and are seized by conscious activity of the composer's mind—that moment is called: musical conception. From this moment on conscious thinking and conscious forming accompanies the whole composing process. The more this process nears completion, the stronger becomes the part of conscious thinking in the musical creation, until critical thinking alone puts the finishing touches to the tone figures. In the case of Beethoven this meant the final, most minute perfection of the dynamic signatures.

With the greatest care Beethoven perfected the dynamics in the last measures of the variations in his String Quartet in C-sharp minor, opus 131. Observe how Beethoven embellished the dynamics of these last bars:

One can see Beethoven mulling, testing, altering in the seven of the twelve pages, the top voice of which is reproduced here. The dynamics are repeatedly polished and refined. This elaboration is a product of reflection and critical thinking. It is conscious perfection.

I.

The first conception takes place differently than conscious formation. It is something elemental. A fount breaks out of the earth. An earthquake changes the surface of the earth. Volcanic masses erupt through the surface.

Whatever had formed in the subconscious thus far now presses toward the light. It may also be something without form. Rhythms, keys. Later such rhythmic movements form themes.

In 1814, when Beethoven re-modeled his "Fidelio" for the second time and gave the work the permanent form that it now shows, he also wanted to re-arrange the "Leonore Overture"—the small third overture opus 138 from the year 1807. Like the two preceding "big" Leonore overtures, this one was in the key of C-major. Now, however, the bright festive E-major broke from Beethoven's subconscious, the key that had only flashed up in the side movement of the two large Leonore overtures. This key took hold of the first half of the overture. Then Beethoven abandoned the work. But the gleaming E-major key continues to be efficacious. After the three Lenore overtures in C-major, Beethoven composed a new overture, the present "Fidelio" overture, in E-major.

Here we have the mood of a key—E-major—that emerges from the subconscious like sunrays that come through the clouds before sunrise. Not until later do the forms of the E-major overture ascend to the light.

The Ninth Symphony shows a similar evolution. Here, too, it is the mood of a key that first obtrudes itself upon the composer. In this instance it is the key of D-minor that emerges like a mass of clouds, before even a theme appears.

In the sketches to the fourth movement of Beethoven's Seventh Symphony one finds the following:

with the notation: "goes first in F-sharp minor, then in C-sharp minor." In the completed work, though, Beethoven did not use the sketched melody. However, he did retain the modulation. Here, in spite of thematic changes, harmonic motion dominates the invention from the subconscious.

In other instances Beethoven shows the rhythmic motion that ascends from the subconscious to be the power that drives the imagination. Before even the thematic sketches to Beethoven's Seventh Symphony make their appearance, we find motifs in the characteristic dactylic rhythm:

The same rhythm out of which the first movement grows—the main theme does not appear until after six pages of work—also takes hold of the subsequent Scherzo. The rhythmic motion in this music had formed in the subconscious of the composer and was now involving themes in strong surges; it was the power that dominated musical fantasy.

It happens to Beethoven occasionally that his musical conception is governed by certain *harmonic modulations* that formed in his subconscious and that now dominate his musical creation. For example, directly preceding the sketches to the String Quartet in A-minor, opus 132, a chromatic motif appears which the composer intended to execute in the style of a fugue. Originally it had this form:

However, this fugue theme disappears soon and makes room for the sketches to the A-minor String Quartet (1824). First the main theme appears in these sketches. Then Beethoven designs the introduction in which a brooding introductory motif appears that pervades the first movement like an "idée fixe." Here is the form of the motif:

Just a cursory glance shows that this chorale-like "idée fixe" descends from the chromatic fugue theme.

But the impulse is not yet exhausted. One year later —1825—Beethoven finished his big B-flat String Quartet, opus 130, which he called his "Leibquartett" (favorite quartet). He ended it with the large fugue which later was detached from the Quartet and published as opus 133. The theme of this fugue first had this form:

and was re-modeled and re-arranged by the composer, provided with counter-themes and condensed until it assumed the shape in which it now appears:

This theme, too, is a descendent of the chromatic fugue theme that appeared in Beethoven's sketchbook in 1824.

However, in the fugue theme of the C-sharp minor String Quartet (the beginnings of which date back to 1825) that was completed in the summer of 1826 and that Beethoven called "the greatest of my quartets," one finds the chromatic turn that had appeared in contrapuntal forms in the A-minor and B-minor string quartets, this time as fugue theme:

It is always the identical musical idea that crops up in different forms between 1824 and 1826: a theme consisting of four notes with chromatic turn. This theme appears either as cantus firmus in the contrapuntal structure or as fugue theme. It controls Beethoven's musical thinking like an "idée fixe."

We are able to follow this theme along part of its way from the unconscious to the top.

Repeatedly Beethoven toyed with the idea of writing a piece of music in honor of Johann Sebastian Bach. As early as 1808 he conceived a string quintet in honor of Bach, ("Quintet in Memory of Johann Sebastian Bach") and dating from that time Beethoven's sketchbooks show notations from parts of Bach compositions. In 1810 Beethoven copies spots from the "Chromatic Fantasy," in 1817 pieces from the "Wohltemperiertes Klavier" and "Art of the Fugue." From 1822 on Beethoven intended to prove his admiration for Bach by composing a "Bach" overture, and up to the year 1825 one finds again and again sketches for a "Bach" overture.

It can be stated that without thoughts of Bach's fugue polyphony, Beethoven's last string quartets would not have been written.

In 1825 one finds sketches for a "Bach" overture side by side with sketches for the big E-flat major String Quartet opus 127 and the grand String Quartet in A-minor opus 132. Thus Beethoven's thoughts of Bach's music wander the same road with his ideas of a new quartet style.

The chromatic four-note motif is also associated with Beethoven's thoughts of Bach and of a Bach overture. This chromatic theme carries polyphonic structures in the A-minor String Quartet, in the B-flat String Quartet and in the C-sharp minor String Quartet, and ought to be called a "Bach" theme; for it is descended from Bach.

Bach himself knew that his surname: B A C H, could be read as a music picture. Transferred into notes, the name B A C H reads:

When Bach composed the great fugue with which he intended to close his "Art of the Fugue," he formed the third theme of this fugue over the notes "BACH":

If death had not prevented Bach from elaborating upon this triple fugue, he would have bequeathed to the world a cathedral crowned with his name in notes. At the peak of the enhancements the theme: "BACH" would have resounded from the organ.

Still, among Bach's piano works we possess one that is likewise a triple fugue. Here a similar "Bach" theme is used as the first of the three themes (C-sharp minor Fugue of the Wohltemperiertes Klavier Part I):

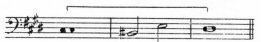

and above this theme a mighty tone structure is erected.

All these "Bach" themes consist of four notes with chromatic turn.

Beethoven, of course, also knew that "Bach" is a musical name. He made musical jokes with this name, as in his letter of August 1, 1824 written to the Viennese lawyer Dr v. Bach. Beethoven addressed the letter:

H. Dr v. Bach

However, Beethoven also used the "Bach" theme for his Bach overture. Among the sketches to the Ninth Symphony dating to the year 1822, the theme of the overture is already to be found:

And in 1825 one finds for the last time in Beethoven's sketches:

In this manner the chromatic four-tone motif that plays a big part in Beethoven's compositions since 1824 is really a "Bach" motif; not merely because it had been used as such by Johann Sebastian Bach himself, but because it is associated with Beethoven's intense admiration for Bach. The motif descends from Bach and signifies: BACH. To Beethoven it was more or less a formula for everything that Bach's music meant to him. It was mysticism, profundity, a glimpse into a fathomless depth. It was a symbol in its simple form, and in its plastic shape.

Thoughts of the Bach art with its polyphony, its mighty chorales and powerful fugues accumulated more and more in Beethoven from 1810 on. In Beethoven's subconscious mind fugues began to ring. As early as 1815 one finds in Beethoven's sketchbooks movements designed in the fugue style. In 1822 it becomes so great that the musical conception of the the fugue material becomes more concentrated in Beethoven's soul. The overture "Zur Weihe des Hauses" is written in fugue style. The Fugue opus 133 is composed, and the idea of a "Bach" overture arises.

Finally the pressure of this polyphonic tone sphere string quartets in A-minor, B-flat and C-sharp minor with their polyphonous and fugue forms follows And from out of all this music sounds the theme "BACH" with the four letters that become four notes, and with its chromatics that are contained in the name "Bach." (In the name BACH B-flat and B-natural (H) are side by side). Many years' accumulation of Bach thoughts and Bach sentiments in Beethoven's subconscious gave the four-tone motif the impetus that changed it into a kind of "idée fixe," into a symbol.

Beethoven would not be Beethoven had not his respect and admiration for Bach associated itself with the sense of his own greatness. It may have been this idea of eternal duration that gave the four-tone motif the chorale-like firmness and magnitude.

II.

As soon as the ideas that emerge from the subconscious of the composers are of larger proportion, they have a longer history behind them by the time they reach the brighter light of consciousness. They have already experienced many destinies. They have wandered a great deal, alone and in conjunction with other musical ideas. They have assumed many shapes.

Nevertheless, the first form in which the musical idea appears is often but a shadow and an indefinite ringing. Schubert, for instance, first designed the following sketch for the third movement of his Piano Sonata in A-minor:

This is already truly Schubertian music, composed out of the piano sound, and quite original in the sequence of a three-bar, a four-bar and a five-bar phrase. Schubertian, too, is the romantic sequence of chords and the accompaniment of the chords in the treble by shadowy triads in the depth.

It was not until Schubert had marked down these chains of chords; harmonies that wander through the night; triads that ring in the dark, that the warm, soulful melody took shape within him from out of the ringing of the chords:

What at first was just an indefinite ringing now becomes definite shape. What first was only a series of harmonies now becomes an expressive form which the dynamic signatures fill with personal sentiment. How expressive is the crescendo of the melody from piano to forte, and then the sudden piano! The melody had already existed in the ringing harmonies. But now it ascends from there like Aphrodite coming out of the ocean; a gleaming body arising from the dark waves.

Beethoven's most beautiful melodies seem to have been poured out in a single flux; yet they originated from temporary designs that show these melodies in a form that is completely uncharacteristic. That which we take for the melodic expression of free sentiment actually was created from many onsets. It took hard work to bring the wonderful prayer melodies into their form.

What trouble Beethoven had in giving the aria of Florestan ("In des Lebens Fruehlingstagen") its form. He begins with small sketches. In these fragmentary sketches, Beethoven attempts to mold the beginning of the aria. After he had already found the beginning of the melody, he discarded it again. He tries again with entirely different, unfamiliar styles. The song "Sehnsucht" ("Die stille Nacht umdunkelt") has quite a similar fate. The melody is pieced together; it takes a good deal of work before the parts fit together. Various measures are tried. Again and again the beginning of the song is tried. There are about twenty different starts in the sketches.

The songs of "Liederkreis an die ferne Geliebte" also originated in this manner. The initial sketches of the first song—written down hastily in pencil on single sheets—are very remote from the later form. This is how the start of the first song appears in the sketch book:

Auf dem Hü- gel sitz ich spä- hend

As yet it shows nothing of the nostalgic line that has so much touching fervour. As yet the song's line does not rise as though it wanted to see in the distance; it falls. At the word "spaehend" the characteristic downward leap is missing which gives the word such strong graphic power. (In the sketches this leap is first mostly a seventh. Later it becomes a sixth). After much labor, expression, declamation and graphic is formed. The song begins to live. The melody fills with feeling.

The first sketches of the solemn-transfigured Adagio of the Ninth Symphony that originated between May and July 1823 also have an incomplete form of melody. The introductory measures that prepare for the divine service of this melody are missing; the individual phrases of the melody are not yet repeated by the wind instruments, as is the prayer of the priest by the chorus of devout. The melody continues to receive new melodic turns until it finally achieves majestic simplicity.

A melody as lovely as that in the final movement of the Piano Sonata opus 90, which seems to have been created in a mold, is interrupted by an eighth rest in its original shape, and does not flow.

Even a melody as popular as "Freude schoener Goetterfunken" in the Ninth Symphony had to undergo many transformations before it attained its permanent form.

Frequently melodies appear in the sketchbooks, their beginnings corresponding to the later form, mature and clear; the endings, on the other hand, lose themselves in the dark. One gains the impression that the imagination of the composer could only hold fast to the first part of the melody. The continuation sinks into the subconscious. It is not able to overcome the inhibitions.

That is what happened with the beginning of the "Fruehlings" Violin Sonata in D-major, opus 24:

The beginning already had its form. The second part is shapeless, as though memory were failing. Only in the second sketchbook do bars 3-6 receive the form in which we know them.

III.

In many cases Beethoven's musical conception does not start at the beginning of a composition, but in the middle.

For instance, when Beethoven conceived the slow movement of the Ninth Symphony, he did not conceive the solemn principal melody that is enhanced with variations and elevated to the heavens, but the charming melody in D-major which is expressly designated as "Theme" in the first sketches. The devout melody that became the chief theme of the movement did not appear in the sketchbooks until later; Beethoven undertook many alterations on it before it re-

ceived its final form. In the initial sketches the finale
of the movement is still incomplete:

Only the motif of the kettledrums was adopted into
the score, albeit in changed form.

Originally, the first movement of the "Waldstein"
Piano Sonata was to include a melody that has no
resemblance at all to the sonata movement as we
know it. Only the bass note was retained in the sonata. With this bass note, the present theme peeks
from behind the originally conceived theme as from
behind the stage wings:

Soon, though, the theme comes out of the wings in
its present characteristic form, and appears onstage.
However, it does not appear in the form as the be-

ginning of the sonata movement shows it; its form is a piece *out of the middle of this movement.* The theme sounds fortissimo in A-flat major, into which key the first movement of the Waldsteinsonata modulates.* In other words, musical conception grasps a piece from the middle of the movement:

and practically hurls it out of the unconscious. Here, large form continuities had formed already, but they had been suppressed by inner inhibitions. What finally broke through this opposition was a piece from the middle which pulled the other parts of the musical form out of the dark recesses of the soul.

Even in a song as small as "Wonne der Wehmut" ('Trocknet nicht, trocknet nicht, Traenen ewiger Liebe') Beethoven's musical conception began *in the middle,* at the words: "Ach nur dem halbgetrockneten Auge, wie oede, wie todt." Apparently this verse attracted strong emotions in Beethoven that lifted the melody across the threshold of consciousness.

---

* The first movement of the Waldsteinsonata modulates from C-major to the upper third key E-major. In order to balance the harmonies, Beethoven later modulates to the lower third key A-flat major. In the exact same manner, he contrasts the modulation from C-major to A-flat major in the big "Leonore Overture" with a modulation from C-major to E-major. His example is followed by Brahms in the F-major Symphony, which swings from F-major to D-sharp major, and from F-major to A-major. In all these cases the harmonies move between the upper and lower third key.

FROM BEETHOVEN TO SHOSTAKOVICH

When Richard Wagner conceived "Meistersinger von Nuernberg," he saw in his mind's eye the, figure of Hans Sachs, hammering at the shoe, and of Beckmesser singing to the accompaniment of the lute: the main scene in the *second* act. And his conception of "young Siegfried" began with the vision of Valkyries riding through thunderclouds. In both instances poetic inventions began in the middle of the works. When Beethoven conceived the "Eroica," his musical invention began with the funeral march, i.e. likewise in the middle of the opus.

In all these cases there is a striking resemblance between the emotional proceeding of musical conception and the emotional mechanism of recollection. In each instance, opposition has to be overcome and inhibitions bridged. Remembering requires a mental exertion. Oftentimes it does not succeed at all, and it is a tormenting sensation to stare down into the dark shaft in which memories have sunk and where they are held down by an emotional force that resists remembering. In trying to surmount this resistance, one begins to search for free associations. One allows oneself to recall part of that which is forgotten. One remembers a word, a character, a scene from the association of recollections. Often memory begins at the end, often in the middle. Once such a fragment of recollection has been found, the rest follows easily.

Plato utilized this similarity between the procedure of recollection and the process of artistic conception most magnificently in explaining the essence of beauty. Beauty is the recollection of the prototypes of existence. Man lives in a dark cave. Here he remembers that which he has seen in a more exalted existence. He remembers gleaming ideas that revolve like suns beyond the world, and this recollection fills his soul with the sense of beauty. Michelangelo expressed similar ideas in his sonnets.

IV.

Among the peculiarities of artistic conception belongs the emergence of pictures, situations and music pieces in an environment in which they do not fit and with which they have no inward connection. The emotional force that sets artistic forms, tones and visions in motion shoves them—like so many illusions —into a totally different sphere of forms from which they do not detach themselves until much later.

Thus it could happen that Richard Wagner, while occupied with "Tristan" toward the close of 1854, saw the figure of Parsifal arising out of the "Tristan" pictures. Parsifal, searching for the Holy Grail, was to enter the castle Tristan's Kareol as a pilgrim, while Tristan lies on his deathbed in agonies of love. With the artistic fantasies for "Tristan" the first plan for "Parsifal" is mingling. Tristan on his sickbed, with the wound in his body, later changes to the wounded Amfortas.* The first "Parsifal" scenes appear thus in the midst of "Tristan" pictures. In 1857 they detach themselves from the "Tristan" composition, become independent poetry and a work by themselves.

A similar observation can be made in Beethoven's sketchbooks. Between sketches of the second and third movement of the String Quartet in C-major, opus 59 No. 3, there appears the graceful theme that later is

---

* Freud would have called this corresponding of the Tristan and Amfortas characters "Condensation."

to become one of the most precious gems of the Seventh Symphony. At that time it seemed to belong to the C-major String Quartet. Six years later it turned independent and made its appearance among the sketches for the Seventh Symphony.

The movement of the big B-flat major Quartet opus 130, superscribed "alla danza tedesca," first appears in a different key among the sketches for the A-minor Quartet opus 132. Later it withdraws from this environment, assumes the key of G-major and becomes part of the B-flat major Quartet.

Before Beethoven wrote his symphony in C-major— the one that now opens the cycle of nine symphonies —he worked on another symphony in C-major. There exist many sketches to the first movement of this symphony, written down on many sheets and single pages. Next to these sketches can be found exercises that Beethoven wrote when he was a pupil of Albrechtsberger; they are exercises in double counterpoint, and a double fugue. The pages were written in 1794 and early 1795. The first movement of the symphony was to have begun like this:

From here this music wanders into the fourth movement of the First Symphony, forming the finale. The reverse happens with the third movement of a sonata on which Beethoven worked between 1819 and 1822. This final movement of a piano sonata that was planned in the same period during which Beethoven worked at the piano sonata opus 110, later became the opening movement of the Piano Sonata opus 111.

In similar manner a melody in F-sharp minor that Beethoven had entered in his sketchbook in 1800 wandered to F-major, and from there into the Violin Sonata opus 24, where it became the final movement. The finale of the Kreutzersonata first appears in the sketches to the Sonata in A-major, opus 30.

In one of Beethoven's sketchbooks which, for the most part, belongs to the year 1803, there is found among sketches to the "Eroica," in addition to unfamiliar marches, a piece for string instruments and the plan for the song "Das Glueck der Freundschaft," this sketch:

This stamping melody finds its place in the "Pastoral Symphony" in 1808: a Breughel-like peasant dance that first appears in the environment of the "Eroica" music with which it has no connection. Not until five years later does it find a suitable spot in the scherzo movement of the Sixth Symphony when the peasants dance to this music at the merry get-together.

The musical forms that took shape in the subconscious wander around there, surge upwards and are absorbed in combinations, whence they are expelled again. Again they sink into the subconscious and are admitted into new combinations. The growth of these forms, and their organization into larger formations proceeds automatically, as it were. The subconscious has a life of its own, and its own powers.

When Beethoven finished an opus, or a movement, new ideas penetrated his fantasy from all sides, as though driven by unseen forces. Some of these ideas were not executed, others wandered around until they found their place, as was the case with the scherzo theme of the Ninth Symphony. This theme first shows up in sketches of the year 1815 and wanders around until 1822, at which time it found the spot upon which it settled permanently. Musical conception opens the gates of the subconscious, and when a composition is nearing completion, sounding forms, themes and musical ideas crowd out of the subconscious. The pressure that had held them there thus far has lessened. Daylight streams through the opened portals, and the musical ideas force their way in swarms from the shadow world to the light of consciousness.

CHAPTER XIII.

The Beginning of Critical Work—The Sketches

I.

UNIFORMLY ORGANIZING FORCES are effective behind all musical thoughts which, at the moment of musical conception, appear on the walls separating the unconscious from the conscious. They are mental forces that embrace the musical ideas. They direct the musical thoughts to their proper place. They combine and they separate; they select and they discard. Without this organizing uniformity art production cannot be created. There is no great musical conception without this organizing power, which is part of nature's formative forces.

Among composers there are some who are closer to nature than others. The musical conception of such musicians as Bach, Haendel, Haydn, Mozart, Beethoven and Brahms is arranged and organized by spiritual forces similar to those that give flowers and trees, animals and men their form. In musicians of this class the musical ideas emanate from a centre; the musical forms expand and grow like organisms. Where these uniform forces are missing, there exist grotesque art works, romantic-arbitrary forms, bizarre music pieces that can be intelligent but are not close to nature.

If musicians do possess such organizing and constructive energy units of the fantasy, but their effect is limited to a narrow space, then affected music works are created. Even a master as great as Brahms shows mannerisms in the dismal harmonies and frequently entwined rhythms.

In any case the root of musical conception already contains the growing and forming forces that decide whether a composer will be a natural genius, an intelligent baroque artist or an artist given to mannerisms.

Whatever applies to the initial musical conception is also valid for subsequent acts, for musical works of art are created by a continuous series of musical conceptions. The execution of musical art works is an extension of the first conception. Séailles spoke of the execution as: "La conception volue, aimée, agissante." We who live in the atom-bomb age can speak of "chain reactions." Conception follows conception. One is kindled by the other in uninterrupted sequence. What applies to the original conception applies to all other conceptions. They all have to be united by uniform forces, and all units have to form a higher unit. Where this is not the case, musical art works show breaks. Despite extreme ingenuity, this sometimes happened to Anton Bruckner. Or we find bizarre accumulations of natural and forced creative power, as in works by Gustav Mahler.

The more the musical work of art progresses, the more the intellectual functions come to the fore, namely: thinking, critique, reflection, conscious forming. Critical thinking must also be absorbed in the process of formation. It is the light carried by the creative fantasy to brighten its path. It is thinking of the imagination, artistic thinking.

There are artists in whom critical thinking — that

shows fantasy the road it has to go—has detached itself from the artistic imagination. Thinking is either not at all, or poorly, united with the creative forces of the soul. It does not help in shaping, but rather retards it. Poets of the highest rank often complained that cold common sense interfered with the activity of their imagination like an unwelcome guest who disrupts the pleasant mood of a stimulated party by being a poor mixer. "Two entirely separate beings live within me," wrote the Austrian poet Grillparzer. "A poet of the most encroaching, even precipitating fantasy, and a matter-of-fact man of the coldest and most tenacious kind."

We are too accustomed to consider musicians purely as men of imagination. That great composers are keen thinkers, and that their critical sense is finely polished, is not sufficiently appreciated. High-ranking composers without strong reflection are unthinkable. It would be entirely erroneous to think of Mozart merely as a naive musician. Even letters written by Mozart in his youth are full of keen observations and critical remarks. Every new opera that Mozart witnessed in Italy is shrewdly characterized. Every person with all his shortcomings is described with wit and cleverness. Eyes bright, the boy peers into the music life of his era, always probing, always thinking.

Whatever Mozart wrote about operas or piano playing is sagacious and lucid. One has only to read the letters Mozart wrote when he was composing "Abduction from the Seraglio" to appreciate how keenly he thought about the fundamental problems of the opera. When Mozart writes: "In an opera poetry must positively be the obedient daughter of music," we have opera aesthetics condensed into

[331]

one sentence. Or, one observes how he controls the work of his fantasy with intellect, for instance in the Osmin aria: "The 'Drum beim Barte des Propheten' is in the same tempo, it is true, but with faster notes; and since his fury mounts continuously, the Allegro assai must—since one thinks the aria is finished—produce the best effect in a different tempo and different tone. For a person who finds himself in such a violent rage naturally transgresses all order, moderation and limit; he does not know himself, therefore the music is not permitted to know itself. However, because passions, whether they are violent or not, may never be expressed to the point of nausea; and because music, even in the most horrible situation, should never offend the ear but give pleasure, consequently must always remain music—therefore I did not give the F (the key in which the aria was written) an alien tone, but an allied tone; however, not the next D minor, but the next further A minor was chosen."

The marvelous psychological descriptions in Mozart's operas, and the realistic portrayal of life in them would be impossible without keen observation and exact thinking.

A "Nozze di Figaro" could only be composed by some one who had observed rococo society well. The boy Mozart watched this society at the court of the archbishop in Salzburgh, in the palaces of the nobility in the German capitals, and in Paris. He was surrounded by it in the palaces in Vienna where he played piano. What he brought to the stage in "Nozze di Figaro," in "Don Giovanni" and in "Cosi fan Tutte" were the men and women of that society who—well and critically observed—came alive in these operas in the same manner as the men and women of the Elizabethan era came to life in Shakespeare's comedies.

Mozart never accepted a libretto without first examining it. Even as a child he undertook corrections in the one-act opera "Bastien and Bastienne." He made changes wherever he thought them necessary in the libretti of "Abduction," "Don Giovanni" and "Magic Flute." In "Abduction from the Seraglio" the original libretto had the harem guard, Osmin, singing only a short song. "So he has been given an aria in act I and he is to have another in act II. *I have explained to Stephanie* (the author of the textbook) *the words I require for this aria.*" And at another place Mozart reports: "The whole story is being altered—and, to tell the truth, *at my own request.* At the beginning of act III there is a charming quintet or, rather, finale, *but I should prefer to have it at the end of act II.* In order to make this practicable, great changes must be made, in fact an entirely new plot must be introduced."

How seriously Mozart thought about the theatre and its requirements! Mozart inserted the deep bass notes in the Osmin aria because he wanted to write effective notes for the voice of the singer, Fischer. ("I have given full scope now and then to Fischer's beautiful deep notes"). Mozart wrote the trio at the end of the first act: "with a great deal of noise, which is always appropriate at the end of an act. The more noise, the better, and the shorter the better, so that the audience may not have time to cool down with their applause."

The wonderful clarity, brightness and the sunny radiance of Mozartian music are equally a product of the most perfect sensuality of Mozartian fantasy as of the greatest lucidity of his intelligence, and the collaboration of imagination and intellect in every second of musical conception was truly a miracle. There was never a moment in Mozart's creative work in which the most beautiful fantasy and keenest intelligence did not work side by side, like a team of dancers.

Among opera composers of our time Richard Strauss has the strongest critical intellect.

Like Mozart, Strauss did not accept an opera text indiscriminately. When Strauss was composing "Elektra" and had written down the first scenes with the new crass naturalism of their dissonances, he sensed, correctly, that now was the time for a moment of quiet and melody. He wrote to Hoffmannsthal (June 22, 1903): "In Elektra, page 77, I need a long pause after the first cry of 'Orestes.' I will insert a gently tremulous orchestral intermezzo while Elektra regards the brother who has been returned to her. I can have her repeat the words 'Orestes, Orestes' stammeringly several times, and of the following, the words: 'Nothing moves!' 'O let me see your eyes!' fit this mood. Could you not insert a few nice stanzas for me?" Hoffmannsthal did write the verses, and thus one of the most beautiful moments in the opera "Elektra" originated at the request of the musician.

The text of "Rosenkavalier" also contains many places that were written in accordance with the composer's requests. Strauss writes to Hoffmannsthal under date of May 16, 1909: "The scene of the baron is ready; but you will have to write a supplement." Strauss wished the baron to "be enhanced incessantly in continued braggadocio of what he could accomplish," if possible in dactylic rhythm. " ... 16 to 20 verses in buffo character. Above that a duet with the Marschallin. In addition Oktavian whom I would like to have explode in a big laugh after the last bragging words of the baron, and who ridicules the baron's comments. That makes for a capital trio mood . . . the music is ready; I only need words for the accompaniment and for a filler." That is how the trio was created that now closes the first scene of the baron.

For the second act Strauss desires the text to have a large "contemplative ensemble after the moment in which a dramatic bomb may have just burst, when action may be at a standstill and everything is lost in contemplation. Such intervals are very important." Later Richard Strauss indicated to the librettist the whole development of the second act, inasmuch as the first composition appeared "dull and flat" and the dramatic enhancement was lacking. As the second act is given on the stage today it is entirely the composer's idea.

The third act of "Rosenkavalier" also had to be altered according to Strauss' directions; he considered it "too broad, too scattering, with everything exploding one after the other instead of together." For the final duet Strauss even gave his librettist the verse scheme.

Strauss also suggested scenes for the text of the opera "Ariadne on Naxos"; for instance the coloratura aria of Zerbinetta with andante and rondo—"parade number with coloratura railleries" as Strauss desired it—and the beautiful ensembles that now belong to the gems of the opera. "Dionysus erleuchte Sie! Ich warte!" (May Dionysus enlighten you! I am waiting!)

Concerning "Frau ohne Schatten," too, Strauss communicated his suggestions to his librettist.

Puccini was another of the opera composers who examined libretti with a sharp critical eye, and who made suggestions and expressed his wishes in regard thereto. Puccini was well acquainted with the popular theatre. He knew this theatre, and he saw the audiences that filled the theatre and he knew what the customers in the loges and the orchestra wanted to see on the stage. He thought of the little people in the galleries, the little shop girls for whom he wrote the sentimental arias of his Mimi and Butterfly. "We must amuse the organ grinder," he wrote to his librettist. "If not, we fail utterly and that must not happen." (September 23, 1914). Puccini never wrote any other music but theatre music. "I have the great weakness of being able to write only when my puppet executioners are moving on the scene ... Almighty God touched me with His little finger and said: 'write for the theatre and only for the theatre.' And I have obeyed the supreme command." (1920).

Puccini made suggestions for the text of "Boheme," and the Musette waltz was his own idea. "Must I blindly accept the fiat of Illica?," he wrote to his publisher, Ricordi. "I have my vision of 'La Boheme,' but it includes the Latin Quarter act, as I said the last time I discussed the matter with Illica. I must have the scene with Musetta which was my idea."

Puccini also made changes in the third act of "Girl of the Golden West."

The critical sharpness of Beethoven's intellect can best be learned from his sketchbooks. Here one sees a fermenting chaos of designs and ideas that required spiritual organization. Every second there are eruptions that jeopardize the formation of the musical works. Beethoven had to exert a maximum of soul force in order to organize artistically this glowing and hissing of fiery masses, this boiling of the material, the eruptive outbursts. All the formative artistic forces: strong morality, extremely keen intelligence, fantasy, ethics and critical thinking had to join hands in order to subdue the artistic world. Even the simplest theme had to be formed with painstaking labor. One has only to glance into the sketchbooks of the "Eroica" to realize with what astute vision Beethoven surveyed the large areas of the symphony, how he abbreviated, condensed, simplified, and unified. He gave orders to his fantasy like the architect of a large dam who distributes the work among his laborers.

When Beethoven theorized, his aesthetic theories were linked to the core of his fantasy. A sentence such as that prefacing the "Pastorale": 'More expression of feeling than painting' is the essence of sagacious aesthetic thinking. No treatise on the limits of tone painting could contain more. But this aesthetic thinking is not abstract, nor is it isolated. It illuminates the deepest recess of Beethoven's fantasy. It is a part of fantasy itself.

Without keen thinking there is no spiritual concentration of the music forces. That goes for Bach fugues as well as Haydn modulations. In order to create the great Bach fugues of the Leipsic period with their themes that compare to the arch of a bridge in their simplicity and magnitude, Bach's thinking had to clear the fugues of his youth of their baroque abundance. Haydn had to lead his romantic symphony music through a clear and well planned school of counterpoint before it became bright, agile and completely logical even in playfulness and humour.

Before Haydn developed his new grand style of symphony and sonata, there appear everywhere in piano sonatas, quartets and symphonies counterpoint forms. Half of the String Quartets opus 20 have a fugue in the finale (1772). One year later Haydn's piano sonatas show a canon finale, and a minuet and trio "al rovescio." In his symphonies, too, more and more counterpoint forms appear, as well as movements in fugue style, canons and double counterpoint.

Inasmuch as counterpoint is the logical school of tonal thinking, Haydn's music now first received its full clarity, and severity of thinking and execution of ideas their lawful mobility. This was considered just as new by Haydn's contemporaries as his popular tone.* Haydn's wit achieved keenness that caused sensational surprise in London and made it necessary to repeat the final movements of the symphonies at all concerts that Haydn gave in London.

This new style of Haydn's that had gone through counterpoint so impressed Mozart that he immediately started writing finales in the fugue style in his string quartets (K. 168.173).

Beethoven's variation style of the grand period is as much a result of energetic thinking as of rich fantasy. To Beethoven varying did not mean playing with musical fantasy. Variations no longer were tone garlands that wound around a theme. No longer decorations that were as fantastic and colorful as Raphael's decorations in the loggia of the Vatican Palace. Variations were necessary, logical re-formations and characteristic new figures. Beethoven's program for variations did not say: invent as many variations on a

---

* Haydn himself was well aware of this novelty in his style. He spoke of his String Quartet opus 33 (1781) as being "composed in an entirely new and special manner."

theme as possible. Rather it meant: as few as possible, but they must exhaust the whole essential value of imaginative thinking. Only a very energetic intellect that commands fantasy could create such variation works and string characteristic variation forms one after the other by selection and contrast.

This was the new technique that Brahms learned from Beethoven. It begins with Beethoven's 32 C-minor Variations for piano and ends with the Haydn Variations by Brahms.

This strength of thinking that organized such variations lessened after Brahms' death. Max Reger's variation works are free fantasies on a theme; they are fantastic byplays and digests of the themes; romantic forests with creepers growing out of the theme's ground. The variations of Bach, Beethoven and Brahms are solid constructions, the outlines of which were drawn by keen logical thinking.

The artistic contemplation of such artists as Schumann, Weber, Berlioz and Liszt is known to us from their writings on music and composers. Here, artistic thinking seems to be separated from actual creation; however, deep down it is connected with creative work. Great musicians always think egotistically. Their thinking radiates from the same centre of their personality as does their work.

No composer's writings can make the claim of setting up generally valid standards as much as those of Richard Wagner. With audacious vision Wagner overlooks millenia of music evolution. His shining eye pries as far back as the days when the Athenians sat on marble benches in the Dionysus Theatre at the Acropolis and heard the chorus of the great tragedies sung onstage. From there Wagner looks into the future. He is prophet, lawgiver. But even when Wagner speaks of Aeschylus, Shakespeare and Beethoven, he always means himself. When he talks about the tragedies of the Greeks, he means his own music dramas. When he speaks about Beethoven, he means his own symphonic music. He muses and philosophizes in order to be clear about his own work.

In like maner Schiller had composed his theoretical essay: "On naive and sentimental poetry" when he became associated with Goethe and wished to draw a line between his style of poetry and Goethe's.

With the clearsightedness peculiar to him, Richard Wagner saw that his thinking was the light radiated by his creative powers in order to illuminate the path of his work. When, after five years of theoretical research, he started work on the poetry and composition of "Ring des Nibelungen," he wrote: "I consider the final undertaking of my artistic plans, to which I am now turning, to be the most decisive moments in my life; between the musical execution of my 'Lohengrin' and that of my 'Siegfried' there lies for me a stormy —but also, as I know—fertile world. I had to clear my whole past life, *had to bring to consciousness everything that was dawning within me; I had to master reflection* that was of necessity awakened within me through itself—through most intimate penetration of its subject, in order to throw mysef with clear, serene consciousness into the most beautiful unconsciousness of artistic creation."

How keenly Arnold Schoenberg theorized can be learned from his "Harmonielehre."* How clearly Stravinsky thought about the problems of his work is evi-

---

* English translation published by the "Philosophical Library", New York.

dent from his "Chronicle of my Life." The great musicians are not just men of grand fantasy, they are also strong art thinkers. One can say that great music forms in the works of Bach, Beethoven and Wagner are just as unthinkable without special strength of theoretical thinking and without far-reaching thought vision, as without strength and originality of invention.

Artistic reflection has three tasks:

First: It can precede creative work. Often enough one finds in Beethoven's sketchbooks intentions, desires or orders noted down—as though they were promissory notes that had to be honored by the subconscious. There is a notation among the sketches for the "Missa Solemnis": "The Kyrie of the New Mass only with wind instruments and organ." At the "Dona nobis pacem" Beethoven writes: "Absolutely simple. Please, please, please." In the sketches for the Ninth Symphony there is a whole series of such directions, such as: "Turkish music in: 'Wer das nie gekonnt, der stehle' (Let him join us, or else weeping steal away to weep alone)"; or: "At: 'Welt-Sternenzelt' (World - beyond all stars) forte trumpet beats"; or at the end of the chorus: "The intensity of the voices (to be supported) more by instruments."

Second: Reflection accompanies work, and revising, regulating and leading the way is its most important function. The absolute work of the unconscious is limited by the criticism of a parliamentary corporation.

Third: Reflection follows work, and applies the finishing touches, erases the superfluous, and supplements. For instance, when Mozart completed the slow movement of the Jupiter Symphony, he ended the movement with these measures:

Not until after completion of the whole work did reflection again begin to shine, and Mozart wrote the eleven final bars as they now stand in the score, to close the movement with the main theme that lets it fade out so wonderfully.

Something similar is found in Beethoven's work. For example, the finale of the first movement in the Seventh Symphony was originally shorter by 34 bars. It is probable that it had its first performance in this form too. Not until later—during the first half of 1814—did Beethoven follow hints of his critical thinking and lengthen the ending, giving it the witty and piquant form that brings the conductor so much applause from the surprised audience.

It was no different with the first movement of the "Eroica." The two chord beats that open the music, immediately giving it the heroic background, were not added to the score by Beethoven until after he had completed the whole movement.

Much critical thinking lies behind this beginning. Beethoven had the idea of starting the movement with marked chords in one of his sketches. He wrote:

However, these chords are not the mighty chords that now introduce the music. They are not triads in E-flat major that hammer down upon the first bars, but dissonances, seventh chords that are irregularly distributed.

Later Beethoven changed the first two measures to

and made the dissonances and rhythms sharper yet. Then the first two bars vanish completely from the sketches, and the idea sinks back into the unconscious whence it had arisen.

However, after Beethoven had written down and completed the entire movement without the introductory chords, his criticism commenced working and fetched the idea back from the unconscious; now it was first in grandest style, in majestic, regular rhythm and possessed of the power of the basic triads.

The measure that preludes the slow movement of the "Hammerklaviersonate" was also written by Beethoven after completion of the composition. Beethoven's critical thinking subsequently demanded a transition at this spot, and Beethoven's fantasy obeyed that command.

Richard Wagner gives us a similar example. When he composed the overture to "Fliegender Hollaender," he concluded it with the theme of the Flying Dutchman and several chord beats, as was customary at the end of overtures. Later, his critical thinking began to work. What the examining eye missed was the fact that the overture closed with storm and thunder and the black garbed seaman under the red sail, and not with the redemption. Accordingly, he changed the ending in the completed overture and added the redemption melody with the light woodwinds and harps that now spreads its heavenly light at the close of the overture. Franz Liszt's "Faust" overture probably inspired him to make this change.

II.

Musical fantasy and critical thinking usually meet in composers for the first time when the composers plan a sketch. All composers design sketches. Poets mark down the progress of action in a novel or a drama, and the preliminary grouping of the material. Painters sketch the distribution of persons in the space, or the distribution of colors. Composers write down themes, ideas, notions, the modulation or disposition of instruments. The sketches establish the first form of fantasy. They are preliminary material for subsequent work. For this reason sketches are almost always written down with an implement that fixes the ideas in a pattern which is easily changed. Painters sketch either with pen or pencil, crayon or chalk, not with the brush. Brunelleschi created the model for the cupola of the cathedral in Florence, that hovers over the city and the Arno valley, from wood, and Michelangelo did likewise with the dome of St. Peter. For his statues, Michelangelo made models of wax that were easily molded into forms.

Composers sketch with pencil, as Beethoven always did in his first sketches. He did not use the pen until later, when the forms were already established.

THE BEGINNING OF CRITICAL WORK

Artists avoid giving their original thoughts a permanent form. They seem to feel that solid material is not mobile enough at first writing, and that in sketching the artistic fantasy should not meet with any resistance of matter.

In all cases the sketch is a primary design. The unconscious says: "My inner work has progressed thus far." Conscious critical thinking probes and chooses and gives advice as to how work is to continue. If this critical thinking is strong, it is also cold and keen. Richard Strauss was right when he said: "I work very coolly, without agitation, without emotion even. One has to be thoroughly master of himself to regulate that changing, moving, flowing chess-board—orchestration. The head that composed Tristan must have been cold as marble."

Even Mozart speaks of "reflecting" and "experimenting" when he talks of his composing.

Sketches are always expedients for further work. They are an inventory of that which already exists and which the artist tests, criticizes and analyzes before his creative imagination moves again. The fantasy of the composer supplements the scant picture of the sketch, which tells him more than the outside observer. Sketches are a stenographic excerpt of fantasy formation rather than a finished picture. They are a directive for the imagination, and only contain watchwords for subsequent work.

This does not hold true for the rare exceptions among composers who, like Mozart, complete the entire work in their imagination, or like Max Reger, who completed the entire contrapuntal construction of the 100th Psalm in his imagination before he wrote down the music.

Like Haendel, Mozart sketched very little. Only in cases where instrumentation was more complicated, for instance in contrapuntal combinations, or sudden harmonic turns, did he sketch his ideas on small sheets, or wherever he found some empty space upon music paper that was already used. Thus Mozart made an exact sketch for the combination of the three dance orchestras in the ball scene of "Don Giovanni," where three melodies in different time coincide. He also sketched the canon that shines like festive candles at the finale of "Cosi fan Tutte." He likewise made sketches for those places in the opera "L'oca di Cairo" that are conducted contrapuntally—the Quartet and Finale.

Only recently the sketch was found in which Mozart wrote the contrapuntal combination of the themes in the Allegro for the "Prager Symphony" before writing down the score, and there is no doubt that Mozart wrote down a sketch for the combination of the five themes at the end of the Jupiter Symphony and that this sketch was lost. In two instances Mozart speaks of "wearisome labor" in the string quartets dedicated to Haydn. That probably means that he had carefully worked out the contrapuntal combinations in sketches. However, in most cases this was the exception rather than the rule with Mozart.

There are but few exceptions to this rule. Among these few is Franz Schubert. Among Schubert's works the Symphony in B-Minor is the only composition for which he wrote a sketch (in the form of a piano score). Otherwise he wrote like an improviser. Music flowed in one stream from his pen. He enjoyed this uninterrupted forming and shaping that was as happy and carefree as the chirping of the birds in the little garden next to the house in which he played as a child. The steeples of the church in which he was baptised, and where he later played the organ, still glitter above the trees of this garden. Even today, when evening comes, the chirping of the sparrows and blackbirds drowns out the droning of the church bells. That was Schubert's world: the garden, the birds, the church bells. He himself was a ringing part of nature, and his music making belonged to the voices of nature.

This type of work is to blame when he did not continue with compositions that he had to interrupt, as happened to his B-minor Symphony—the "Unfinished"—after the first bars of the Scherzo. He preferred to invent new music rather than return to old music. He always lived in the happy enjoyment of the present.

Schubert began his symphonies improvisatorially. Even the measure was not decided upon when he began writing, as in the "Tragic Symphony," but was changed during the process. Occasionally even the theme of a symphony was altered when the work was already completed.

This is how the main theme of the first movement of the Symphony in B-flat read when Schubert wrote down the movement, carefree as one who, in a good mood, whistles a tune:

Not until Schubert reached page 67, bar 14, did he change the rhythmic setting of the theme:

It is more Schubertian yet that Schubert wrote the theme of the whole first movement in the big C-major Symphony in the following shape:

Wherever the theme appeared, it had this form; even on page 16, when it is played by the violoncellos, and shortly thereafter, in the inversion. It wasn't until the whole movement was completed that Schubert changed the theme to its present form:

Schubert also scored chamber music right away. It could happen occasionally, during such improvising, that Schubert lost the combination of the keys and went astray, like a wanderer in the woods. In Schubert's music sketch and composition are confluent. That is what gives Schubert's music its freshness and makes it a blooming garden.

Schubert approached the composition of his lieder with similar music enjoyment. Here too, there are instances where the measure or the key was not yet established when work was begun. Schubert wanted to write the "Fruehlingstraum" of "Winterreise" in G-major. After he had composed the prelude he first decided upon the lighter key, A-major, which seemed to him to fit the character of the piece better as it unfolded in his mind.

For most of his songs Schubert planned the melody with great swiftness, and it was almost always settled in all details; contrary to Beethoven who formed a melody with much painstaking work and in phrases. Simultaneously, he wrote outstanding figures of accompaniment, or such passages as were harmonically important. Then he filled out whatever had to be added. If he was not satisfied with the form thus created, he threw the whole creation back into the crucible and re-formed it. (In similar manner Goethe's "Werther" had "to return to the womb" in 1782). Songs such as "Erlkoenig" and "Forelle" exist in four different readings.

Only one of Schubert's many songs originated like Beethoven's music: in fits and starts, in repeated onsets. It was "Der Gesang der Geister," and was designed in 1816 as a song with piano accompaniment. In 1817 it was arranged for four male voices. In the spring of 1820 it was written as a male chorus with piano accompaniment, and in the winter of the same year it was composed with the accompaniment of deep stringed instruments. In this way it expanded more and more, and grew in depth.

In later years Schubert felt his improvising to be a weakness, and wanted to study "strengen Satz" (strict composition) under Simon Sechter, who later taught Anton Bruckner, in order to concentrate his music fantasy. Beethoven's strict logic seemed to be the ideal he wanted to achieve. However, Schubert would not be Schubert without this carefree, blossoming manner; his music would not be lyric singing, nor his melody the song of heart and nature.

Among the composers who did not require sketch work was the reformer of the opera, Gluck. Gluck was no contrapuntalist. His musical fantasy contained neither particular wealth of harmonies nor special wealth of orchestral colors. His musical invention was tied to the words of the text. Thus he did not need sketch work, or at least not in any great measure, and the report of Burney, who visited him, may be considered reliable: "Finally Gluck consented to sing himself . . . from a French opera, "Iphigenie," after Racine. True, he did not put one note of this opera down on paper; but he had perfected it in his head to such an extent that he was able to sing it almost from start to finish, as though he had the fair copy of a score before him."

Sketching music was much too slow a procedure for Haendel. It would have required a system of musical stenography to catch up with his stormy fantasy.

Haendel would start writing his big chorales with all the voices. But as the work progressed he dropped first one, then another voice, and finally he wrote only one voice or merely the bass. His imagination had simply run away with him and he attempted to catch up with it.

In composing operas, Haendel lacked the patience of Gluck who, before putting down the music, worked for a full year on each act and then digested the complete text. Oftentimes Haendel composed the act of an opera without knowing its continuity. Often he didn't allow his librettist sufficient time to write the continuation. In the introduction to "Rinaldo," text and music of which was completed within a fortnight

(1711), the librettist Rossi remarks that Haendel did not give him time to write the text. The librettist of "Belzazar" was also too slow in sending Haendel the text; in order to occupy himself during such lulls, while awaiting the libretto, Haendel composed his "Hercules" (1744).

Haendel's working tempo makes one's head swim. In January 1736 Haendel composed "Alexandersfest." In February and March he conducted oratorio concerts. In April he wrote "Atalanta" and "Wedding Anthem." During April and May he conducted a season of opera. From August 14 to September 7 he composed "Giustino," from September 15 to October 14 "Arminio." In November he again conducted opera.

From November 18 to January 18, 1737, he composed "Berenice." In February and March he conducted operas and oratorios. Then he suffered a stroke, necessitating the "Kur" in Aachen.

Early in November of 1737 Haendel returned to London. On November 15 he began to work on the composition "Faramondo." On December 7 he started to compose the "Funeral Anthem" and had it performed on the 17th. On December 24 he completed "Faramondo."

On December 25 he began composing "Serse" and finished it on the 14th of February 1738. On February 25 a new Haendel 'Pasticcio,' "Alessandro Severo" had its first performance.

Several months later Haendel started work on "Saul"—from July 23 to September 27, 1738. On October 1st he began composing "Israel in Egypt," and on October 28 the great oratorio was completed. In the same month his first volume of organ concerti made its appearance, and during that same period he sent his publishers seven trios.

All this was accomplished within two years, during which time Haendel was sickly and almost came close to death.

While Haendel was composing, he isolated himself from the world. No visitor could get through to him; he locked himself in so that he could be alone with his ideas. He took notice of no one, and talked out loud to himself. He sobbed when moved by some text. Often the servant who brought Haendel his morning chocolate found him sobbing aloud, tears wetting the sheet of music he was writing on.

Haendel wept while composing the Christus aria "He was despised." About the "Halleluja" of his "Messiah" he observed: "I know not whether I was within my body or without when I wrote it; God alone knows."

It took blindness and ill health to destroy Haendel's energy, his obsession, the storm of his imagination. In 1751, still in good health, Haendel began to compose "Jephta." He put down the first act, as was his habit, in one sweep; in twelve days it was finished. In the second act the writing changes; it becomes indistinct and shaky.

While writing the choral finale of the second act he has to stop working. "Got this far on Wednesday, Feb. 13. Am prevented from writing more on account of my left eye."

He suspended work for ten deys. On the eleventh day he makes this entry: "Feb. 23 (it was Haendel's birthday). I feel better. Have taken up my work again."

In five days he completed the big chorus which describes the dying light and the break of night and which must have deeply moved the musician who was growing blind.

For four months the work lay untouched. Then, on June 18th, the third act was taken up again. The work drags along, with interruptions; the final five numbers require more effort than an oratorio usually needed. On August 30, 1751 the work is completed, but the eyesight of Haendel is enveloped by night.

III.

The fantasy of every great musician has its own manner of using sketches. We possess many sketches by Haydn, Beethoven, Wagner and Bruckner, but the purpose of these sketches is different, and the relation of sketch and final music form is varied. The fantasy of every great musician has its peculiarities; in each case the relation of inspiration and critical thinking is different; in each case the pressure that opposes the rush of unconscious springs is different. Every one of them has a different strength of tone memory and energy by which the tone masses of the subconscious are held together.

Composers like Bach need sketches only for the very large compositions; for their inner music wealth is so great that during their whole life it breaks forth into the mightiest forms, and never weakens. Such composers are like great organs, from the pipes of which the most powerful tones roar in uniform fullness. In addition, these musicians encounter no difficulties in transforming their fantasy into musical forms. Unlike modern musicians, they do not need their intellect for the solution of technical problems.

FROM BEETHOVEN TO SHOSTAKOVICH

The harmonies are established. They are ancient doctrine and law.

The forms into which their fantasy flows are known quantities. The forms of organ preludes, organ fantasies, passacaglias, choral variations, Easter and Christmas oratorios, cantatas, passions and concertos that Bach used were over one hundred years old; the fugue form had a history that went back as far as the early middle age. All the Protestant masters before and around Bach: Pachelbel, Buxtehude and Boehm, employed the forms of organ music that Bach then adopted; all the music masters of the 17th and 18th centuries used the forms of choral music. The operas that Haendel wrote, his "concerti grossi" and oratorios were the music forms of his time. Bach and Haendel never shook the traditional forms as Beethoven did. Their mighty fantasy poured into these forms without inhibition, without resistance, without delay. It resembled a huge stream flowing serenely between its embankments.

Only in the summer could Bach and Haendel create such a large number of works, a number which never again has been attained. Only a music fantasy of this sort could flow unhindered by formal problems. For very expansive works, Bach was satisfied with a very few notations. As a rule he retained the design for a tone piece without changes, once it was established.

To a composer like Bach, a sketch meant something else than it did to Beethoven. It was the first notation of the composition; a stop on the road before creative fantasy, which had gone this far and taken a moment's rest, continued energetically on the same road. Beethoven's sketches serve a different purpose.

Beethoven had to overcome strong inner inhibitions

[354]

before everything that stormed in his soul was sublimated artistically. He was the new man of the revolutionary era, whose personality, like that of Lord Byron, was entirely self-centered. He was not limited by a firm religion, like Bach and Haendel were limited by a faith that penetrated the entire life in German cities, so that the musicians in these towns all seemed to be alike: all good bourgeois people with quiet dignity, living simply in their houses, begetting many children, dealing in music as though it were a solid trade.

Beethoven was surrounded by revolution of all conditions in society, by a new spiritual life, a new science and new poetry. The destinies of the people became more colorful, appreciation for the peculiarity of the personality became stronger. People relied upon their own strength. This meant heavy inner conflicts, an intensified realization of one's own inner world. Only now poetry became possible such as the subjectivistic poems of Lord Byron, the psychic narratives of Rousseau's "New Heloise," the melancholia of Goethe's Werther and the cosmopolitanism of his "Faust." Only now was a philosophy possible such as that of Kant which made the world a creation of the human mind. Napoleon rose to fame and marched through Europe, revolutionizing all conditions.

Beethoven was the first subjectivistic musician of this era; he relied upon his own strength and turned all the conflicts in his soul to music. This meant stirring up all the depths of his soul, as well as the dark abysses where all the destructive and elemental forces of the soul were held prisoner ere they broke the dams.

Werther's suicide, as described by Goethe, would be a common occurrence in our days. But at the close of the 18th century it was something that frightened the world, because it first showed the abysses of human nature from which, later, the writings of Dostojewsky and Strindberg emerged. In opening the First Symphony with a dissonance, Beethoven manifests himself in his youth already as the composer who shapes the discordant soul life of his era in music. He was the first great musician of the modern era who could say of himself, in the words of St. Augustine: "Thou hast created us for Thee, O Lord, and our heart is uneasy until it rests in Thee."

All subjectivistic music of the 19th century is descended from Beethoven: Schumann's reveries, Chopin's nocturnal poetry, the fantastic ecstasy of Hector Berlioz, the love and death music of "Tristan and Isolde," Bruckner's religious struggles and Mahler's satanism that cries to God from the depth of the earth. The storm in Beethoven's soul created the surging waves in all music of the 19th century.

Music does not flow from a soul of this kind in a calm, broad stream, as it did in Bach and Haendel, nor in harmony of all soul forces, as exemplified by Haydn and Mozart; it erupts like a cataract. For this reason Beethoven needed sketches, so that he could catch the eruptions of his fantasy and let the boiling tone masses cool off. Sketching is a part of his fantasy work itself as was the case with no other composer.

That was so in his youth already, and later became even more necessary in order to transform the volcanic outbursts of his imagination from destructive powers to formative forces. "The way I write now," Beethoven told Wegeler in a letter dated June 29, 1800, "I often do three or four things simultaneously." This means that Beethoven's musical fantasy jumped restlessly from one work to another, like a flickering flame. Beethoven worked simultaneously at the Quartet opus 130, the Fugue opus 133, and all the more extensive movements of the Quartet opus 131. When Beethoven composed the three Rasumoffsky String Quartets, he worked on the last movements of the first quartet and on the second quartet at the same time, and also simultaneously on the second and third quartet. Even when Beethoven was working on just one composition, his fantasy skipped back and forth among various movements. Thus he worked simultaneously on all of the first three movements of the Seventh Symphony, and among the plans for the first three movements one finds sketches for the finale. Sketches for the last two movements of the Pastoral Symphony are likewise written down promiscuously. Sketches for all three movements of the Piano Sonata opus 4, No. 1 are found in confusion.

Beethoven also labored at the four movements of the Piano Sonata opus 27 at the same time. The Violin Sonatas in A-minor and F-major grew on the same field; the ideas for both sonatas grew side by side and promiscuously.

His work on sonatas and symphonies was always interrupted by ideas for different music. For instance, among the sketches for the Piano Sonata in A-flat major, opus 110 there are plans for other sonata movements, one of them being the beginning of the Piano Sonata in C-minor. If anybody has ever stood at the brink of a volcano and looked down into the smoking, flaming, boiling crater, then he has an idea of what went on in Beethoven's fantasy.

Beethoven's sketch books show the process of his fantasy. It was altogether different from the work of Mozart's fantasy, which shaped music like some one who draws water from a stream and sees the water forming into a gleaming ball. Beethoven always has stormy weather. He always experiences eruptions of the imagination. While he was working on the String Quartet in C-major, the Adagio of the Seventh Symphony broke out of fiery streams of metal; while forming the first movement of the Seventh Symphony, ideas for the Scherzo began to whisper.

Beethoven was overwhelmed by his musical fantasy. In this manner of work he is akin to the Hebrew prophets, in whose heated minds visions arose; words bubbled, and they often "spoke with tongues." This accounts for his abstraction while composing, explains his yelling and muttering, his stormy wanderings through the woods. But it also explains the form of his sketches, the hasty scrawl of notes that are barely legible and that he later entered into another sketchbook in ink in order to give them firm shape.

It is easy to follow the work of his fantasy in Beethoven's sketchbooks, and to observe how it becomes calmer and more conscious. Beethoven needed the sketches in order to have a firm station in the storms of his fantasy from where he could survey his work. When music was boiling in his fantasy; when sudden eruptions of new ideas penetrated with destructive power his work on other compositions; when his fantasy jumped from one work to another, and from movement to movement: then Beethoven needed his sketches to retain the feeling of uniformity that united the musical thoughts of a piece of art. Beethoven's strict logic required sketch work, and in a movement such as the first movement of the Fifth Symphony one can sense beneath the iron logical form the violence of an agitated imagination that was tamed and subdued by him.

That is what Nietzsche meant when he said: "Grand style originates when the beautiful carries the victory over the enormous"; or when he states in the aphorisms in his work "Der Wille zur Macht": "To master chaos means: to force one's chaos into becoming form; to be logical, simple, ambiguous, mathematics, law — that is the great ambition here."

In the sketches Beethoven unfolds his moral and logical powers. He makes order, clarifies his work; he surveys "the road from chaos to formation, which is the essence of the artistic process" (Gundolf, Goethe) with undaunted eye. Only some one who has made a minute study of Beethoven's sketches for the "Eroica" knows how the magnificent style of this music originated. Whereas for other composers the sketches are an inventory of what they have invented thus far, to Beethoven they are the process of composition itself and an implement of compositorial work.

No other great musician had to overcome such strong inner opposition in order to liberate himself with music, as did Beethoven. His psychic underworld, with all its passion, with its dark powers, with its storm of revolutionary impulses and with its resistance against pressure, was that of a titan. Now he was Werther, now Mirabeau; now Danton, now Napoleon. Goethe, who was the greatest poet of the same era, freed himself of the titanism of his youth through classical antiquity, through the beauty of Italy and by studying nature. Beethoven stood alone and fought his way through with his ethical strength. His sketch books show these struggles; they are a weapon in the conflicts. They liberate his unconscious by absorbing everything in their pages that streams toward Beethoven from his subconscious. They are diary pages of his inner wrestling.

In Mozart's case, musical creation did not signify liberation from the tempestuous powers of his inner self and victory over titanic soul forces, but natural growth of a wonderful soul. In Mozart, all moods transformed themselves into sensual timbre. Whatever was in his subconscious was sublimated with divine facility and streamed into the melodies, into harmonies and into the timbre of the instruments. This does not mean that Mozart was free of darkness and a sense of the tragic. No great nature is. Beethoven even learned from Mozart's passionate C-minor Piano Concerto; he played it often as a young musician, and wrote cadenzas for it. But in spite of its agitation and sadness, music such as the first movement of the D-minor Piano Concerto, the Piano Fantasy in C-minor, the String Quartet in D-minor, the G-minor String Quintet and the G-minor Symphony is still enveloped in gracefulness. The pathetic and elegiac in Mozartian music dissolves in harmony; and the buffo laughter of Leporello invades the Hereafter music of "Don Giovanni."

The nocturnal dark that emerges from the unconscious mind in such music is also just a part of Mozart's rich inner world; it expands with the same perfection and ease as all other moods. Only in this way was it possible for Mozart to write the cemetery scene in "Don Giovanni" in the radiant key of E-major and in the "Allegro con brio" tempo without impairing the mood of the cemetery and the Beyond.

Such perfect harmony explains the naturalness and lack of inhibition in Mozart's creative process, where invention and formation coincided. With the exception of instances already discussed, Mozart did not require sketches, for his inner working process went through all stages with the greatest ease and sureness, until that work was completed. Only Raphael and Shakespeare can compare as far as forming is concerned.

When Mozart wrote the score for whatever he had completed in his mind, he first wrote the part of the first violin and the bass. In the systems of the wind instruments, he only marked those places where the instruments were to stand out independently. Then he went on to the complete execution and supplement of the design that was finished in his head. Rarely did Mozart make subsequent changes in the instruments. In "Don Giovanni," Leporello's aria was originally to have had trumpets and drums. But when Mozart was ready to complete the opera, they were subsequently cancelled. In the G-minor Symphony Mozart had first intended to employ four horns; after several bars he limited them to two.

It was a bigger change, though, when Mozart wrote down trumpets and drums in the Magic Flute right from the start and then crossed them out again; his purpose was to give more radiance to the entrance of the three ladies, at which point now the trumpets and drums are employed for the first time. Similarly, Mozart first wrote out the horns completely in a comic aria in "Cosi fan Tutte," and then crossed them out. And in Magic Flute, he exchanged the string accompaniment to Pamina's words: "Ich muss ihn sehen" in the second finale for the gentler wood-winds.

However, such alterations were rare. As a rule, whatever sounded in Mozart's fantasy immediately had the wonderful orchestral coloring, the real Mozartian golden tone.

Hesitation, fumbling and altering is a rare happening in Mozart's work. It occurs only in the garden aria of Susanna in "Marriage of Figaro" which required painstaking work before it achieved the perfect beauty of line and the delicate arc.

The overture to "Nozze di Figaro" originally was to have a slow middle movement in D-minor. Mozart left it out when he saw that this center movement would slow down the lively flow of the "crazy day" music. However, this, too, is an exception. If ever Mozart made changes during his work, they were trivial.

When it came to opera, Mozart was very good at subsequently inserting a few touches that imparted greater vigour to the characters. By adding four measures of coloratura, the aria of the count in "Marriage of Figaro" attained greater elegance; the aria of the countess in the same opera was given seven additional bars, which, with their modulation to C-minor, gave the countess the profound grief and impressive longing.

In the vengeance aria of Donna Ann in "Don Giovanni," the lady originally urged her betrothed to take revenge with the following melody:

Or sai chi l'o-no-re   ra-pi-re a me volse

This did not seem strong enough to Mozart. So, with a very slight change, he syncopated the accents, thus giving the aria more rage, pathos and energy:

Or sai chi l'o no-re   ra-pi-re a me volse

Mozart always completed the actual artistic work even before the first sketch. Writing the score was merely the establishment of the already developed whole. Even compositions that were not entirely perfected by Mozart, such as movements of the Mass in C-minor and the Requiem, already have their definite form. In many of Mozart's compositions the original form, and the subsequent execution, can only be recognized by the difference in the color of the ink. This is the case in the score of the overture to "Zauberfloete." However, the first form is always completely developed. It is never the result of sketch work.

Josef Haydn did not use sketch work to any great extent until after his return from England. Until then he had worked out his compositions in his head and only wrote down the details after perfecting them. "I never wrote hastily," Haydn told Griesinger, "but always composed diligently and deliberately and set nothing down until I was quite sure of what I had to say."

It may not have been just a greater sense of responsibility that induced Haydn, following his London trip, to employ sketches. He probably was not as sure of his memory as he had been in younger days. This seems to be indicated by the notice written down on the first page of sketches for "The Creation": "So that I shall remember."

A small trio for two flutes and cello was composed during Haydn's second London sojourn (1794). Here he re-wrote the finished middle movement twice, which is another indication of a greater wavering and pondering. Extensive sketches of "Creation" show the care with which Haydn labored at this huge work. The chorus "Gesegnet sei des Herren Macht" was worked out in three sketches: the first sketch is in minor, the second sketch brings the music in the major key. The solo soprano stands out stronger and the chorus simpler; but then the chorus first achieves the devout, humble prayer tone.

There are two sketches of the introductory piece "Das Chaos." It is only in the second sketch that the orchestra is furnished with all the picturesque details of timbre; the first violin sings its lonely song, the tone of the orchestra becomes shadowy. But even here, the sixteenth accompaniment of the bassoon in the second part is missing and was not sketched until later.

After his return from England, Haydn never tired of making corrections in completed compositions, and polishing them before publication.

Richard Wagner repeatedly discussed the manner of his work. Poet and musician were combined in his romantic fantasy. The choice of his operatic material was determined by the music that resounded within him. "For the time being," Wagner wrote to a friend under date of January 30, 1844, "no material can attract me other than such material as presents itself to me simultaneously in its poetic as well as in its musical significance. Before I attempt to write a verse, I am intoxicated by the musical aroma of my creation; I have all the tones, all the characteristic motifs in my head so that, when the verses are finished, and the scenes arranged, the actual opera is likewise finished. The musical treatment is more or less a calm and circumspect retouching which was preceded by the actual moment of producing."

Often the chief moments of the action appeared in Wagner's fantasy in dreamlike, hallucinatory form before he sketched the real action. Before he began working at the poetry of Nibelungenring, the picture of the valkyries, riding through the clouds in storm and thunder, emerged from Wagner's subconscious. In unison he heard the music of the ride of the valkyries with the precipitating violin figures and rhythms of the wind instruments.

Three years before Wagner even touched the score to the last act of Walkuere, he had marked down the song of the valkyries (November 12, 1852). Work on the last act of Walkuere began in November 1855.

Wagner always first designed a sketch in prose for the text of his music dramas, and then executed it in verse. With that, music resounded. "The musical phrases," Wagner wrote when he was working on "Young Siegfried," "develop from these verses and periods without my having to make any effort; everything grows out of me like wild. I already have the beginning in my head; also several plastic motifs, such as Fafner."

Similarly, when Wagner prepared for the composition of "Ring des Nibelungen," he wrote in a letter to Liszt that the music would progress very easily, for it was "merely execution of something already completed." Concerning "Ring des Nibelungen," Wagner wrote: "I am thrilled by the prospect of setting all this to music; *as far as form is concerned,* it is entirely finished within me, and I was never so much in agreement with myself about the musical execution as I am now with respect to this drama. I only require the important life incentive to reach the indispensable cheery mood whence the motifs should sprout joyfully."

The composition sketches, up to the third act of "Siegfried," are predominantly single-lined. On the second empty music line chord sequences were noted here and there, or directions for instrumentation According to these sketches the orchestra score was written. Only "Rheingold" was executed in score right away. "Now I am going to write 'Rheingold' directly in the score, with the instrumentation. I could not find any way of writing the prelude (Die Rheinestiefe) distinctly as a sketch; so I got the idea of writing the full score. Only it takes me much longer."

The "Rheingold" score was written down without any correction. One typographical error, one ink spot sufficed, and Wagner discarded the page he had started.

Wagner usually wrote his sketches in pencil, which is the reason for his calling them "Bleistiftereien (Pencillizing). From these sketches Wagner wrote down the score, without corrections, without erasures. It looked like lithography in its uniform beauty. When Wagner showed Meyerbeer the score of the "Flying Dutchman" in Paris, the clean writing was greatly admired by Meyerbeer. Wagner was proud of the beauty of his scores, and when Mathilde Wesendonck presented him with a golden pen, he wrote: "The score will be my most perfect masterpiece in penmanship. I *must* write clean score as long as I shall live."

One of Wagner's peculiarities consisted in his drawing the bar lines before entering the notes in the scores. These lines were always drawn in such a manner that the notes fitted perfectly in the space between two bars, without crowding or pushing.

While Wagner was working on "Ring des Nibelungen," he wanted to have an assistant who could copy the score from his sketches; for he was afraid of losing too much time with copying of the score. "Can you find me a person who is suited to write a clean score from my wild pencil sketches?", Wagner wrote to Liszt. "Without such a skilled person I am lost." However, several weeks later Wagner was convinced that he himself would have to undertake the copying. "It is just too difficult to make it (the copy) according to my wishes, especially since the sketches are so horribly mixed up that only I can make heads or tails out of them."

In the "Meistersinger" Richard Wagner again used Hans Richter as the copyist of his score. Wagner sat in his villa in Triebschen, on the first floor, and from there sent the sketch of the score to Hans Richter, who sat in a room on the ground floor and copied the score. Anton Seidl served in a similar capacity in the "Parsifal" work.

We are especially well informed about Wagner's work on the "Meistersinger." Wendelin Weisheimer tells how Wagner hummed characteristic motifs during his walks. "The next two days were spent waiting until Wagner's domicile—in Bieberich on the Rhine—was sufficiently in order that he could think of picking up his pen. Sitting at the grand piano, he wrote down, above all, the introduction to the "Meistersinger" in the form of a very exact sketch that looked like a piano score, but contained all duplications and middle voices the way he intended to execute them for orchestra. He would say: 'The more exact the sketch, the easier and surer the instrumentation' . . . 'Youth frequently makes the mistake of working too hastily' . . . 'Actually, to be really exact, one ought to give each of the wind instruments a system of its own' . . . 'Writing two each woodwinds to one system is often detrimental to free expansion of the melody'."

According to Weisheimer, Wagner wrote about six pages of score daily.

The "Ring of the Nibelungen," too, was invented during walks, with Wagner's dog his sole companion.

Forenoon was the time when Wagner's fantasy was most active—"in heat," as Wagner termed it. Composing and inventing filled Wagner with warmth, with fanatical ardour and with happiness. "For the artist producing is really an enjoyable and satisfying activity, not work." he wrote. And on June 3, 1854, having completed "Rheingold," he wrote to a friend: "I have just finished a new score. If you only knew what work means to me now! It is a fanaticism that does not let me look left or right to observe anything else."

"I am becoming more and more convinced," Wagner wrote to Liszt, "that people like us should really never feel well except in moments, hours and days of productive excitement; but then we also enjoy and relish more than any other person."

In such hours of artistic agitation Richard Wagner lived and suffered with the characters of his fantasy. When he wrote that Lohengrin had to leave Elsa, he shed tears; and in regard to "Walkuere," he wrote to Praeger that he would see "what a superlative vein of heartache, anguish and despair branches through the whole work," and how "profoundly and painfully the work had gripped him." "I don't believe that I could ever again create anything similar. However, when it is finished and stands before me as a completed work of art, it is something entirely different and it gratifies." The sketches, of course, do not give the slightest conception of such sentiments, of the artistic agitation, or of the ecstatic condition of the artists' soul that is oblivious to the world. In the sketches begins the working process of the artists, conscious forming that becomes increasingly brighter.

*   *   *

THE BEGINNING OF CRITICAL WORK

What a varying significance a sketch can have for a composer is shown very distinctly by the different uses which Johannes Brahms and Max Reger made of such sketches.

Brahms possessed the fantasy of an architect. He created solid structures, and a sketch of Brahms' was a totally perfected foundation. It had a firm base to support the musical construction. For his lieder, Brahms first sketched the solid frame: melody and bass. He was not interested in the modern singing middle voices, and when he was shown songs, he covered up the middle voices with his fingers. "I am only interested in the treble and the bass. If these two are all right, everything is all right," he used to say. The middle parts were not considered by Brahms as tone, but as musical lines. The rolling of the clouds in "Feldeinsamkeit," the stormy emotion in "Wie bist Du meine Koenigin," the shadows of death in "Immer leiser wird mein Schlummer," the grave mood in the song "Am Kirchhof" are drawn with firm lines.

The sketch for the "Haydn Variations" (for two pianos) is already the completed work. Here and there Brahms marks figures under the bass; for instance, at the end of the seventh variation of the Passacaglia:

At one place in the third varation he added one voice in order to logically prepare the triplet motion of the following development. Originally, the development in 4/4 movement stood directly next to the following development in triplet movement:

(Now the triplet move-
ment begins in the last measure of the preceding variation) :

But these are just minor details. The picture of the
whole work was right before Brahms' inner eye when
he wrote the sketch. He wrote it in ink, and merely
added the small alterations with pencil. The sketch
already had a definite character, and was more than
merely a first plan.

For instrumental works Brahms usually prepared a
sort of piano score in which he entered all parts and
wherein the important instruments were already indicated.

Compare the sketch work of Brahms, in which all
the essentials were written down clearly and firmly, with
the sketch work of Max Reger. Reger's musical fantasy
was practically deluged with music. His sketching could
not keep pace with his imagination. Thus, they are
only assistants to his memory, a kind of stenographic
excerpt.

When Reger composed his piano quintet in Wies-
baden in 1898, he only wrote down the first seven bars.

All the rest is just indicated. He marked down the melodic thread, and occasionally the bass, the thematic skeleton. Sometimes the sketch expands like an unregulated river: two, three, often four score lines are written down. Sometimes there are directions, such as: "Fine harmonizing! Veil with light eighths! Change the rhythm to triplets, or even faster!" These were commands which thinking gave to the quickly passing fantasy of the composer.

A few notes such as these:

are the sketch for:

The line in the sketch stands for the sixteenth (1/16) figures; the notes in the upper staff mean the end of these figures, the notes in the lower staff represent the basses of the pedals. That is all.

The "Benedictus" for organ was sketched by Reger in the following manner:

To him, this means:

Often, Reger cannot even hold on to the music roaring within him with this indicative kind of sketching. In that case, he immediately wrote down in score whatever cascaded out of his mind. That is what happened with the double fugue of the 100th Psalm and with the last movement of the "Hiller Variations" for orchestra.

Carl Goldmark, the great orchestra colorist with the oriental glowing fantasy, designed a small score for his compositions in which the principal parts of the orchestra were inserted. Then he settled down to the execution of what he had sketched.

THE BEGINNING OF CRITICAL WORK

Among composers of our time, Richard Strauss is the most diligent writer of sketches. He himself explains his manner of composing: "I compose everywhere, walking or driving, eating or drinking, at home or abroad, in noisy hotels, in my garden, in railway carriages. My sketchbook never leaves me and as soon as a motif strikes me, I jot it down. One of the most important melodies from my opera 'Der Rosenkavalier' struck me while I was playing a Bavarian card game.* But before I improvise even the smallest sketch for an opera, I allow the text to permeate my thoughts and mature in me at least six months or so, that the situation and characters may be thoroughly assimilated. Then only do I let musical thoughts enter my mind. The sub-sketches then become sketches. They are copied, worked out, arranged for piano and re-arranged as often as four times. This is the hard part of the work. The score I write in my studio straightway without troubling, working at it 12 hours a day."

Into the little sketchbooks that Strauss could easily carry in his pocket, he jotted the notes in pencil with a dainty hand. They show how deliberate Strauss is in writing his compositions, and how clear is his critical thinking.

When I visited Strauss in Garmisch in 1924, he handed me the text of the opera "Die Aegyptische Helena" for perusal which the poet Hoffmannsthal had sent him shortly before. Various places along the margin of the manuscript were marked with the main

---

* Strauss likes to play the popular German card game Skat. To my question why he enjoys playing Skat so much, he answered: "When playing Skat, I at least do not think of stupid music." But it seems that stupid music has been visiting him at the card table.

[373]

motifs of the opera as they had occurred to Strauss during the reading of the text. The libretto had obviously put him in a musical mood. However, there was a stoppage of the creative forces in the second act, just as there had been during composition of the scene between Elektra and Klytemnestra in the opera "Elektra."

At that time Strauss undertook a journey to Greece. There, on the soil of Argus, the figure of Klytemnestra stepped toward him when he saw the prehistoric Cyclopes' walls, the gold masks in the museum of Athens, and the barbaric friezes of the Acropolis museum with their loud colors and snake figures.

This time he travelled to Spain in the search for the colors suitable to his desert king Altair.

There were librettos, though, that caused music to flow out of Strauss in a broad stream. Such was the case with "Rosenkavalier." "Received first act yesterday; am simply delighted," Strauss wrote to the librettist, Hoffmannsthal, on May 4, 1909. "It is really charming beyond measure: so fine, almost too fine for the masses, but that does not matter . . . The final scene is grand, have already experimented on it today." And on May 16, 1909, Strauss wrote to Hoffmannsthal: "My work runs like the Loisach (the river near Strauss' home). I am composing every little bit."

When Strauss was to compose the ballet "Josefslegende," he did not have the feeling that the text evoked and enhanced his composing faculties. True, he considered this composition merely as an intermediary work, but even as such it did not interest him: "Josef is not progressing as fast as I thought. Chaste Josef is not to my taste, and when something peeves me, I find it hard to invent suitable music. Such a Josef, seeking God—for that I have to force myself terribly."

One of the modern composers who doesn't care for sketchwork is Dmitry Shostakovitch. In accordance with his easy-flowing fantasy, Shostakovitch is an improvisator rather than a tone philosopher. The composer's wife, Vina Vasilevna, says that he never writes sketches: "He always knows exactly what he wants and practically never touches his compositions after putting them down on paper. Examining the original score of the Ninth, I found only two brief episodes crossed and rewritten."

Despite this ease of producing, Shostakovitch made three different starts of the Ninth Symphony, which may be adopted into later works. By no means is Shostakovitch one of those composers who have to overcome many inner inhibitions in order to form music. That he should have required six weeks for the first movement of his Ninth Symphony is unusual. He wrote the second movement in only one week, the third movement in eight days, the fourth and fifth movement in five days each. He just shakes music out of his sleeve.

Writing sketches serves a different purpose for each composer. For one, it is a means of setting fantasy in motion. For another, it is a technique for surmounting opposition from the subconscious. Some use sketches as a preliminary establishment of the tone picture, as the outline of an idea; some as a foundation upon which they continue to build. In any case the sketch is the first moment at which the conscious forces of the soul test and examine the musical ideas and forms, and prepare to begin their work.

Critical thinking of great musicians is either combined with their sense of beauty—as represented by

Bach, Haendel, Haydn and Mozart — or with their moral strength, as demonstrated by Beethoven, or with their logical severity, exemplified by Brahms. Critical thinking is the light that strikes the work of fantasy, without which the world of fantasy would remain dull and formless.

CHAPTER XIV.

The Composition Process

I.

ACTUAL COMPOSITION work is accomplished in a regulated coordination of unconscious forming and critical thinking, of inspiration and work. This harmony of the creative forces is the most difficult part of compositorial work. It may be disturbed at any moment, and requires an uninterrupted balance of the conscious and unconscious faculties. When Mozart did not complete works he had begun, but preferred to start afresh on something new, it was because collaboration of fantasy and work demands a certain warmth which had cooled off. Works with large forms, such as Bach fugues, Beethoven symphonies and Wagner's music dramas cannot be created without long lasting coordination of mightiest musical fantasy and greatest spiritual strength. Nor was this co-ordination on the great bridge arcs of musical work permitted to be less perfect for even one second. Similar masses melt only in the biggest smelting furnaces.

We are astonished to learn that Haendel wrote his oratorio "Israel in Egypt" in two weeks, or that Schubert wrote eight songs in a single day—October 15, 1815—and another seven songs four days later. This calls for such perfect union of inspiration and work that their cooperation takes place without pause and without restraint. A composer like Beethoven had to struggle hard with formation, and required four large sketches and numerous side sketches before a composition such as the first movement of the "Eroica" assumed its powerful shape. This meant that the control of elemental tone masses by thinking, which organized these masses, had to expand over large tone areas, and that the common work of conscious and unconscious forces had to retain the same strength over a long period.

The spiritual strength with which inspiration and critical thinking were held together during the formation of the greatest musical works of art—such as the St. Matthew Passion of Bach, or Beethoven's big symphonies—such spiritual strength had the same mightiness as the spiritual strength with which the architects of Gothic cathedrals held boldest fantasy and greatest clarity of construction together. Even in the great Gothic domes such as the Cathedral in Rheims, or the Dome of Cologne, boldest and freest fantasy had to be transformed into geometrical forms, and be organized by mathematical laws through pointed arches and pillar groups, through buttresses and window rosetttes, despite the fact that this fantasy soared from the ground heavenwards and grew over the roofs of the houses in Rheims and Cologne into the immeasurable.

The same was the case in great philosophical structures, such as Spinoza's "Ethica" or Kant's "Kritik der reinen Vernunft." In such works boldest inspiration unfolded in logical forms and formulas. In Spinoza's work exuberant mysticism went through axioms, definitions, postulates and propositions on its way to God and eternal love; in Kant, scholastic thinking went to God, liberty and immortality. Such spiritual strength, which combined fantasy and thinking, is absolutely equalled by the spiritual strength of composers such as

Bach, Haendel and Beethoven; for they, too, combined logical thinking, mathematical clarity and geometrical form with daring fantasy and transformed them into great patterns.

Just as this joint inventing and thinking emanates from a single center in great philosophical thinkers, so, too, in great composers. In his "Essai sur l'Imagination créatrice," Ribot establishes a "principe d'unité" that holds together all the details of a musical piece of art as a kind of idee fixe, or as a fixed emotion. Such a principe d'unité, that combines fantasy and critical thinking and lets them grow till they produce the perfect form in a composition, is contained in all music by Bach, Haendel, Haydn, Mozart and Beethoven. It is weaker among the romantic composers than among the classic composers, and symphonic works of Hector Berlioz most certainly do not have the same strong, uniform center as Mozart's or Beethoven's symphonies, no matter how bold the romantic music of Hector Berlioz may be.

The perfect musical form originates only where all tone forms emanate from such a center in which invention and formation unite, and fantasy and thinking are connected. Great musical art production is based upon an "intuition" comparable to that which Henri Bergson exhibits in the philosophy of Berkeley and Spinoza. "The philosopher did not arrive at unity, he started from it." The great composers, too, start from unity.

When Goethe said that "his nature always drove him toward unity," the same can be applied to all great artists. In Mozart's letter, quoted in another chapter, he describes how he envisages compositions "as though they were a beautiful picture or a handsome person" and how he "hears everything together."

Richard Wagner also describes very beautifully, in a letter to Mathilde Wesendonck, the feeling of unity that animates him when working and does not let him rest until the most intimate combination of all parts of the art work is established: "My finest and most profound art I should now like to call 'the art of transition'; for my whole artistry consists of such transitions. The rough and the tough go against me; often it is unavoidable and necessary. But even then it should not occur without the mood being so definitely prepared for the sudden transition that it demands this transition by itself." (Paris, October 29, 1859).

In the "principe d'unité" lies the difference between a free fantasy and a musical work of art.

In free fantasy, the imagination of the composer rules completely unrestrained. The composer with the free fantasy yields entirely to the blissful play of his artistic faculties. When Mozart or Beethoven improvised on the piano, Mozart's inventions were Mozartian: graceful, singing, full of light; Beethoven's inventions stormy, dramatic, powerful. When Mozart or Beethoven improvised free fantasies, the music and the ideas were the same type of music that we know from their compositions. But in compositions by Mozart and Beethoven was a unity of thought that united all ideas. In free fantasy there was variety, color, a wealth of ideas; but the logical union created by strict thinking was lacking.

This does not mean that Mozart's or Beethoven's free fantasies were lacking in form. Mozart liked to improvise—or, as he called it, "play out of his head" —in the form of variations in order to demonstrate the intellect and wealth of his invention. On March 11,

1783, he gave a concert in Vienna's National Theater. Because the Emperor was present, as well as Gluck, to whom he wanted to prove his mastery of the severe arts in music, Mozart began his free improvising with a fugue and continued with variations. He played variations on an aria by Paesiello and, in honor of Gluck, variations on an aria by Gluck.

At a concert in Leipsic he played variations; in Prague he improvised variations on his favorite aria: "Non più andraï" from "Marriage of Figaro." One of the musicians present at this concert reported: "His improvising surpassed everything that one could expect of piano playing, for the highest degree of compositorial art was united with the most perfect dexterity of playing."

As a musician, he improvised in a convent in Augsburg. (October 24, 1777). A priest gave him a theme that he worked into a fugue; then he began to joke. He returned to the fugue theme—"to the posterior," as he playfully wrote; which, in uncouth language means in the inversion—and finally ended with the jocular theme in fugue form.

The Piano Fantasies in D-minor and in C-minor indicate how Mozart may have improvised: melody follows melody.

Beethoven, too, improvised frequently in the form of variations, according to the custom of the period. The composer Johan Schenk, who heard Beethoven in 1792, tells that he began with free tone playing and ended with variations. "To each of these Variations he gave a particular mood and all of them demonstrated passionate feeling in a personal way and in original forms."

Carl Czerny described for us the forms of Beethovenic

improvisations: 1.) Sonata form or Rondo with free finale. 2.) Free variations. 3.) Potpourri or Allegro fugue. However, in most instances Beethoven improvised in such a way that he started with storm and lightning and worked his way through to peace and heavenly rest—as exemplified by the piano introduction to the Choral Fantasy. Even free improvising was a battle for him; a wrestling with demons, a longing for ease of mind.

Even where Mozart and Beethoven needed firmer forms, their improvising has the character of fantasy: they were concerned with free expansion of their musical forces and with the wealth of ideas; they gave way to the stream of their inventions, and enjoyed the plays of their imagination. They did not develop their thoughts from a center, as they did in their compositions, and these thoughts are not united by such a center.

It was something else again in the era of Bach and Haendel. When they improvised, they did so in contrapuntal forms. It was the natural form of thinking in that period. In free improvising Bach employed only one single theme. First he used this theme for a prelude and a fugue with organ register. Then he demonstrated his prowess at the registers in a trio or a four-part movement, followed by a choral prelude. As the finale, he played a fugue on the old theme. Forkel reports that Bach's organ compositions that were handed down to us cannot give a proper conception of the magnificence of his improvisations.

Such improvisations were an old art of organists. Every organist of the 18th century who applied for a position just vacated, had to demonstrate his ability at this art of choral elaboration and the fugue.

THE COMPOSITION PROCESS

As a rule, Haendel improvised double fugues at the cembalo. During intermission at performances of his oratorios, Haendel played the organ and improvised "Capriccios" or "Voluntaries" on the royal instrument. Mattheson reports about Haendel's improvising: "I have never met anybody among the younger composers who showed such dexterity in improvising double fugues as Herr Kapellmeister Haendel; not just in composing, but in extemporizing as well, such as I have heard hundreds of times with the greatest astonishment." Still, even while improvising in strict forms, it was most important to show wealth and lustre of fantasy. The contrapuntal technique was just the means for achieving the purpose.

The last of the great improvisators was Anton Bruckner. I often heard Bruckner improvising at the organ, in the court chapel in Vienna and in the convent of Klosterneuburg. He always crowned his fantasies with a mighty fugue enhancement that unfolded all the glory of the organ. The final movement of Bruckner's Fifth Symphony can give us an idea of this art of enhancing, of solemnly developing tone masses and leading them to the summit with a fugue. Nevertheless, the finished work of art has a logical unity that had never been the purpose of a free fantasy. A work of art has its limits. Free fantasy has none. In a Beethoven fantasy the duration of a movement is determined by the first theme. Transition, second theme, coda, development: all this is dependent upon the first theme, just as the breadth and height of a Gothic dome depends on the size of the pointed arches. Free fantasy has no such inner lawfulness; it is unrestrained.

In the great work of art, something else is added to fantasy: it is artistic, logical thinking, a surveying of the whole; organic growth of ideas. A work of art is developed by its inner forces; it grows the way a tree or a living being grows out of a seed. It develops out of a single "intuition" which Bergson calls "indivisible and indestructible unity" and is "indivisible in spite of what is added at every instant, or rather, thanks to what is added."

Every artistically invented melody is a complete unity, and every movement of a symphony is one single, big melody. The second act of "Tristan and Isolde" likewise is a single melody that swells, expands, is enhanced. And the entire operas "Salome" and "Elektra" of Richard Strauss are such melodies in symphonic form.

It is the task of compositorial work to form such melodies out of great bulks of tones and tone figures, and to make intellectual order out of them.

The painter Albrecht Duerer said a painter "is full of figures inside"; similarly, a great composer "is full of tone figures inside." Not all these tone figures are of equal importance, and Friedrich Nietzsche is correct when he says: "In reality the fantasy of the good artist or philosopher continually produces some things that are good, some mediocre and some bad; but his judgment, highly experienced and sharpened, makes the selection, knots together."

A glance into Beethoven's sketchbooks proves the truth of this sentence. However, it is not just judgment and critical thinking that makes a selection from many varying musical ideas; there is also an inner power that groups the musical ideas around a center. Among the musical ideas which Beethoven wrote down in his sketchbooks are many that are valuable, but that were not executed. One is the theme of a piano concerto in

D-major, of which we possess 50 sketches, written down
between 1814 and 1815:

How truly Beethovenic is all this music. Big, energetic, heroic, just like the music of the Piano Concerto in E-flat which originated in the same period.
What impetus in the piano passages that roll from the
descant to the bass and storm back to the treble! What
power in the trills! Even the orchestra sounded in Beethoven's fantasy, as shown by the indication of the instruments. And yet work stood still, probably because
the preceding concerto in E-flat had a similar mood.
The creative impulse was exhausted therewith. The
strength that shapes material from an inner center was
too weak. It could no longer carry the work through
the many stages that a great opus has to pass. Beethoven always transformed new experiences into music,
and new battles, new moments of his development. This
made possible the formation of new artistic power cen-
ters, whence new life radiated.

Every one of Beethoven's symphonies is an artistic
world in itself, with its own mood, own form and own
instrumentation.

It is different in Anton Bruckner's symphonies. They
all have the identical musical form because again and
again Bruckner converted into tones his religious experience, which filled him completely. The path from
world to God was the purport of life to him. He was
a saint, not, like Beethoven, a fighter. His symphonies
are prayers, not pages out of a diary. How different

is the instrumentation of the Eroica, with the three radiant horns, from the broad tone areas of the Fifth Symphony; or from the delicate, chamber music—like colors of the Pastorale, which the trumpets and the small flute of the tempest music invade. How different is every reprise in Beethoven's music: in the Eroica, the victorious entrance of the principal theme in E-flat major, F-major and D-flat in irresistible rhythm, with the jubilation of victory; the lovely tone garlands of the violins in the Pastoral Symphony; the rhythmic storm of the Seventh Symphony; the tragic battles, the turmoil of dissonances, the droning drums in the Ninth Symphony! Always everything is new, shaped from an experience.

Every large work of Beethoven's emanates from a new power center that had formed in the subconscious and attracts the tones. This is the core around which unconscious experiences have crystallized. Beethoven is altogether different from Johannes Brahms, who frequently composed two works of like form in consecutive order: two symphonies, two piano concertos, two overtures, two serenades, two string quartets, because one work alone did not exhaust the contents of his soul. After completion of a composition of great form, sentiments and moods were left unformed in Brahms' soul, and they grouped themselves around a new core. In Beethoven's creation every work attracted everything in Beethoven's soul that wanted to turn to music.

Beethoven's creative instinct, which grew out of a single root, selected from the bulk of music within him whatever was usable for the formation of a new world. The useful material that had vitality was re-formed over and over again in the light of his critical thinking until it fitted into the great combinations and its shape was crystallized clearly and sharply.

Critical thinking accompanied the entire process of fantasy with its advice and wishes. It surveyed details and the whole. It looked down into the depth out of which the musical ideas formed like pots and vases from the clay that the potter kneads. It grasped with one glance the whole breadth of the form. Just as the "principe d'unité" reached into the depth and held the musical ideas together, so did conscious thinking hold the musical ideas together and give directions that removed everything that did not conform to this unity. It regulated all conditions, brought all details into one single harmony.

When Lessing said: genius is diligence; and Voltaire, that inspiration is the equivalent of daily, untiring work, this can be applied to the conscious formation of music material. Many different figures stream out of the subconscious of great composers without cessation. Through the open gate of the underworld of fantasy pours a glowing mass that is to be molded. Conscious critical thinking guards this gate, permitting only those ideas to be free that fit in with the organism of art work to be formed.

For the aria of Florestan, Beethoven wrote 18 beginnings; ten beginnings exist to the melody: "Wer ein holdes Weib errungen," and there is a whole pile of sketches for the duet "O namenlose Freude." In the sketchbook for the first arrangement of "Fidelio"— at that time still titled "Leonore"—can be found eight full pages and just as many partly filled pages of notes, which were actually three pages of music for the small trio of Marcelline, Rocco and Pizarro that came before the Pizarro aria in this original form of the opera. The sketches for Beethoven's C-minor String Quartet occupy three times as much space as the entire opus. This means an uninterrupted critical selecting and sifting.

Even Mozart, who almost always allowed his big compositions to mature in the protective mantle of his inner self, accompanied the inner formation process incessantly with his keen critical thinking. (There are many examples therefore in the chapter: "The Fragments and the Process of Creation" in Einstein's "Mozart" book.) His critique demanded simplification of the themes, so Mozart's fantasy simplified; or it demanded a better balance between the individual movements of a sonata, and Mozart created this balance.

The theme of the first movement of one of Mozart's Haydn String Quartets (K458) originally read like this:

Mozart's critical sense told him that the copying voice at the beginning of the "vivace," which comes in at the fifth measure, did not belong at the beginning, and that such counterpoint plays must be saved for the modulation; thereby the theme was given the necessary simplicity of a jocular beginning.

In other instances Mozart removed the most beautiful melodies if they did not fit into the continuity of the whole. The Larghetto of the C-minor Piano Concerto originally started:

This appeared to Mozart's critical sense to be not calm enough after the storms of the first movement, which had already heralded Beethoven's coming, and before the passionate agitation of the last movement, and so Mozart wrote the new, intimate melody:

Mozart's wonderful clearness was as much a product of a perfect purity of fantasy as of perfect lucidity of his thinking.

In all great musicians fantasy and critical thinking

are a pair of twins, grown in the same womb. During the entire working process, and in all phases of formation they have an equal share in forming music.

In the years 1800 and 1801, Goethe and Schiller discussed in an exchange of letters the question as to whether artistic creation was a conscious or an unconscious process, and this discussion has general significance.

Schiller wrote: "You will be surprised to read (in a new magazine) that true production in arts must be completely unaware, and that your genius is especially credited with acting wholly without consciousness. Therefore, you are very wrong in continuing your restless efforts of working with greatest circumspection and trying to clarify the process. Naturalism is the true sign of mastery, and that is how Sophocles worked." (July 7, 1800).

Goethe replied: "I believe that everything that genius does as genius, should happen unconsciously. The man of genius can also act rationally, after due deliberation, out of conviction; but all this happens just incidentally. No work of genius can be improved and freed of its errors by reflection and its next consequences; but through reflection and deed, genius can gradually raise itself to the point where it produces exemplary works." (April 6, 1801).

This whole discussion was continued by great composers of the present. When Stravinsky said "there is no such thing as inspiration," or "work brings inspiration," he was thinking of conscious forming. When Richard Strauss claims "he works very coolly, without agitation, without emotion even," he likewise thinks of the awareness of work. Neither of them considers that unconscious and conscious, fantasy and intelligence, in-

vention and critical thinking are associated with one another in the personality of the creating artist. None of
these soul forces is able to produce creative work by
itself. Together they are only alternating phases of a
uniform process of fantasy.

Schiller came to the same conclusion when he finally
wrote to Goethe: "The unconscious combined with
reflection makes the artist."

II.

Many different activities of the imagination and
thinking are necessary to give great works of art their
final shape. Composers who design sketches compare
these sketches with an inner picture, remove whatever
does not conform to this picture, add what seems to be
unclear or undecided, simplify anything that does not
express the picture plastically enough; they bring all
tone forms into proper proportions, create contrasts that
distribute light and shadow correctly, and smooth and
polish the finished work to give the surface a gleam.

The first conception, the first idea, is absolutely the
work of the subconscious. Often it is a crystallization of
many divers figures that exist in the subconscious;
a kind of crystallization whereby unformed material
winds around an axis and forms a regular body.

Gustav Mahler's third symphony originated in this
manner. "When I arrived this noon," reports Natalie
Bauer Lechner—"Justi (Mahler's sister Justine) ran
to meet me. 'Just imagine, Gustav has completed the
sketch for the first movement!' And as I stood there,
speechless, Mahler called out of his room: 'Natalie,
Natalie' and told me how, to his extreme surprise, he
had suddenly finished the sketch today of which he had

spoken as though it would still take him weeks. He was so happy about it that he could hardly control himself. 'How did that happen, how is it possible?', I asked him. 'I don't know myself; of course, the stones were there, but that all of a sudden a whole should come out of it must have been like a picture puzzle. After trying a long time, in vain, to find the design from the chaos of individual pieces, suddenly one finds the correct grouping of a few puzzle pieces, one part leads to another, and the picture is there! Now, of course, I have only the skeleton; all the flesh and blood and the vitality are missing and it will take me a good four weeks to gain them'."

After the work had crystallized in this way, instrumentation was begun, and Mahler was surprised to see that he had already made all instrumental inventions. Then came execution of the hundreds of sketched pages on which he had jotted down turns of a motif, or modulations. After finishing the orchestral sketch, Mahler took a few days' vacation in order to face his work fresh and capable of judgment—just as a painter steps back from his picture so he can survey and correct it.

At one place he tortured himself and could find no solution. "There, in my sleep, I heard a voice calling to me (it was the voice of Beethoven or Wagner, with whom I have been keeping company at night—not bad company, either!): 'Let the horns begin three bars further on!' And with that my difficulty was solved in the most simple and wonderful manner, I could hardly believe my eyes."

When everything was completed, Mahler still altered the introduction to the work, which was to become greater and more monumental: "I admit I had to proceed like an architect who plans the forms of his building in the proper proportions to one another. By doubling the number of the starting bars (i.e. by slowing them by half through an adagio tempo) . . . this part now has the weight and length that was indispensable."

An inner picture regulates the whole composition process on its way from the subconscious to the light of consciousness. It has already been pointed out how invention of themes, as well as formation in big dimensions, creates the impression of remembering. It seems altogether as though the whole work of art had been forgotten by the artist, and he would make an effort to recall this memory. First the recollection is unclear. Pieces of the forgotten make their appearance. The pictures are not coherent, they are pale, often distorted. They come from everywhere, from the beginning, from the middle, from various movements of a composition or from pieces that are utilized later. The compositorial process itself resembles the psychoanalytical method with which the psychiatrist draws the forgotten and repressed out of the subconscious.

Once a piece is found, it pulls along other parts that are connected with it. In the most profound depth is an adventure, a desire, some suppressed emotion around which all thought formations encamp and build. Above that are various layers in which "condensation" and "displacement" link picture to picture as in a dream, the affinity of which to art work was recognized in olden times. The goal of artistic work is "making the unconscious conscious." Artistic intellect that arranges and organizes the formations of the subconscious; that files them in ingenious continuities, clears and brightens them, is the tool that digs into the depth.

Beethoven's composition process always begins with the notation of single ideas. Whatever larger combinations have formed in Beethoven's subconscious are not strong enough, at the start of the composition process, to break through the barriers of the subconscious. They have the character of repressed memories. They have to overcome inhibitions. What comes to light first are only fragments, individual themes and ideas from various parts of the larger form. In similar manner archeologists start excavations by digging shafts into the ground, from which individual objects—marble pieces, vases and statues—belonging to a buried house, are brought to light. Then they first make their plan for excavating the whole house. That was the method of Schliemann in Troy and Mycenae, and of the men who excavated Pompeii and Herculaneum; and Beethoven used the same method.

In the sketchbook—to be found in Paris—that contains the plans for the Piano Concerto in E-flat major by Beethoven, the first pages are filled with innumerable repetitions of the principal theme of the first movement. Beethoven tries repeatedly to give the theme a new shape, first the first half:

and then the second half:

The themes appear singly, not in a combination. However, there is proof that such a combination existed in Beethoven's mind; for on one page that contained both parts of the main theme in different variations, there suddenly appears a piece out of the greater continuity (page 78 and 79 of the score):

Then the total form first emerges from the subconscious. The Tutti of the first movement is written down in its entirety, in parts exactly as it appears in the finished opus. The modulation passage is also established. Only the piano part belonging to this orchestral music is not yet written down, or only fixed with occasional indications. But it surely was in existence in Beethoven's fantasy, for it is symphonically linked with the orchestra part.

Work continued to progress. Whatever could not be used because it did not fit into the intellectual context was crossed from the sketchbook. Frequently the word "or" lets us know that Beethoven considered, wavered, and sought other figures. But always the total picture of the movement stood before Beethoven's mental eye. Prominent passages from the larger context were noted, such as the repetition of the beautiful passage of wind instruments with the piano trills from measure 381 and 382:

The more Beethoven occupied himself with the themes, the larger and broader became the form of the concerto. New foundations are required by the big dimensions; some are discarded, some are used. The movement continued to grow.

In the second movement, too, the first theme appears
first; then the parts are fixed in combination. At first
the sketch resembled an indistinct memory of the theme,
rather than the theme itself. How much work was still
necessary to give the soulful song of the theme its form
is indicated by the sketch:

Then Beethoven begins to work on the melody of
the piano. Again fragments from the combination appear: the transition from the orchestra to the solo part:

The piano trills are intimated. The orchestra also sounds
already. Once the horn is marked. Simultaneously,
the first theme progresses to its symmetrical form, on
which Beethoven keeps polishing.

All other great works by Beethoven originated similarly: in a long, laborious, never interrupted remembering of a never forgotten figure that was drawn from
the unconscious. Inhibitions and oppositions are subdued. First come themes and ideas that are washed up
on dry land like sea-weed brought up by ocean waves.
Next come larger forms. Then, with constant criticism
by conscious thinking, the form is molded. The ideas

attain clarity, become plastic; the form assumes large proportions. The work grows high and wide.

The greater the composition, the more intensive is this process, in which fantasy and thought participate alternately. It is an incessant inventing and shaping, whereby awakened consciousness always controls the work of the unconscious.

The first total sketch of the "Eroica" shows the music in the following pattern:

[399]

One can see that the most important themes are written down: the chord beats of the beginning, the first theme, are almost entirely in their permanent form, (with the exception of the third repetition, which later stays in the chief key). There is the intimation of the second theme with its coda; the jagged figure that leads to the third theme, which is still shapeless in the sketch; and the tone phrases of the end part.

Nevertheless, one is still far removed from the large dimensions of the work. The sketch contains 99 measures. The same part of the finished work has 151 measures. It has almost doubled in size. How much

work had to be done by Beethoven before this movement achieved its grand heroic style can be ascertained
from three other large sketches and numerous auxiliary
sketches. The whole first part, from the chord beats
of the beginning to the third reprise of the first theme
was spread out in the key of E-flat major in order to
put the music on its powerful pedestal. The second
theme had to be shaped as a contrast to the chief theme,
had to be an episode of lament following the victorious
advance of the beginning.

The doleful third theme, too, was elaborated upon to
form a special episode, with a new enhancement, with
the dramatic syncopated chords and with the arising of
the first theme from the depth. And at the end the
principal theme had to re-appear. In all parts the rhythms were heightened. Broad tone areas were created.
Powerful beats rained down as though they would burst
the rhythmic structure; syncopes opposed the victorious
rhythm. An heroic world emerged from the first sketch
with new battle. Violent outburst lent tension to the
music. All details had to fit into the large proportions
of the whole.

The same thing happened in the development, which
had been prepared by the first part. Here, too, powerful intellectual work had created, out of small beginnings, a picture of heroic battles, courageous advance
and soulful lament, mighty swelling of passion and slow
pacification. The middle part is sketched, with its
great enhancement, its battle of dissonances and its decline; but how small it appears in the first sketch in
which it is found. It storms against discords, and the
tragic music weakens, until the first theme is sounded
by the horn as from a distance.

[401]

Every detail was the starting point for new work and new forming. No matter how strong the passion of the volcanic composer, his critical thinking was powerful enough to control the outbursts of emotion. The first sketch shows the rising bass line that storms to the peak as the Titans may have stormed Mt. Olympus. It is opposed by dissonant chords until the battle abates and nothing remains but the rest of a buzzing low dissonance, above which is heard the call of the horn in the basic key. In this sketch, a violin roulade was to lead to the main theme:

Beethoven's critical thinking saw at once that this violin passage would destroy the declining arch of the music. It would have lent agitation to a music that was supposed to lose strength. At this spot the giant struggle was finished. The hostile combatants had been beaten in heavy fighting. Not the slightest resistance was possible any more, and quiet had settled upon the battlefield. Nothing more than a gentle agitation could echo in the violins. Only two tones of a dissonant chord buzzed around in the air, and from the distance came the sound of the triad of the horn. Beethoven crossed out in the sketch the violin passage that disturbed this mood.

In like manner he worked out to full clarification every single moment of the tone poem. He was inventor and philosopher in one.

III.

The work of the composer, which fills the work of the imagination more and more with the light of consciousness, can be embraced in the following individual activities:

1) Condensing and simplifying. If the sketched form contains more than is suitable to the idea of the work of art, and to the inner picture of fantasy, then it has to be shortened, condensed and simplified as far as possible. "The pen is not just for writing, but for crossing out as well," Brahms used to say. This faculty of condensing is not dependent upon the composer's taste alone, which desires to create the clearest, most symmetrical musical form; it is equally dependent upon the lucidity of his thinking and the force of his will power. What is termed grand style is the result of such concentration and simplification.

Bach first found his grand style in his Weimar and Leipsic time. In Weimar he learned from Italian masters like Corelli and Vivaldi how to construct large forms. The themes of his Weimar fugues become simple and unadorned, and the music is built out of massive notes. The extravagant and the fantastic disappear; all the runs and enjoyment of masterful play make way for greatest simplicity of themes and form. Out of the dazzling virtuoso develops the strict architect who, during his stay in Leipsic, erects fugues in the manner of wide bridges with mighty arcs.

In long concentrated work Bach created the A-minor organ prelude from a three-part piano fugue. The theme of the organ fugue with its calm plasticity is a product of the work that condensed and simplified:

This symmetrical musical line lifted itself out of the restive piano fugue:

The apparently spontaneous naturalness of melodic expression that we admire in Haydn's "Creation" like-wise is the result of hard work which concentrated and simplified. This applies to the choruses as much as to the arias. We admire the magnificent description of the eagle's flight in Gabriel's aria in Haydn's "Creation," and the simple line of the melody that soars from earth heavenwards with wide wings:

The eagle's flight to the sun cannot be described grander or simpler than it is done here with the run from G to high A.

However, the two pages of sketches for this aria prove that such popular simplicity is the result of an energetic simplification:

And cleaves_the_air in swift - - - - - - - - - - - test flight in the swift-est flight and cleaves the air and cleaves the air in swift - - - - - - - - - - - - - - - - test flight to the blaz - - - - - - - - - ing sun to the blaz- ing sun

How restless the majestic flight of the eagle in the numerous 1/16 runs; here, the eagle even trills like a lark.

In the sketch, Haydn had designed the aria in 3/4 time:

Later he changed this to 4/4 time, which has much more symmetrical balance of accents and therefore is better suited for the flight of the eagle; with light changes he made the melody calmer and more uniform:

With the changed tempo, and with very light retouching, everything here becomes larger and broader; the fluttering of the wings, and the take-off.

The greatest master of concentration was Beethoven. In his condensing of musical thoughts his intellectual and moral energy shows itself.

Themes like the first theme of the Fifth Symphony are an agglomeration of musical forces in a clenched fist. Michelangelo is a kindred spirit in a different field of art. The mighty gesture of creation with which God parts the clouds on the plafond of the Sistine Chapel, and separates light from darkness, or casts the sun upon the firmament, or imparts life to Adam, receives its majesty from the simplicity of the contours.

The World Judge in "Last Judgment," jumping up enraged, attains a gesture the simple line of which imparts majesty and subjugating power. In Michelangelo's statues expression of soul was brought into such simple cubic form that, to use the artist's words, the statues could have been rolled down a mountain without breaking. The magnificent lines of St. Peter's dome comprise the most powerful ascending forces in the simplest form.

The

is a musical form of the same type. It is as short and intense as a clap of thunder. Masses of energy are stored therein. In the shortest formula it already contains the entire further development of the first movement.

Beethoven carried the rhythm of this theme around with him for many years. It is already present in the first outline of his F-major String Quartet opus 18, No. 1:

It throbs audibly in the G-major Piano Concerto and in the Appassionata, until finally, in the Fifth Symphony, it is given its most concentrated form.

Many other themes of Beethoven's originated similarly through condensation.

For instance, the first theme of the F-major String Quartet originally had the following shape:

By leaving out whatever was superfluous, it first obtained this marked form:

Only at this point, by condensing four measures, does the theme become a personality that one does not forget. It receives its inward tension. Its energy. Its willpower.

Or, to cite another example: Every music lover is familiar with the ending of the great "Leonore" aria, in which the melodic line rises to high B with heroic elan:

Everything here appears natural and matter of course: the mounting of the vocal line, in which Leonore's expression of love is intensified more and more; the powerful roulade as musical expression of victorious jubilation and devotion. One assumes that this is the way it has to be.

But in the first outline of "Fidelio," the big aria ended in the following maner:

How detailed, how rich in tones, and yet how much less effective is this roulade of triplets, which first sinks to the ground twice before it works itself back up! The energy with which Beethoven expresses enthusiastic jubilation, heroic trust and love that surmounts all obstacles was produced only by condensation of the melodic line. There are fewer notes, but now Leonore first lives.

Condensing and simplifying not only gives themes

greater inner strength and more personality, it also augments the tension in large forms.

Here, too, Beethoven is the greatest master. In the Second Symphony Beethoven already employs condensation of the melodic material in order to enhance the inner emotion of the first Allegro. In the sketches for this symphony, the principal theme of the first movement—which pushes forward so courageously—is brought three times in its entirety. Three times it rises step by step in its complete form:

Only by condensing did Beethoven achieve the courageous flow of the music. Now the theme appears only twice. Only part of the theme is used for the transition, thereby accelerating it. The movement is strengthened and receives a new inner enhancement.

Something similar takes place in the sketchwork for the first movement of the "Eroica." In the first large sketch of the "Eroica" (see pages 398, 399, 400), the chief theme is presented three times; twice in E-flat major and once in B-flat major. In subsequent sketches it appears three times in E-flat major and a fourth time in B-flat major. In the final form, it passes only three times, each time in E-flat major. With this abbreviation a broad, harmonic E-flat major surface is established; an energetic uniform exposition of the heroic tone sphere of this symphony.

The B-flat major is saved for the incidental movement, and the contrast between the first part and the incidental movement is accentuated. Against the big E-flat major background of the first part, the syncopated rhythms, the beats against the measure and the dissonances seem even more grandiose than before. Condensation and simplification produces the great style of this music.

At another point condensation accents the dramatic tension of the music. The story of its origin, which can be learned from the sketchbooks, belongs to the most interesting parts of the history of this grand work.

As indicated by the sketchbooks, Beethoven wanted to have parts of the main theme ascending from the depth before the end of the first part. One comes across this rising passage in all the sketches. (See bars 83—87 p. 400). In the second of the big sketches, this movement has the following form:

The great enhancement reaches its peak in:

This passage shows up in the third and fourth large sketch in similar manner.

Later, Beethoven, in another sketch, arrests the idea of opposing the chord beats that seem to break the measure before the ending, with this passage that comes from the depth:

Before closing, there was to be a final assault. The main theme was to gather its strength before breaking down with lyric lament at the end of the movement. After the heroic battles of the first movement, this was to be the last.

In the completed work, Beethoven condenses this episode into the tightest form. Only one bar from the principal theme appears piano, a gentle, last lament a last weakening rearing:

But how much more gripping has this artistic vision now become! How much nobler is the idea expressed that the chord beats in straight measure batter the 3/4 measure of the first movement and decide the victory; and that one bar of the chief theme rears itself once more like a dying soldier on the battlefield before his blood is drained! The many bars that appear in the sketches are replaced by a single bar, the mood was concentrated; but just because of such epigrammatical condensation of the contrasts, the artistic idea became stronger and more plastic.

One of the most magnificent examples of Beethoven's power of concentration is the big "Leonore Overture."

As is well known, this classical work originated from a re-arrangement of the overture that had been played at the initial performance of "Leonore" in 1805. This first overture had been an outburst of romantic fantasy that had frightened the conservative audience. "The overture . . . displeased throughout because of the incessant dissonances," one critic wrote; another established that "never was anything written in music that was so incoherent, shrill, confused and insulting to the ear."

THE COMPOSITION PROCESS

When Beethoven re-wrote the opera in 1806, he also subjected the overture to a revision. By re-modeling, he changed a romantic work of art into a classic piece of art. The passion of the music was transformed into grand style, the immense agitation of the Beethovenic imagination tamed through breadth and moderation.

Condensation and simplification plays the greatest part in such remodeling. In the first design, the introductory Adagio had 57 bars; in the new form only 36.

The Adagio leads into Florestan's cell, where sighs are heard. The touching grievance of the Florestan aria sounds ("In des Lebens Fruehlingstagen"). Then quiet and dreariness again settles upon the dark chambers. Alone! Forsaken! A ray of distant light that pierces the dark of the dungeon heralds the approach of liberation. That, approximately, is the mood of the picture.

Into the dungeon depth leads a descending passage that begins fortissimo and dwindles down to pianissimo.

In the first overture, this passage begins twice, and twice tapers off to a pianissimo:

In the second setting we have but a single melodic arch, a stylistic, expressive line that sinks down into the darkness of the dungeon:

The graphic power of the line becomes stronger, and the mood more uniform.

The same thing happens in the further course of the opera. The bold modulation that follows Florestan's aria; the tightening chord movement from A-flat major to E-major and back again to A-flat major with the use of enharmonic permutation, requires the space of 26 bars in the first setting. In the new form, only 21 bars.

The gripping fortissimo outburst of the orchestra that follows is also concentrated through simplification.

The first design brings this part twice: the broadly stretched harmonies of the wood-winds and brass, besieged by the 32nd run of the first violins and violas. The second setting brings this part only once in triple forte, which sounds mightier; this despite the fact that Beethoven employs only two horns here instead of four, because the roll of the kettle-drum and the triplet motion in the low strings augments the elemental eruption. The whole violin section is taken unisono, the chord of the wind instruments more powerful because it is distributed differently among the wood-winds, and the three trombones blow the A-major triad in the most sonorous pitch. The phrase is made mightier by simplification.

The concentrating ability of the artist can also be admired in the beautiful ending which is already penetrated by the mood of hope, although it is as yet weak. Here we have a noble melody that descends into the dungeon with gentle third passages of flute and oboe, to promise consolation to Florestan. The melody seems to come straight from the heart, its emotional line is so simple:

And yet, a glance at the first overture shows that this simplicity and fervour was created only by critical sifting of a very complicated, jagged melody:

The bars leading to the Allegro also required simplification before attaining their classic outline. Quite novel is the poetic trait as the agitation of the whole quivers in the thirds of the flutes and oboes like a small flame in a breeze.

IV.

The reverse of condensing and concentrating is the *expanding of ideas and forms,* which constitutes a second important phase of composition work.

It may be that the sketch contains less than the artist had in mind. Then the fantasy of the composer unfolds breadthwise and depthwise. In discussing the "Eroica" sketches, mention was made of how whole phrases in the first Allegro originated through this process of expansion. How the growth of a lyric phrase required a compensation by a greater dramatically agitated part. How, as the lyric expression deepened, the dissonances became more violent, the conflicts were heightened.

When Beethoven designed the "Appassionata," he sketched the chief movement completely in F-minor. The stormy and the sombre dominated, the contrast of the mild and gentle was missing. Not until later did the music in the sketches expand into the sphere of lightness. The part in A-flat major is worked out in order to establish a balance and to achieve a development toward emotional mildness in the tragic music.

Expansion also created the famous pedal-note that forms the transition from the Scherzo (Allegro) of Beethoven's Fifth Symphony to the victory march of the finale. In the sketch the mysterious transition that causes so much suspense comprises 17 bars; in the score, 50 bars.

Beethoven first sketched the drums that softly hammer the rhythmic motif of the Scherzo in the low registers, and swell continuously toward the end:

This hammering and droning of the kettle-drums continued to grow breadthwise. Increasing the tension,
mysterious harmonies entwined themselves around the
drums. The transition waxed larger, more exciting.
Inasmuch as the victory music assumed ever greater
proportions—440 measures—the preparation to this
movement also had to increase in size. Tension was
augmented by the expansion of nocturnal cloud
masses. The great episode that subdues with gigantic
energy the dismal forces in Beethoven's soul leads from
the demonic plays of the Scherzo to the lustre of the
finale.

In other of Beethoven's works, expansion serves to
intensify expression of soul. Compare, for example,
the bars with which Beethoven modulates from E-
major to A-flat major in Florestan's aria. In the first
outline of the aria it read like this:

How different in the second setting! Here, the same modulation is executed broadly with chromatic "Stimmfuehrung." Voice and orchestra participate, and the moving expression of the music is enhanced with this amplification. The emotional value of the words: "Das Mass der Leiden" is augmented to an extraordinary extent by the enlarged melodic line and the expressive harmonies. Florestan's characteristic achieves a new, touching trait. Beethoven must have sensed deeply the sad fate and distress of mind to be able to sketch such a detail. In great composers every detail is animated by the idea of the total:

Nothing is more characteristic of Franz Schubert's music-happy nature than the fact that he liked to expand his themes. He was the lyric singer who enjoys revelling in music, rather than a strong logician like Beethoven and, later, Brahms, who mostly aspire to conciseness.

In the first sketch for the Schubert B-flat Symphony, the second theme of the first movement shows this form:

But in the finished symphony, it has doubled in breadth:

[421]

It was similar in the large C-major Symphony of Schubert, when Schubert began to write the second main idea in the sketch for the final movement:

No sooner was the melody written down, than it grew in width. Even in the Symphony Schubert does not disavow his pleasure in easy sauntering.

In addition to expansion in area, however, compositorial work also shows an expansion depthwise. This type of extension of the musical idea is not intended to give the thoughts of the composer greater distinctiveness, form and power of emotion, but, instead, a deeper background. It does not serve musical drawing as much as it tends to make the music plastic. In the stead of work in relief steps work at the block.

I can think of no more beautiful example of this work that penetrates to the depth, than the sketchwork for the first of Beethoven's "Claerchen" songs.

Shortly before the year 1809 drew to a close, Beethoven started to compose the music for Goethe's "Egmont," and in Beethoven's sketchbooks of the same year there appeared sketches to the two songs of Claerchen that are sung in the Goethe epos.

The first of the two songs: "Freudvoll und Leidvoll," is sung in the first act. It was written for Toni Adamberger, the young and beautiful actress who played Claerchen in Vienna at the first performance on May 24, 1810, and not for a singer. For this reason the song was originally to have been simple. "Nur huebsch munter und frisch weg" (Just lively and fresh away), says Claerchen when she wants to intone the song. "It is a soldier song, my favorite piece."

The first melody appears in Beethoven's sketchbooks as a simple soldier song:

It is a lively march tune. But Beethoven would not be Beethoven had not his fantasy experienced stronger vibrations from the Goethe drama. Even before 1809 Beethoven had set a Goethe poem ("Nur wer die Sehnsucht kennt") to music four times. He was an admirer of Goethe's, and in his fantasy the music of this song expanded into the depth.

The music was given a larger background. Beethoven heard the soldiers' drums on their way to battle, and the fifes that blow a march music, and he combined the melody of the song with this background.

The fifes of the soldiers blow the following march
tune as intermezzo:

However, even this was not enough for Beethoven.
He visualized the picture of the marching soldiers,
heard the drums and pipes louder and louder. The
fifes sounded more and more into the girl's song, and
she begins to march along:

Finally, as indicated by the instruction "Sempre diminuendo" at the end of the sketch, the marching soldiers vanish in the distance together with the marching girl. The whole picture had become plastic. It was
a realistic portrayal.

All this was external description. Not until the very end did Beethoven provide this music, which outgrew the theatre for which it was intended, with depth through psychological mood. As a gay soldier's song the tune was originally written in F-major. But "Egmont" was a tragedy, and a tragic shadow lay over the scene in which Claerchen sings the song. So Beethoven substituted the major with minor, and thus it remained in the sketches of the year 1810 and in the completed composition.

Now the song, which had grown in depth, first combined everything: emotional description, portrayal of the situation, realistic detail, the mood of tragedy. It portrayed the heroic girl who marched alongside of her lover's soldiers, and it pictured the atmosphere of the Netherlands filled with the noise of war.

V.

Even more important than condensing and expanding is the elaboration and intensification of every detail. Accenting the expression. Augmenting the clarity of the picture. All this digesting of all details to the limit of expression is associated with the other intellectual operations of the composer, and all this forming and shaping grows out of a single root of the imagination.

Bach worked at his themes like an architect in order to give them the strongest plastic form, frequently with one stroke that changed them completely.

For instance, according to Mattheson in his "Gene-

ralbassschule," the theme of the great organ fugue in
G-minor had the following form in 1725:

In this form, Bach may have performed the fugue for
the old organ master Reinken in Hamburg, perhaps
as homage for the composer since the theme is patterned after a theme by Reinken. But later Bach made
a slight change in the theme:

This way it first attained the powerful, calm shape
and uniformity of form.

In the Bach cantata "Ach liebe Christen seid ge-
trost" there is a chorus the music of which, in confor-
mity with the text, paints the sowing of wheat seeds:

THE COMPOSITION PROCESS

We are in possession of a sketch to this music, which demonstrates Bach's picturesque fantasy. The theme occurred to Bach while he was working on the introductory chorus. He was afraid of forgetting it, and jotted it down on an empty line of the score:

With but a very light rhythmic change, the graphic of the theme was worked out of the sketch: the swinging arm, the sowing, the triple scattering of the grain.

No composer struggled harder than Beethoven at giving his ideas plastic shape.

Often when his themes appear they seem indistinct. Frequently they have something general and impersonal. It takes a lot of work to give them outstanding features. For instance, the Scherzo of the "Fruehlingssonate" has the character of a pretty general minuet in the first sketch:

With a very light rhythmic re-formation Beethoven gave the music its present teasing, graceful, dainty character:

[427]

It is particularly interesting to observe how an accentuation created the gripping phrase in Beethoven's "Fidelio" which is the dramatic climax of the opera. It is Leonore's outcry: "Toet' erst sein Weib" (Kill first his wife) that evokes the maximum of tragic emotion. It is the moment that taught young Richard Wagner what tragic effect means, when he saw the great tragedienne Schroeder-Devrient in "Fidelio." Ortrud's elemental grandeur in "Lohengrin"; Isolde's violent passion and Kundry's ferocity in "Parsifal" are all descendents of this moment. The entire modern naturalism of theatrical expression reverts to this moment. Never before had there been a similar naturalistic keenness on the operatic stage, or a similar pathos, a comparable eruption of sentiment.

This new expression of sentiment is not stylized; it is all blood and nerves. In the sketches for this phrase one can see how Beethoven reached that expression step by step by reinforcing it continuously. Originally, Beethoven wrote:

Then he strengthened the high B-flat to the more intense B.

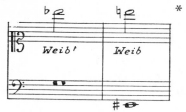

And finally he heightened the outburst with a harsh dissonance:

Thus the outcry first became the most violent cry of passion!

Another instructive point is contained in Beethoven's String Quartet opus 18, No. 1 in F-major. It is little known that there exists an original design of this quartet that differs from the present form in many places. Beethoven presented this first outline to his friend Karl Ferdinand Amenda, with whom he was very intimately associated in 1798 and 1799, when Amenda was in Vienna. Beethoven requested him by no means to give the quartet any further which he had presented to him because he had changed it greatly, having just learned how to write quartets. Com-

---

* Here we have the same fifes that are heard in the victory fanfares of the "Egmont Overture" composed toward the end of 1810.

parison of the two settings of the F-major String Quartet shows what Beethoven considered good in the quartet and what he thought was bad.

Essentially, the first design of the quartet is less condensed and less concentrated. The development of the first movement experienced most of the re-modeling. One of these re-formations shows what detail work, accentuation of expression and inner enhancement meant to Beethoven.

It is the moment when the development presses toward the return of the first part; it is the most important moment of the sonata movement, in which the first theme re-appears in its original form and with intensified significance after many transformations. Following its many adventures on its journey, its return is to be surprising and impressive. There should be logic in its reappearance, not arbitrariness.

In the first form, a big enhancement leads from F-major to the return of the F-major theme on the extended dominant:

All this is full of suspense: the mounting chords in the violins, the tempestuous motion in the viola and cello, the imitation in the low voices, the strong rhythmic accents. Everything urges toward the end. These tensions have to be resolved in the appearance of the principal theme.

Still, this was not enough for Beethoven. He gave the same phrase the following shape:

Here, the accents are still heightened, inasmuch as the first violin and viola are set in syncopated motion, therefore push forward even more dramatically. At the same time, the stormy movement in the second violin and the cello assume an even more tense character. Here Beethoven for the first time makes use of counter movement with which he later produced enhancements so often. The two voices move in divergent directions, not in the same direction like in the first version. They wrestle with one another, they press the harmony to the extreme limit, and would tear the chord apart if the artist did not compress the two voices with an iron hold.

The artistic idea of this part of the development: the creation of a tension that makes the entrance of the main theme appear necessary and logical, is perfected with even greater decisiveness and energy in the new version.

VI.

In great compositions this condensing, expanding and accentuating takes place incessantly upon broad tone areas and in deep tone spaces. The whole composition work, which is now consummated in the light of conscious forming, is a large organizing of the tonal masses and the bulk of sentiments and experiences that stream from the subconscious to the higher strata of soul life. That which is called the technique of a composer is merely the tool with which these masses are formed.

At first this technique is only what the great composers have learned from the masters of past times. It is the old heritage, the old experiences of listening, the handicraft of the past. This was the technique that Bach first learned from the organ masters of the 17th century, from Sweelinck, Pachelbel, Buxtehude, Boehm and Reinken, and which he studied from Corelli, Geminiani, Vivaldi. Mozart absorbed the whole technique of his era which had been created by the Mannheimer Symphoniker, by Johann Christian Bach, by French opera composers, Italian buffo masters and German operetta composers. His technical learning was encyclopedic and comprised the total music of his period. Beethoven learned from the Mannheimer Symphoniker, from Philipp Emmanuel Bach, from Cherubini, J. J. Fux, from Bach and from Haendel. Wagner, from Karl Maria von Weber and Franz Marschner, from Meyerbeer and Halevy, Bellini and Donizetti.

The greater a composer, the larger the old foundations upon which he constructs his music. Schoenberg absorbed the technique of Brahms and Wagner's "Tristan and Isolde," of Liszt and Beethoven's last quartets; Stravinsky that of Rimsky-Korsakoff and Tschaikowsky, before they ventured out on new paths.

Every great composer experiences the moment in which he begins to give this inherited technique a personal transformation. Whatever was inherited technique and experience of the past is reformed by his own fantasy and made expression of this new fantasy. The more great composers became aware of their peculiarity, the more they filled the technique with their own personality. Melody, harmony, tone and rhythm became something else than what they had been in the past.

When great composers studied the works of the old masters, it was not to copy them, as artisans do who have no ideas of their own, but to get acquainted with their own new personalities, and to remodel these forms in accordance with this new personality. Beethoven, for instance, copied and studied Bach's works since 1810, because he wished to expand his personality and saw in polyphony a means of taming the wealth of his moods and the many contrasts in his inner mind. The Bachian fugue form turned out to be something else than what it had been with Bach: it became the form in which Beethoven portrayed his inner battles. The Bach fugue had been law and cosmic order; Beethoven's fugue became the subjective expression of his struggling.

This same form, in the hands of Robert Schumann, became a means of expressing romantic dreaming. For Bruckner it was religious ecstasy, for Arnold Schoenberg a construction designed to suppress romantic sentiment.

In every truly creative composer the faculty that we call technique is an expedient in bringing to consciousness whatever streamed toward him from his subconscious. It is not an outside addition to fantasy, in order to organize and clear this fantasy; in every creative musician it is the form of his fantasy proper, and the spiritual form of his personality.

The great form of classical creation is also a personal force. Here, too, that which was inherited is given a personal transformation. The symphonies of Haydn, Mozart and Beethoven developed out of the form of the Mannheimer Symphoniker and of Philipp Emmanuel Bach; but every symphony by Haydn, Mozart and Beethoven is the expression of his personality, and has the rhythm, the harmonies and the timbre of that personality. Even when a C-major symphony of Haydn, Mozart and Beethoven begins with the identical chord, this chord sounds different; it has a different inner tension, a different energy, different life mood. The same applies to the form of symphonies in general. It contains a varying sense of order and organization of the music material; a different survey, a different feeling for proportions, contrasts and tensions. Similarly, a renaissance palace by Bruneleschi, Raphael and Sangallo was different in each structure, though the same architectural forms were used.

The greatest genius of composers is the survey over the great form; it regulates the fantasy process. Composing of grand style is regulated by this sense of form which joins all details in harmonic proportions, as an inner picture, as it were. All condensing, expanding, accentuating and plasticizing of ideas and forms would still not produce a perfect work of art if the sense of great form would not distribute these thoughts properly, distinguish them by contrasts, enhance them in logical perfection.

In transforming his Piano Trio opus 8, Johannes Brahms showed what this feeling for form meant. Over thirty years separate the first and second version of this music. Brahms was twenty years old when he wrote down the first setting. This was the romantic period in his life; the time when, as a slender young man, with long blond hair, he serenaded a lady of the nobility in a moon-lit night in Hildesheim, and dreamily roamed through the Rhineland. Therefore, he wrote genuine romantic music in this work; free, fantastic and colorful. The quotations of Schubert's melody: "Wir sassen am einsamen Fischerhaus" in the Adagio of the work, and of a Beethoven melody from "Liederkreis an die ferne Geliebte" are reminiscent of adventures of the soul, of which his youth is replete. The music is broad, the moods vary, the form is rich in many interpolated episodes.

Brahms was 58 years of age when he re-formed this piano trio. He had become the master who had composed his greatest works: the four symphonies, two string quartets, concertos, and the "Deutsches Requiem." He looked back at the romanticism of his youth as upon a distant time from which he had turned in his search for classicism. That he reviewed his youth with longing is indicated by the re-formation of his piano trio. That he had acquired the great form perspective that he had lacked earlier, is proven by every bar of this re-formation. The fantastic work became severe in form. The music was held together with strong logic. It became more concise and more energetic.

Of the first movement the old maestro left only 62 bars. All the rest is new, forceful, virile. With impressive uniformity new themes are created out of the material of the first theme group. From this material the new incidental movement originates, as does the development and the Coda. Counterpoint takes the place of fantastic liberty. The manifold moods of the first version are displaced by uniform thinking work. The form becomes big, classical, energetic.

The Scherzo is given a new ending with improved enhancement. The ecstatic Schubert quotation is removed from the Adagio, as is the bizarre insertion of the first version that had interrupted the solemn Adagio mood. Thus this movement, too, became uniform.

Of the final movement only 54 bars remained. All episodes vanished; the wonderful F-sharp major cello cantilene that sings so soulfully of love disappeared. The chromatically winding main theme is confronted by a diatonic theme as artistic contrast. A calm, clear eye surveys the final movement, which now is really an ending, not a broad enlarging of changing moods.

As the re-formation shows, it was not feeling that changed in Brahms; although it is repressed more strongly, it nevertheless remains romantic feeling. The change was in the perspective, in more severe artistic thinking, the ability of disposing in large spheres. He comprises, instead of expanding sentiment; he condenses instead of joining one colorful episode to another; he shapes uniformly, not motley and fantastically. His understanding of large surfaces and big form had grown.

* * *

Beethoven remodeled the "Leonore Overture" of 1805 into the "big" Leonore overture of 1806 in a similar process of thinking in large proportions.

In the original version, the Allegro of the Leonore Overture had the following proportions:

Version I:

Statement	*Development*	*Repetition*
First part:	148 bars	Second part:
186 bars		140 bars

One can see at a glance that the second part with its 140 bars—which, incidentally, is not uniformly bound, but consists of individual, separate episodes—cannot hold its balance either against the development with 148 bars, or against the first part with 186 bars. The form is reminiscent of a bridge that starts with big arches, but breaks off before reaching the shore, and is completed with an auxiliary bridge. If the bridge is really to give a monumental effect, the arches would have to be continued. It would have to rise and sink symmetrically. It would have to become a large symmetrical form.

That is what Beethoven made it in the second setting. Now the work first received its third part that has the mighty, broadly arched form that is equal to the first part and the development.

The proportions now are these:

Version II:

(*Statement*)	(*Development*)	(*Repetition*)
First part:	80 bars	Second part:
155 bars		367 bars

The new development is shorter. It is now organized more clearly. Large contrasts appear. Light and shadow are evenly distributed. The regular sequence of four-bar groups lends a greater style to the development.

One meets this new style in the trumpet fanfare that was reshaped by Beethoven. In the first version it is jagged:

In the new arrangement, it is simple:

There is the same simplicity in every detail, as well as in the large form. A new poetic reprise, in which the melody of the flute trills like the song of a lark in the breeze, leads to the reprise; for now Beethoven

repeats the Allegro in order to create a powerful symphonic arch. The key of C-major spreads above the
main and side movements, mostly in the strong basic
chords. Once again the characters of the drama pass
by, enveloped in radiance: Leonore in her courage,
her sense of heroism, her loyalty; Florestan with his
plaint which sounds transfigured in flute, oboe and
bassoon toward the end, while the kettledrums sound
the rhythm of the liberating fanfare as from the distance. Then the assault of the strings, which had 10
bars in the first version and now has 20 bars, leads to
the lavish finale.

By broadening the theme, Beethoven now gives it a
strong heroic soul. In the first outline there were two
bars:

Now he extends it to four measures:

The measure becomes broader too: 4/4 instead of the
Alla Breve. Likewise the accompaniment of the
strings: marked fourths instead of rustling eighths.
The chords of the wind instruments are stretched further. Everything becomes mightier.

Altogether new is the great pedal point enhancement that leads to the rapture of the finale and to the ecstasy of the Leonore theme. Contrary to the original version, where Florestan appears at the end, we have Leonore in the final scene. Her exultation winds up the work.

The grandeur of this style showed itself in the new proportions of the overture, in the broad disposition of the whole and in the architecture. But Beethoven did not achieve this style until he had ennobled the passionate fanaticism of the first overture by his artistry. He surveys the music from a high position. The first version was a glowing eruption. In the second version this glowing mass first takes shape. However, in competitions of such great style forming means: organization of fantasy by superior artistry; even control over the tone masses; grand structure; invention in large spaces; clarification of fantasy through intellect.

Creation of large proportions as they exist in Bach's "Matthaeus Passion," in Mozart's Jupiter Symphony or in Beethoven's Ninth Symphony, in which strongest musical fantasy is subjected to the strongest sense of art, is the final, top step of compositorial work. Only the greatest musical minds can reach that step.

VII.

The various activities that propel the musical work of art into the full light of consciousness all work simultaneously, in a uniform rhythm and according to the same basic plan. This plan might be termed the "idea" of the composition, and the composer does not rest until this idea is worked out perfectly clear in all forms. The whole work is an analogy of a world creation, whereby spiritual forces and physical powers, thoughts, laws and order are linked with matter and natural forces to the same extent as they are associated with tones in the work of a great artist.

When the composition has been completed, there follows a final revision of the result achieved. This revision smoothes the surface of the form in the same manner as the sculptor does when he again walks around the completed statue and corrects little flaws with a fine instrument; or as the painter does who adds a few highlights to his picture.

Bach never ceased correcting finished compositions. Near the end of his life he wrote the variations on the Christmas Carol "Vom Himmel hoch da komm ich her," in which gay Yuletide joy plays with the carol. The engraving of this music, which we possess in addition to an original manuscript that is of later date than the engraving, shows that Bach even made corrections on printed compositions. We find the same thing in the "Achtzehn Choraele" which Bach composed either in Weimar or in Koethen, and revised in Leipsic. We have in our possession 15 older editions from the estate of Philipp Emmanuel Bach that show how Bach elaborated upon these compositions.

Bach's last work was the revision of the chorale "Wenn wir in hoechsten Noethen sind" which remained incomplete in the original. Ill, and almost blind, he dictated the revised chorale to his pupil, Altnikol, in the darkened room. The notes, written behind curtained windows, are in ink; from day to day they become more watery, and can hardly be deciphered. With the tones of this transfigured chorale, which Bach now titles "Vor Deinen Thron tret ich alhier," Bach passed into the Great Beyond.

Neither Haydn nor Mozart did much correcting on

completed compositions. Among Mozart's works, only the six string quartets dedicated to Haydn—which Mozart himself defined as "the fruit of long and wearisome labor"—show many corrections in the score; several of them may possibly have been made after completion of the composition. In the score of the big G-minor Symphony Mozart subsequently changed the chords in the violas when he saw that the original version contained a forbidden harmony (concealed fifths) that had escaped him.

Beethoven was different. After completing his compositions, he labored ceaselessly at bagatelles which he wanted to bring out more sharply. In particular he was always working on an improvement of the dynamics.

Beethoven undertook many subsequent changes in the score of "Missa Solemnis." In the manuscript of the score, the flute melody that describes symbolically the alighting of the Holy Ghost originally was simpler. Other points in the Credo were also altered subsequently. Thus, in a later version, Beethoven did not let the trumpets enter until the words: "Judicare vivos et mortuos."

Many times great composers made changes after the performance of their works, if they were not satisfied with the timbre after hearing the work, or if they desired changes for other reasons.

Bach's "Johannespassion" had a different shape at the first performance (1723). At that time it started with the chorus: "O Mensch bewein die Suende gross," which now ends the first part of the Matthew Passion. At the second performance (1727) Bach replaced three of its arias with others. At the finale stood the chorale: "Christe, du Lamm Gottes." He also composed the big entrance chorus "Herr unser Herrscher" for this performance. Likewise new was the end chorus. For a still later performance, Bach made corrections in the voices and changed orchestral details. Phrasings and dynamic directions were also added; proof of how important it was for Bach, whose music now so often swims in a grey color which is considered Bach style.

Mendelssohn was one of the most careful workers. The lovely line of his music, which has an almost Mozartian perfection, is the result of tireless work.

Mendelssohn's Italian Symphony did not attain the form and timbre which we now admire until after its performance in London (1833); they did not originate until 1837. On June 26th Mendelssohn wrote to his friends Ignaz and Charlotte Moscheles: "The other day Dr. Frank, whom you know, came to Duesseldorf and I wished to show him something of my A-major Symphony. Not having it here, I began writing out the Andante again, and in so doing I came across so many errata that I got interested and wrote out the minuet and finale too, but with many necessary alterations; and whenever such occurred I thought of you, and how you never said a word of blame, although you must have seen it all much better and plainer than I do now. The first movement I have not written down, because if once I begin with that, I am afraid I shall have to alter the entire subject, beginning with the fourth bar—and that means pretty nearly the whole first part—and I have no time for that just now."

Mendelssohn was never satisfied with the finale in its first form. Its alteration postponed the publishing of the score until after the composer's death (1851). The first performance of the symphony in its new form also took place only two years after Mendelssohn's death (Leipsic, 1849).

Brahms was another composer who made changes after completing his scores. Sometimes, after having heard a new work performed, he made corrections right before printing.

The same was true of Anton Bruckner. We have almost all of Anton Bruckner's symphonies in various versions, and find changes between the last manuscript and the printed score that raised the legend that Bruckner's pupils altered the scores. Whoever knew Bruckner's stubbornness, and whoever knows, besides, how little Bruckner's pupils—all young people, then, with an almost religious esteem for their master— would have dared to change any of Bruckner's music —that person will understand the senselessness of such a legend. The only changes made were in the score of the Ninth Symphony, done by Ferdinand Loewe because Bruckner had passed away before its completion and could not revise the music himself, as he had done often enough in other symphonies.

Richard Wagner made changes in the instrumentation of the "Parsifal" score after it was finished. The orchestra was to have a solemn, transfigured timbre in this work, and so, when the tone appeared to him to be too material, after having heard his music, he made alterations.

For instance, Wagner wrote the instrumentation for the prelude to "Parsifal" in November and December 1878—while still working on the third act of the work —because he wanted to perform this prelude in his house "Wahnfried" for Cosima's birthday. He invited the Meininger court orchestra to play the festive music, which first resounded on December 25th and was repeated the next day for a larger audience. Following this performance, Wagner changed a chord in the prelude. "When I heard it," Wagner said later, "I told myself: all well and good, but this chord it not going to stay!" This chord was too sentimental to suit him, too earthy. He also changed a high tone of the trumpet that appeared several times in 6/4 measure and had given the trumpeter of the Mannheimer orchestra some difficulties. The trumpeter had told Wagner: "The tone is too ticklish." Wagner replied: "But I have often heard this tone played by the military band!" However, he finally did change the part.

Even during rehearsals of the orchestra in the Bayreuth Theatre Wagner made changes in the timbre of "Parsifal." He had always been afraid of "too strong an instrumentation." Even in festive moments he desired to have the "Parsifal" tone soft, not pealing. Thus, in order to soften the tone for the entrance of Parsifal in the third act, he adds horns to the trombones and trumpets. "For Parsifal's entrance," said Wagner, "I have horns and trumpets; horns alone I considered too soft, not solemn enough; trumpet alone is too brassy, too noisy—so, one has to *find*."

The customary instruments, especially wind instruments, did not seem sufficient for this score, in particular not for the final scene. At the first orchestra rehearsal, he omitted the wind instruments that did not appear fitting to him. But it was not until after this rehearsal that he added the drum roll for Parsifal's coronation.

It is an exception, though, when Gustav Mahler completely re-formed the entire orchestration of the Fifth Symphony after the first performance in Cologne (1904). Mahler must have had a feeling of uncertainty as to whether the new and frequently shrill tones of his music sounded the way he wanted them to. When he had finished a new symphony, he regularly arranged a private performance of the new work, after which he made changes in the instrumentation. But never was he so much in doubt as after the Fifth Symphony. Even after its first performance in Vienna he made omissions in the timpani.

Had Ahasverus been a composer of symphonies, he too might have changed and re-changed the orchestra, restless and dissatisfied, thus shrieking his despair into the world.

CHAPTER XV.

RETROSPECT
The Path of Musical Imagination
The Musical Work of Art

I T IS A LONG ROAD that leads to the perfection of
great musical art production. This path leads from
the dark regions of unconscious soul life, where the
roots of instincts reach deep into the psyche of man,
to the realm of light where intellect arranges, organizes and joins the ideas. At the start of this path are
the natural instincts, the titanic underworld which
mankind subjugated in the course of cultural development, be it through total conquest or through transformation into new forms and spiritual figures. Of
these instincts the most important one is eroticism,
which gives lustre to the timbre of the music. It exists
in all art creation. This is the instinct that gives the
characters of the poet their brightness and celestial
gleam. It gives sensual form to plastic pictures. The
power of the word that even today is a magic formula
when it comes from the pen of poets such as Shelley,
Keats, Stephan George, Paul Verlaine, Stéphane Mal-
larmé, Carducci and D'Annunzio, has the colors of
erotic vision. Music, which still is considered magic
by the listeners, is eroticism in sounding form.

These erotic forces are joined by an impulse of aggression, which has a long history and many shapes.

It is present in all the noise and blare of primitive music; it is spiritualized in the rhythm; it exists in every dissonance; it manifests itself in every effect of music upon the masses. Inverted, it turns to melancholy moods, to depressions, to pain. When strong impulses of aggression turn against the interior itself, they cause in many artists the hours of sadness that occur so frequently among the very great artists, thus originating the fable of the artist's insanity. Michelangelo's melancholias, his brooding, his gloom and his sudden fits of fear; the eight years of growing gloominess in Shakespeare's life, to which we owe "Hamlet," "King Lear" and "Timon of Athens"; the 'black hours' of which Mozart speaks, and in which "Don Giovanni," the C-minor Piano Concertos and the G-minor Symphony were born; and the mighty reveries indulged in by Beethoven at abysses—all of these are of one genus.

Only powerful artists know such hours in which the aggressive impulses that give their work passion and tension dig their way into their inner self. Without them, great tragic creation that represents destruction, ruin and death is inconceivable. The enjoyment of such destruction by the great tragic poet is the pleasure granted by the satisfied instinct of aggression. Schiller appropriately called the end of a tragedy: "the feast of the dramatist." Every great artist derives pleasure even from the depressions with which the soul appears to be destroying itself. In writing the storm scene of "King Lear"; in painting "Judgment Day" and in composing adagios (such as the sobbing song of the Cavatine in the B-major String Quartet), Shakespeare, Michelangelo and Beethoven, respectively, found pleasure in pain. Beethoven, in loosing the storms of the "Appassionata," was as happy in the appreciation of his creative power as Shakespeare was when he let the thunder storm across the heath and rage around Lear, Edgar and the fool. Were it not for this enjoyment of pain, the third act of "Tristan and Isolde" would no more have been written than Goethe's "Werther" or Lord Byron's "Manfred."

Another important instinct is the play impulse, which even exists all over the animal world, and which blusters and laughs in all nurseries during the childhood of man. Here, to play means living in an imaginary world, pleasure in re-forming and in dreams, free molding of adventures. All the primitive stories, fables and myths originated from such enjoyment of play. The more childlike traits are retained by musicians, the stronger is the pure play impulse within them. Haydn's enjoyment of musical story-telling, Mozart's pleasure in the play of tones are both transformations of the childlike play impulse.

One of the most important forms of music: the variation, resulted from the play instinct. In it is preserved the child's pleasure in reshaping things; and this pleasure expresses itself just as much in childish distortions of the language and gay garbling of words as in the desire to transform and disguise oneself, and in playing with dolls. Mozart's childlike traits manifest themselves in every letter in his enjoyment of nonsense and the twisting of words. It also shows in the pleasure with which Mozart invented fairy tales. The same childishness manifested itself in his music as merriness, tone pleasure and play with tones and tone figures. This combination of tone impulse and erotic instincts makes the happy type of artist. The play impulse motivates the forms, eroticism gives them gleam and color.

Repression and sublimation of the instincts, made to serve culture, form the personality of the artist. These battles may continue through the years of maturity. Artists like Beethoven and Michelangelo remained fighters to their old age, battling with the dark forces of their interior. However, there are also pathological artist natures who do not succeed in subduing and organizing their personality. Berlioz can be called the greatest composer of this type. Lord Byron has similar traits. These are artists who are overwhelmed by their dark underworld, are cast around and driven about, while stronger artists like Beethoven or Shakespeare control such powers of the night.

There are artists who completely sublimate their instincts and play with music, among them Haydn, Mozart or, to name modern musicians, Hindemith and Ravel. And there are artists who battle the primitive powers of their instincts and conquer these powers, like Beethoven and Wagner, Michelangelo and Rembrandt. Inbetween these two groups there are artists like Bach and Haendel or, in other fields, Shakespeare and Rubens, in whom the passionate underground of their soul is extremely strong. However, they themselves are so strong that they are able to organize all their storm and stress in complete artistry and arrange it in such perfect form as otherwise only the child-type musician can achieve. These are the valiant natures who, by virtue of their strength and calm control, reduce even the greatest passionateness to lawful form. Their music contains epic magnitude rather than dramatic contrasts and struggles that threaten to uproot their art.

FROM BEETHOVEN TO SHOSTAKOVICH

Childhood, youth and manhood are mixed more strongly in great composers than in other people. All these life periods may be of different strength in various composers, so that Haydn and Mozart appear childlike, Chopin and Schumann youthful, Bach and Beethoven manly; but this only indicates different combinations of identical talents. Even though the music of Haydn and Mozart has the lustre and playful wealth of childhood, it likewise possesses the ecstasy of youth and the superior clearness of manhood. The proportions of the combination differ; the component parts are the same.

In all great musicians the path of formative and creative forces leads from the subconscious, from instincts and emotions, to consciousness: to lucidity, to thinking and logical shaping. On this path, the creative forces absorb all the memories and sentiments of many years. Every new experience is reinforced by old recollections. Just as every musical tone has many tone particles that all swing together and give the tone its color, so does every experience that turns to music in the hands of the composer consist of many experiences. All the joy and grief of many years strengthens the music created by great artists. Every amorous adventure of Beethoven's awakens sentiments experienced in old adventures of the same kind, as far back as childhood experiences. Every type of buffo music that Mozart composed is reinforced by the playfulness and gaiety of his happy childhood. The memories of his youth were always vivid in Shakespeare; the forest scenery of Stratford-on-Avon appears in a magic light as the forest of Arden in "As you like it"; the Castle of Warwick, near his birthplace, returns in "Henry IV" and "Henry VI," and the period in which young Shakespeare

[452]

slaughtered animals in Stratford is reflected in numerous similes in "Henry VI."

Strong recollection of old sentiments and old experiences is an important ingredient of artistic fantasy. It is easily possible that the artist is not only richer than other people in these old sentiments and moods, which strengthen every one of his future adventures, but that these sentiments and moods are more mobile and more loosely connected. They were not so greatly repressed during the artist's development as being useless, as they were by the average human being who can make no practical use of these recollections. They are ever present, and every new experience is capable of reviving them.

More important yet: in the soul of the artist is a free floating sensuality that envelops and penetrates all memories, all sentiments, all images and all figures, so that this soul life becomes radiant and colorful. Ordinary people may consider this forming and shaping of sensuality unsuitable, though it sometimes inspires them to daydreaming; and they are able to sense it only occasionally, usually only in youth or in a period of infatuation. Otherwise they exclude it from their life that is dedicated to practical purposes. The artists, however, live on these inspirations, plays and visions of their sensual fantasy. This sensuality flows around the tones that a musician hears.

Inasmuch as it is the aim of all eroticism to comprise living substance into larger units, it may well be that such sensuality participates in the actual forming of the artist, not merely in the tone to which it lends color. At any rate the whole inner life of the artist is permeated by spiritualized and re-formed sensuality. It is the sensuality that joins every old emotion and every recollection; it unites in varying forms with all impulses of the unconscious; it gives light and warmth to the artist's imagination, and it isolates the artist's world of fantasy from every day life, which looks gray in comparison. Sensuality also participates when stormy passion, death and destruction, melancholy moods and grief fill the composer with sensations of happiness while he is portraying such pictures of the soul. His ear, its sensuality irritated, experiences joy while his heart is bleeding.

The inner development that releases such forces of the soul, that blends them in varying proportions and makes them grow, takes place either in conflict or in harmony with the world and the age in which the musician grows up. The present time offers the great musician the musical forms which the composers, past and present, have developed. The creative musician first combines his fantasy with these forms when he is a pupil. Within these forms he recognizes his own powers and becomes conscious of his particular personality. Shakespeare first re-shaped theatrical pieces by recognized dramatists of his time; as assistant to Verrocchio, Leonardo da Vinci first painted at pictures of his master. Raphael worked in the style of Perugino, Beethoven in the style of Haydn and Mozart, Brahms in the style of the German romanticists. Bruckner's orchestra evolved from the Wagnerian orchestra; Schoenberg first composed in the style of Brahms and Schumann, later in the Tristan style. Stravinsky wrote in the style of Rimsky-Korsakoff; Gershwin learned rhythm from jazz music.

But within the given styles of art, which mediocre artisans copied all their lives, the creative composers found their own personalities. In working on forms that were handed down to them, they developed their peculiarities. The angel that Leonardo da Vinci painted into Verrocchio's picture "The Baptism of Christ" when he was the latter's assistant, already carries Leonardo's smile. In romantic pieces of Henrik Ibsen's youth ideas are expressed on marriage, women and personality that are quite Ibsenic; and the future "Hedda Gabler" is already in existence in the romantic Viking play "The Vikings at Helgeland." Beethoven's dramatic passion erupts already in the Haydn-Mozartian sonatas of his youth, and even the first of his symphonies, written in the Haydn and Mozart style, begins with a dissonance. Similarly, in Schoenberg's Wagneresque "Verklaerte Nacht" Schoenberg's individuality shows itself and penetrates the musical construction, the tone and harmonics.

However, the present does not just surround the composer with music forms which he makes use of to develop his own personality. It also envelops him with its new sphere of education, its new ideas and its problems. It furnishes him with intellectual material, from which he chooses whatever he considers suitable to his personality and which he then combines with this personality. The humanistic ideas of "Age of Reason" are digested by Haydn, Mozart and Beethoven; Schopenhauer's ideas by Wagner. To this are first added the adventures that meet the artist and motivate his imagination: important men, women, travels, friendship, love, struggles. From there the artist makes his selection of whatever matches his individuality and development. From there his particular style gets its form. His fantasy recognizes more and more what it is. Just as plants draw materials from the earth and from the air which they need for their growth and which they digest for their special form, so, too, do great musicians draw spiritual and emotional matter from the life in which they have been placed, and work it into art production. They choose incessantly, instinctively they segregate the essential from the non-essential. Little people are objects for life; great men are the subjects of their experiences, architects of their personality.

Just as electric waves are intensified in a radio tube, so, too, all experiences are intensified in the soul of a great composer. It is as though a whole column of related experiences, its foundations laid in the subconscious, would start vibrating. It is this vibration of all experiences: old sentiments, repressed events, forgotten memories, dreams, fantasies, erotic sensations and primitive instincts, that gives the melody of great composers its profundity. Beethoven's melodies do not expand in surface only; they grow in depth. Bach's melodies distinguish themselves from those of minor contemporary composers by their depth dimension. A simple tune such as Haydn's "Kaiserlied" contains Haydn's whole religious feeling; from the time of his childhood, when he sang in the choir of the church at Hainburg, to the piety of his old age which extols the might of God in the music of "Creation" and "The Seasons." Therefore Haydn was able to work this melody into magnificent variations that bring to light all the spiritual value contained in the melody.

In Wagner's ecstatic "Tristan" love music are all the longing and passionate love emotions that had accumulated within him since his youth and were never fully gratified. Wagner recognized this fact when he wrote: "I am pouring into my art all my love desires that were never stilled in life," and: "Since I have never really enjoyed the happiness of love in my life, I wish to erect a monument to the most beautiful of all dreams, in which from beginning to end this love should grow real intense: I have designed a Tristan and Isolde in my mind."

To be sure, all this urging, the abundance of inner adventures, the transformations of the contents of the subconscious, sublimation of the instincts and the growth of individuality would still not lead to art production were it not for the fact that all this ascends from the soul to light, clarity and thought. It is the joint work of unconscious and conscious forces that first forms works of art. In art creation, as in every other type of intellectual work, lies the whole evolution of man which first had to learn to control, subdue and subjugate the instincts before it became civilization and conscious formation of life. All art creation is based deep in the past, in primitive and childlike soul life which is especially strong in the artist. Fantasy and play, through which art originates, come from the deepest layers of soul life. Here, too, everything that is charm and magic in art is at home. The whole evolution of mankind, from a primitive, magic era to an era of great religions and the age of philosophy, which is a metamorphosis of religion, and to the age of science, lies in modern art.

Conscious forming in music in the highest and brightest layer of fantasy has the clarity and logic of scientific thinking. The thought structure of a symphony belongs to the greatest organizing accomplishments of thinking and was actually created in the period that replaced the religious moyen age with the scientific age of Galileo, Newton, Locke, Hume and Voltaire. Great musicians are also strong thinkers: Bach had knowledge of mathematics, and Mozart also liked mathematics as a child. Beethoven's logic is akin to Kant's. Scholastic divinity taught the mass composers of the moyen age how to work a cantus firmus artistically and severely. The intellectual work of enlightenment, of French encyclopedists, of English philosophers and of Kant gave classical music its clarity and order. Haydn, Mozart and Beethoven absorbed these ideas with the air that blew into their room. They did not have to read this in books, although Beethoven's library contained Kant's "Naturgeschichte und Theorie des Himmels" and he had read books by Plato and Aristotle.

There is surely something of the technical-scientific spirit of our time in modern musical constructivism, and the Bergson philosophical idea of "change and motion" as sole reality of a certainty influenced French impressionism, which read in Bergson texts: "Reality is mobility. There do not exist things made, but only things in the making, not states that remain fixed, but only states in process of change."

Every beautiful melody is a psychic condition that is illuminated by the light of consciousness. Hence its organization, its symmetry and its regulated fluency. But even the largest musical work of art, be it a Bach fugue, a movement from a Beethoven symphony, or an act from a Wagnerian drama, can be considered a single melody that develops, grows and mounts, although the proportions are much bigger here. All good music is an organism that unfolds, its construction as organized as the build of a plant or an animal. Just as there is not only growth, but also shape in all phenomena of nature; not just vitality, but a spiritual form as well: so does a musical work of art consist of both vital strength and order. What vitality in art production is cannot be defined scientifically. It belongs to the mysteries of creation and can no more be explained than the growing of a plant. Kant said that it would never be possible "to explain, according to the laws of nature, the growth of a grass blade, but that one must utterly gainsay the insight of man" (Kritik der Urteilskraft). However, whatever is spiritual order in a work of art is certainly related to thinking. It is light from the light of thought.

Neither can it be explained how all sentiments, all moods, all experiences, past and present, can crystallize around a core or an axis in the musician's soul, and change into a musical form that has a life of its own, that attracts substance and grows; for this also belongs to the mysteries of creation. We can say, though, that an external incident in the life of the musician gives the impetus that suddenly starts the masses of unconscious emotions, instincts and sensual forces moving and turns them into musical form which, at first, is imperfect but becomes increasingly lawful and clear, expands, organizes and takes on meaning. This external incident apparently has the strength to intensify all inner experiences so that they attain sufficient energy to tear themselves loose from the subconscious and to overcome any resistance opposing them, until consciousness can absorb and digest them. This inner work turns to music when the forces of the soul, that aspire to form and shape, set the sensuality of the ear in motion, which then transforms them into tone.

Eros, which in all life is the generative and creative principle, created music. And conscious artistic thinking, which gives music clarity and shape, and regulates and manages the entire creative process of the composers, is but the finest metamorphosis of Eros. This explains why critical thinking by composers differs from every other kind of thinking, and always remains associated with the creative forces of fantasy. Artistic

[459]

thinking, be it ever so keen and logical, as in Bach's counterpoint or in Beethoven's symphonies and sonatas, is always a function of creative fantasy. One could say that the creative powers begin to shine themselves in order to see their way. It is sensuality itself that begins to radiate, like a lighthouse that rises up on the coast of a rough sea.

No composer can create with consciousness alone. Thinking of composers is a part of their fantasy proper that turns to light at the peak of its path. In this respect, too, artistic creation is reminiscent of a process in world creation, and of the "Let there be light." Great musicians, like every creative personality, are bringers of light. They transform into lustre, clearness and beauty whatever exists in the depth of the soul in a shapeless mass of instincts, impulses and emotions that moves in darkness.

It is a long road that leads to such heights. I wanted to describe the stations of this path of musical fantasy as far as they can be ascertained by scientific analysis. Entirely unavailable to scientific analysis are the secrets of creation, creation itself, the inner development of imagination. It is enough to establish where science has its limits. All science is limited to experience and the description of that which can be learned. What lies beyond experience is unknown. But the creative power of the artist is a part of the spiritual forces that shine into the phenomena of the world and become visible as universal laws and laws of living forms, as visions of ethical life and as great personalities.

Great creative musicians—a Palestrina, an Orlando Lasso, a Bach, a Mozart, a Beethoven, a Bruckner— are linked to such spiritual forces. Their work, too, contains something of the mysterium of world creation;

there is something of a celestial light in their lustre. And when Beethoven lets the chorus at the end of the Ninth Symphony sing: "Ahnest Du den Schoepfer Welt," every one senses that the composer did surmise as he wrote the overpowering music.

What aspires to the light in such music, from out of the night of unconsciousness, is a piece of life that wants to become a higher existence.

The compositorial work that has been described here is probably related to all earthly work; but the light that strikes this work through thinking is a part of the gleam beyond, that idealizes the form, that combines the tone figures in lawful order and makes the musical work of art a world creation, a bundle of spiritual strength that moves through the universe like a planet.

At the border of this mysterium of forming, growing and shaping, science has to make a halt.

Index

INDEX

INDEX

INDEX

INDEX

INDEX

INDEX

[471]

INDEX

INDEX